SUPREME COURT WATCH 2010

Highlights of the 2007, 2008, and 2009 Terms
Preview of the 2010 Term

DAVID M. O'BRIEN
UNIVERSITY OF VIRGINIA

W • W • **NORTON & COMPANY** • NEW YORK • LONDON

W. W. Norton & Company has been independent since its founding in 1923, when William Warder Norton and Mary D. Herter Norton first published lectures delivered at the People's Institute, the adult education division of New York City's Cooper Union. The firm soon expanded its program beyond the Institute, publishing books by celebrated academics from America and abroad. By mid-century, the two major pillars of Norton's publishing program—trade books and college texts—were firmly established. In the 1950s, the Norton family transferred control of the company to its employees, and today—with a staff of four hundred and a comparable number of trade, college, and professional titles published each year—W. W. Norton & Company stands as the largest and oldest publishing house owned wholly by its employees.

Composition by Cathy Lombardi.
Manufacturing by Courier—Westford.
Project Editor: Justin Hoffman.
Production Manager: Benjamin Reynolds.

ISBN: 978-0-393-91215-9

W. W. Norton & Company, Inc., 500 Fifth Avenue, New York, NY 10110-0017
www.wwnorton.com

W. W. Norton & Company Ltd., Castle House, 75/76 Wells Street,
London W1T 3QT

1 2 3 4 5 6 7 8 9 0

Contents

Preface

Supreme Court Watch 2010 examines the changes and decisions made during the Supreme Court's 2007, 2008, and 2009 terms. In addition to highlighting the major constitutional rulings in excerpts from leading cases, I discuss in section-by-section introductions other important decisions and analyze recent developments in various areas of constitutional law. The important cases that the Court has granted review and will decide in its 2010–2011 term are also previewed. To offer even more information in an efficient format, special boxes titled "The Development of Law" and "In Comparative Perspective" are also included.

The favorable reception of previous editions of the *Watch* has been gratifying, and I hope that this twentieth edition will further contribute to students' understanding of constitutional law, politics, and history, as well as to their appreciation for how the politics of constitutional interpretation turns on differing interpretations of constitutional politics and the role of the Supreme Court. I am most grateful to Aaron Javsicas for doing a terrific and expeditious job in producing this edition.

D.M.O.
July 1, 2010

SUPREME COURT WATCH 2010

VOLUME ONE

2

LAW AND POLITICS IN THE
SUPREME COURT:
JURISDICTION AND
DECISION-MAKING PROCESS

Continuing a decade-old trend, the Court granted and decided by written opinions less than 1 percent of its total docket of around 9,000 cases (see the "Inside the Court" boxes in this chapter). In its 2007 term the docket fell slightly from the prior term of over 10,000 cases to 9,602 cases, and in its 2008 term fell further to 8,966 cases. Still, the Court heard oral arguments and decided less than 80 cases. As usual, the Court more often reversed than affirmed the decisions below, as indicated in the following table.

On April 30, 2009, Justice Souter, at age 69, announced that he would retire after eighteen terms on the Court. President Barack Obama anticipated filling one or more vacancies on the high bench even before his election, and in December directed a small group of White House staff to begin the process of narrowing the pool of potential nominees. In mid-April the administration learned privately that Justice Souter intended to retire at the end of the term and staff—led by White House Counsel Gregory B. Craig and Ronald A. Klain and Cynthia Hogan of Vice President Joseph R. Biden's office—began assembling more names and reviewing their backgrounds. From a pool of about forty potential nominees, the list was narrowed to nine and, then, to a final four—Second Circuit Court of Appeals Judge Sonia Sotomayor, Seventh Circuit Court of Appeals Judge Diane P. Wood, Solicitor General Elena Kagan, and Homeland Security Secretary Janet Napolitano—all of whom the president subsequently met with in the Oval Office. Although he knew Judge Wood from their days teaching at the University of Chicago, and appointed Kagan and Napolitano to positions in his administration, Obama had not met Judge Sotomayor until an interview on May 21, 2009. President Obama then announced her nomination on May 26th, observing that she would bring a diversity of experience to the Court and had a compelling personal background and an impressive legal record. Judge Sotomayor, age 54, grew up in the Bronx, the daughter of immigrants from Puerto Rico and then went to Princeton University and Yale Law School, where she was an editor of the *Yale Law Journal*. After spending five years as a prosecutor in Manhattan and then working in private practice, she was appointed in 1992 to the federal district court by Republican President George H.W. Bush upon the recommendation of Democratic Senator Daniel Patrick Moynihan, and later elevated to the Court of Appeals for the Second Circuit by Democratic President Bill Clinton in 1998. In announcing her nomination, President Obama aimed to receive the Democratically-controlled Senate's confirmation by the beginning of the Court's term on the first Monday in October. The Senate Judiciary Committee recommended her confirmation by a thirteen to six vote in late July, and in August the full Senate confirmed Sotomayor as the 111th justice, the first Latina, and third female justice to serve on the Court; she also brought the number of Catholics serving at the same time to six, the highest number in the history of the Court.

Almost a year later, Justice Stevens announced that he would retire at the end of the 2009–2010 term. Appointed by Republican President Gerald Ford in 1975, Justice Stevens was the fourth-longest serving justice in the history of the Court. Although appointed as a noncontroversial moderate, at age 90 Justice Stevens became the leader of liberals on the Court, following the retirements of Justices William J. Brennan (in 1990) and Thurgood Marshall (in 1991). Speculation that Stevens would retire circulated for months. Prior to announcing his nominees, Obama met with Judge Wood and Solicitor General Kagan, again, along with appellate court judges Merrick Garland and Sidney Thomas. But, in fact Obama's selection team contacted Kagan about serving on the Court more than a month before Stevens announced that he would retire. And two days before Stevens made his announcement, Vice President Biden and a White House team met with Kagan. Kagan grew up on the upper west side of Manhattan, New York. Born in 1960, she received her B.A. from Princeton (1981), an M.Phil. from Oxford University (1983), and her J.D. from Harvard Law School (1986). Subsequently, Kagan clerked for Justice Thurgood Marshall, practiced law for three years, and then taught at the University of Chicago Law School, before serving (1995–1999) in the Clinton administration. Afterward, she taught at Harvard Law School and became dean before Obama appointed her solicitor general in 2009. Her few prejudicial publications focused primarily on the First Amendment, administrative law, and tributes. A fight with Republicans over her confirmation ensued, but Obama had calculated on her confirmability, while some liberals complained that a more liberal justice was not named, and conservatives attacked her lack of judicial experience. Nonetheless, at age fifty, Kagan became the 112th justice, fourth woman, and eighth Jewish justice.

The Court's Disposition of Appeals in the 2009–2010 Term

	AFFIRMED	REVERSED OR VACATED
First Circuit	1	2
Second Circuit	1	6
Third Circuit	3	2
Fourth Circuit	1	4
Fifth Circuit		4
Sixth Circuit		7
Seventh Circuit	1	10
Eighth Circuit		3
Ninth Circuit	4	11
Tenth Circuit	2	
Eleventh Circuit	2	7
Federal Circuit	1	
District of Columbia Circuit		2
Other Federal Courts		1
State Courts and Other	1	6
*Totals:	17	65

*Excludes cases decided on original jurisdiction or dismissed for lack of jurisdiction and remanded.

B | *The Court's Docket and Screening Cases*

■ INSIDE THE COURT

The Business of the Supreme Court in the 2009–2010 Term ★

SUBJECT OF COURT OPINIONS	SUMMARY	PLENARY
Admiralty		1
Antitrust		4
Bankruptcy		
Bill of Rights (other than rights of accused) and Equal Protection		8
Commerce Clause		
1. Constitutionality and construction of federal regulation		1
2. Constitutionality of state regulation		
Common Law		
Miscellaneous Statutory Construction		25
Due process		
1. Economic interests		1
2. Procedure and rights of accused	8	10
3. Substantive due process (noneconomic)		
Impairment of Contract and Just Compensation		
International Law, War, and Peace		1
Jurisdiction, Procedure, and Practice	5	16
Land Legislation		
Native Americans		
Patents, Copyright, and Trademarks		2
Other Suits against the Government		1
Suits by States		1
Taxation (federal and state)		1
Totals	13	72

★Note: The classification of cases is that of the author and necessarily invites differences of opinion as to the dominant issue in some cases. The table includes opinions in cases whether decided summarily or given plenary consideration, but not cases summarily disposed of by simple orders, opinions dissenting from the denial of review, and those dismissing cases as improvidently granted.

H | *Opinion Days and Communicating Decisions*

■ INSIDE THE COURT

*Opinion Writing during the 2009–2010 Term**

OPINIONS	MAJORITY	CONCURRING	DISSENTING	SEPARATE	TOTALS
Per Curiam	13				13
Roberts	8	3	1	2	14
Stevens	6	11	12	2	31
Scalia	8	14	4		26
Kennedy	9	7	4		20
Thomas	8	13	4	1	26
Ginsburg	9	2	4		15
Breyer	8	6	6	1	21
Alito	8	9	5		22
Sotomayor	8	2	3	2	15
Totals	85	67	43	8	203

*Note that court opinions disposing of two or more companion cases are counted only once here. In addition, this table includes opinions in cases disposed of either summarily or upon plenary consideration, but does not include cases summarily disposed of by simple orders, dismissed as improvidently granted, and concurring or dissenting opinions from the denial of *certiorari*.

I | *Impact of Supreme Court Decisions: Compliance and Implementation*

The Roberts Court, again, reconsidered the doctrine of retroactivity of its decisions, established in *Linkletter v. Walker*, 381 U.S. 618 (1965) (excerpted in Vols. 1 and 2, Ch. 2), *Griffith v. Kentucky*, 479 U.S. 314 (1987) (excerpted in Vols. 1 and 2, Ch. 2), and *Teague v. Lane*, 489 U.S. 288 (1989). Under *Teague*, an old ruling applies both on direct and collateral review, but a new rule, overturning a precedent, applies only to cases still on direct review and applies retroactively in collateral proceedings only if (1) it is substantive or (2) a watershed ruling bearing on "the fundamental fairness and accuracy of the criminal proceeding." In *Whorton v. Bockting*, 549 U.S. 406 (2007), writing for a unanimous Court, Justice Alito reaffirmed *Teague* in holding that a new ruling, which is neither substantive nor a watershed, does not apply retroactively to cases on collateral review in federal courts. However, in *Danforth v. Minnesota*, 128 S.Ct. 1029 (2008), Justice Stevens held that under *Teague* state courts were free to apply broader retroactivity, observing that *Teague* serves to "limit the authority of federal courts to overturn state convictions—not to limit a state court's authority to grant relief for violations of new rules of constitutional law when reviewing its own state convictions." Chief Justice Roberts dissented.

3

PRESIDENTIAL POWER, THE RULE OF LAW, AND FOREIGN AFFAIRS

C | The Treaty-Making Power and Executive Independence

In its 2007–2008 term, the Roberts Court rebuffed President George W. Bush's broad assertion of executive power with respect to the enforcement of interpretations of treaty provisions. In 2004, the International Court of Justice (ICJ) ruled against the denial of certain procedural rights under provisions of the Vienna Convention. Subsequently, President Bush issued a memorandum directing Texas state courts to comply with the ICJ's decision, but they balked and held that the president exceeded his constitutional authority over the conduct of foreign affairs and intruded on the independence of state court proceedings. On appeal in *Medellin v. Texas* (2008) (excerpted below), six members of the Court rejected the administration's interpretation of the Vienna Convention and position on presidential power. Writing for the majority, Chief Justice Roberts held that the convention was a non-self-executing treaty, requiring further congressional legislation to make the ICJ's ruling binding on domestic courts; in contrast to self-executing treaties that have immediate binding legal effect. In addition, he held that President Bush's order had no binding legal effect because it exceeded his authority under the treaty-making provision of the Constitution. Non-self-executing treaties require congressional legislation to force interpretations of their provisions. Thus, neither the ICJ's decision nor President Bush's memorandum, in the absence of federal legislation, compelled state courts to alter their procedures for granting writs of *habeas corpus*. Justice Stevens filed a concurring opinion. Justice Breyer issued a dissenting opinion, which Justices Souter and Ginsburg joined, countering that the Vienna Convention was a self-executing treaty and had binding legal effect.

Medellin v. Texas
128 S.Ct. 1346 (2008)

Jose Medellin was convicted of murder and sentenced to death in Texas. He filed in state courts for a writ of *habeas corpus*, contending that he had a right as a foreign national to consult Mexican authorities, under the Vienna Convention on Consular Relations, and he had not been informed of that right at his trial. After his appeal was dismissed, Mexico filed a suit against the United States in the International Court of Justice (ICJ), which has jurisdiction over disputes arising from the convention and other treaties. Mexico contended that Medellin and fifty other Mexican nationals had been denied their procedural rights under the treaty. The ICJ, in the *Case Concerning Avena and Other Mexican Nationals (Mex. v. U.S.)*, 2004 I.C.J. 12 (*Avena*), held that the nationals were entitled to reconsideration of their convictions and sentences in the United States.

Medellin appealed his conviction, relying on the ICJ's *Avena* ruling. But a federal appellate court dismissed his petition, holding that he was procedurally barred from *habeas* relief because he had not raised the claim during his original trial. He in turn appealed that decision and his death sentence to the Supreme Court. While the Court was considering his appeal, in February 2005 President George W. Bush issued a memorandum announcing that the United States would comply with *Avena* "by having state courts give effect to the [ICJ] decision in accordance with general principles of comity filed by the 51 Mexican nationals addressed in that decision." Subsequently, the Court by a five-to-four vote dismissed Medellin's appeal in an unsigned decision to allow Texas courts to comply with the presidential memorandum. Medellin once again appealed to the Texas courts, contending that they should comply with the ICJ's ruling and Bush's memorandum. But in 2006 the Texas Court of Criminal Appeals dismissed his petition and held that the ICJ's ruling was not binding on state courts. The state appellate court also held that President Bush exceeded his constitutional authority over foreign affairs and intruded on the independent powers of state courts. Medellin, again, appealed to the Supreme Court, which granted review.

The state appellate court's decision was affirmed by a six-to-three vote. Chief Justice Roberts delivered the opinion for the Court. Justice Stevens filed a concurring opinion. Justice Breyer issued a dissenting opinion, which Justices Souter and Ginsburg joined.

☐ *CHIEF JUSTICE ROBERTS delivered the opinion of the Court.*

The International Court of Justice (ICJ), located in the Hague, is a tribunal established pursuant to the United Nations Charter to adjudicate disputes between member states. In the *Case Concerning Avena and Other Mexican Nationals (Mex. v. U.S.)*, 2004 I. C. J. 12 (Judgment of Mar. 31) (*Avena*), that tribunal considered a claim brought by Mexico against the United States. The ICJ held that, based on violations of the Vienna Convention, 51 named Mexican nationals were entitled to review and reconsideration of their state-court convictions and sentences in the United States. This was so regardless of any forfeiture of the right to raise Vienna Convention claims because of a failure to comply with generally applicable state rules governing challenges to criminal convictions.

In *Sanchez-Llamas v. Oregon*, 548 U.S. 331 (2006)—issued after *Avena* but involving individuals who were not named in the *Avena* judgment—we held that, contrary to the ICJ's determination, the Vienna Convention did not preclude the application of state default rules. After the *Avena* decision, President George W. Bush determined, through a Memorandum to the Attorney General (Feb. 28, 2005), (Memorandum or President's Memorandum), that the United States would "discharge its international obligations" under *Avena* "by having State courts give effect to the decision." . . .

In 1969, the United States, upon the advice and consent of the Senate, ratified the Vienna Convention on Consular Relations (Vienna Convention or Convention), the Optional Protocol Concerning the Compulsory Settlement of Disputes to the Vienna Convention (Optional Protocol or Protocol). . . . Art. 36(1) provides that if a person detained by a foreign country "so requests, the competent authorities of the receiving State shall, without delay, inform the consular post of the sending State" of such detention, and "inform the [detainee] of his righ[t]" to request assistance from the consul of his own state. . . .

Under Article 94(1) of the U.N. Charter, "[e]ach Member of the United Nations undertakes to comply with the decision of the [ICJ] in any case to which it is a party." The ICJ's jurisdiction in any particular case, however, is dependent upon the consent of the parties. The ICJ Statute delineates two ways in which a nation may consent to ICJ jurisdiction: It may consent generally to jurisdiction on any question arising under a treaty or general international law, or it may consent specifically to jurisdiction over a particular category of cases or disputes pursuant to a separate treaty. The United States originally consented to the general jurisdiction of the ICJ when it filed a declaration recognizing compulsory jurisdiction under Art. 36(2) in 1946. The United States withdrew from general ICJ jurisdiction in 1985. By ratifying the Optional Protocol to the Vienna Convention, the United States consented to the specific jurisdiction of the ICJ with respect to claims arising out of the Vienna Convention. On March 7, 2005, subsequent to the ICJ's judgment in *Avena*, the United States gave notice of withdrawal from the Optional Protocol to the Vienna Convention. . . .

Medellin first contends that the ICJ's judgment in *Avena* constitutes a "binding" obligation on the state and federal courts of the United States. He argues that "by virtue of the Supremacy Clause, the treaties requiring compliance with the *Avena* judgment are already the 'Law of the Land' by which all state and federal courts in this country are 'bound.'" Accordingly, Medellin argues, *Avena* is a binding federal rule of decision that pre-empts contrary state limitations on successive *habeas* petitions.

No one disputes that the *Avena* decision—a decision that flows from the treaties through which the United States submitted to ICJ jurisdiction with respect to Vienna Convention disputes—constitutes an international law obligation on the part of the United States. But not all international law obligations automatically constitute binding federal law enforceable in United States courts. The question we confront here is whether the *Avena* judgment has automatic domestic legal effect such that the judgment of its own force applies in state and federal courts.

This Court has long recognized the distinction between treaties that automatically have effect as domestic law, and those that—while they constitute international law commitments—do not by themselves function as binding federal law. The distinction was well explained by CHIEF JUSTICE MARSHALL's opinion in *Foster v. Neilson*, 2 Pet. 253 (1829), overruled on other grounds, *United States v. Percheman*, 7 Pet. 51 (1833), which held that a treaty is "equivalent to an act of the legislature," and hence self-executing, when it "operates of itself without the aid of any legislative provision." When, in contrast, "[treaty] stipulations are not self-executing they can only be enforced pursuant to legislation to carry them into effect." *Whitney v. Robertson*, 124 U.S. 190 (1888). In sum, while treaties "may comprise international commitments . . . they are not domestic law unless Congress has either enacted implementing statutes or the treaty itself conveys an intention that it be 'self-executing' and is ratified on these terms."

A treaty is, of course, "primarily a compact between independent nations." *Head Money Cases*, 112 U.S. 580 (1884). It ordinarily "depends for the enforcement of its provisions on the interest and the honor of the governments which are parties to it." Only "[i]f the treaty contains stipulations which are self-executing, that is, require no legislation to make them operative, [will] they have the force and effect of a legislative enactment." *Whitney*.

The interpretation of a treaty, like the interpretation of a statute, begins with its text. *Air France v. Saks*, 470 U.S. 392 (1985). Because a treaty ratified by the United States is "an agreement among sovereign powers," we have also considered as "aids to its interpretation" the negotiation and drafting history of the treaty as well as "the post ratification understanding" of signatory nations. *Zicherman v. Korean Air Lines Co.*, 516 U.S. 217 (1996).

As a signatory to the Optional Protocol, the United States agreed to submit disputes arising out of the Vienna Convention to the ICJ. The Protocol provides: "Disputes arising out of the interpretation or application of the [Vienna] Convention shall lie within the compulsory jurisdiction of the International Court of Justice." Of course, submitting to jurisdiction and agreeing to be bound are two different things. A party could, for example, agree to compulsory nonbinding arbitration. Such an agreement would require the party to appear before the arbitral tribunal without obligating the party to treat the tribunal's decision as binding.

The most natural reading of the Optional Protocol is as a bare grant of jurisdiction. It provides only that "[d]isputes arising out of the interpretation or

application of the [Vienna] Convention shall lie within the compulsory jurisdiction of the International Court of Justice" and "may accordingly be brought
before the [ICJ] . . . by any party to the dispute being a Party to the present
Protocol." The Protocol says nothing about the effect of an ICJ decision and
does not itself commit signatories to comply with an ICJ judgment. The
Protocol is similarly silent as to any enforcement mechanism.

The obligation on the part of signatory nations to comply with ICJ
judgments derives not from the Optional Protocol, but rather from Article
94 of the United Nations Charter—the provision that specifically addresses
the effect of ICJ decisions. Article 94(1) provides that "[e]ach Member of the
United Nations undertakes to comply with the decision of the [ICJ] in any
case to which it is a party." The Executive Branch contends that the phrase
"undertakes to comply" is not "an acknowledgement that an ICJ decision
will have immediate legal effect in the courts of U.N. members," but rather
"a commitment on the part of U.N. Members to take future action through
their political branches to comply with an ICJ decision."

We agree with this construction of Article 94. The Article is not a direc-
tive to domestic courts. It does not provide that the United States "shall" or
"must" comply with an ICJ decision, nor indicate that the Senate that ratified
the U.N. Charter intended to vest ICJ decisions with immediate legal effect
in domestic courts. In other words, the U.N. Charter reads like "a compact
between independent nations" that "depends for the enforcement of its provisions on the interest and the honor of the governments which are parties
to it." *Head Money Cases.*

The remainder of Article 94 confirms that the U.N. Charter does not
contemplate the automatic enforceability of ICJ decisions in domestic courts.
Article 94(2)—the enforcement provision—provides the sole remedy for noncompliance: referral to the United Nations Security Council by an aggrieved
state. . . .

If ICJ judgments were instead regarded as automatically enforceable
domestic law, they would be immediately and directly binding on state and
federal courts pursuant to the Supremacy Clause. Mexico or the ICJ would
have no need to proceed to the Security Council to enforce the judgment
in this case. Noncompliance with an ICJ judgment through exercise of the
Security Council veto—always regarded as an option by the Executive and
ratifying Senate during and after consideration of the U.N. Charter, Optional
Protocol, and ICJ Statute—would no longer be a viable alternative. There
would be nothing to veto. In light of the U.N. Charter's remedial scheme,
there is no reason to believe that the President and Senate signed up for such
a result.

In sum, Medellin's view that ICJ decisions are automatically enforceable
as domestic law is fatally undermined by the enforcement structure established by Article 94. His construction would eliminate the option of noncompliance contemplated by Article 94(2), undermining the ability of the
political branches to determine whether and how to comply with an ICJ
judgment. Those sensitive foreign policy decisions would instead be transferred to state and federal courts charged with applying an ICJ judgment
directly as domestic law. And those courts would not be empowered to decide whether to comply with the judgment—again, always regarded as an option by the political branches—any more than courts may consider whether
to comply with any other species of domestic law. This result would be particularly anomalous in light of the principle that "[t]he conduct of the foreign
relations of our Government is committed by the Constitution to the Execu-

tive and Legislative—'the political'—Departments." *Oetjen v. Central Leather Co.*, 246 U.S. 297 (1918).

The ICJ Statute, incorporated into the U.N. Charter, provides further evidence that the ICJ's judgment in *Avena* does not automatically constitute federal law judicially enforceable in United States courts. To begin with, the ICJ's "principal purpose" is said to be to "arbitrate particular disputes between national governments." Accordingly, the ICJ can hear disputes only between nations, not individuals. More important, Article 59 of the statute provides that "[t]he decision of the [ICJ] has no binding force except between the parties and in respect of that particular case." The dissent does not explain how Medellin, an individual, can be a party to the ICJ proceeding. . . .

The pertinent international agreements, therefore, do not provide for implementation of ICJ judgments through direct enforcement in domestic courts, and "where a treaty does not provide a particular remedy, either expressly or implicitly, it is not for the federal courts to impose one on the States through lawmaking of their own." . . .

Our Framers established a careful set of procedures that must be followed before federal law can be created under the Constitution—vesting that decision in the political branches, subject to checks and balances. U.S. Const., Art. I, Sec. 7. They also recognized that treaties could create federal law, but again through the political branches, with the President making the treaty and the Senate approving it. Art. II, Sec. 2. The dissent's understanding of the treaty route, depending on an ad hoc judgment of the judiciary without looking to the treaty language—the very language negotiated by the President and approved by the Senate—cannot readily be ascribed to those same Framers.

The dissent's approach risks the United States' involvement in international agreements. It is hard to believe that the United States would enter into treaties that are sometimes enforceable and sometimes not. Such a treaty would be the equivalent of writing a blank check to the judiciary. Senators could never be quite sure what the treaties on which they were voting meant. Only a judge could say for sure and only at some future date. This uncertainty could hobble the United States' efforts to negotiate and sign international agreements.

In this case, the dissent—for a grab bag of no less than seven reasons—would tell us that this particular ICJ judgment is federal law. That is no sort of guidance. Nor is it any answer to say that the federal courts will diligently police international agreements and enforce the decisions of international tribunals only when they should be enforced. The point of a non-self-executing treaty is that it "addresses itself to the political, not the judicial department; and the legislature must execute the contract before it can become a rule for the Court." . . .

Our holding does not call into question the ordinary enforcement of foreign judgments or international arbitral agreements. Indeed, we agree with Medellin that, as a general matter, "an agreement to abide by the result" of an international adjudication—or what he really means, an agreement to give the result of such adjudication domestic legal effect—can be a treaty obligation like any other, so long as the agreement is consistent with the Constitution. The point is that the particular treaty obligations on which Medellin relies do not of their own force create domestic law. . . .

In sum, while the ICJ's judgment in *Avena* creates an international law obligation on the part of the United States, it does not of its own force constitute binding federal law that pre-empts state restrictions on the filing of successive *habeas* petitions. Nothing in the text, background, negotiating and drafting history, or practice among signatory nations suggests that the President or Senate intended the improbable result of giving the judgments of an international tribunal a higher status than that enjoyed by "many of our most fundamental constitutional protections."

Medellin next argues that the ICJ's judgment in *Avena* is binding on state courts by virtue of the President's February 28, 2005 Memorandum. The United States contends that while the *Avena* judgment does not of its own force require domestic courts to set aside ordinary rules of procedural default, that judgment became the law of the land with precisely that effect pursuant to the President's Memorandum and his power "to establish binding rules of decision that preempt contrary state law." Accordingly, we must decide whether the President's declaration alters our conclusion that the *Avena* judgment is not a rule of domestic law binding in state and federal courts.

The United States maintains that the President's constitutional role "uniquely qualifies" him to resolve the sensitive foreign policy decisions that bear on compliance with an ICJ decision and "to do so expeditiously." In this case, the President seeks to vindicate United States interests in ensuring the reciprocal observance of the Vienna Convention, protecting relations with foreign governments, and demonstrating commitment to the role of international law. These interests are plainly compelling.

Such considerations, however, do not allow us to set aside first principles. The President's authority to act, as with the exercise of any governmental power, "must stem either from an act of Congress or from the Constitution itself." *Youngstown* [*Sheet & Tube v. Sawyer*, 343 U.S. 579 (1952)].

Justice Jackson's familiar tripartite scheme provides the accepted framework for evaluating executive action in this area. First, "[w]hen the President acts pursuant to an express or implied authorization of Congress, his authority is at its maximum, for it includes all that he possesses in his own right plus all that Congress can delegate." *Youngstown*. Second, "[w]hen the President acts in absence of either a congressional grant or denial of authority, he can only rely upon his own independent powers, but there is a zone of twilight in which he and Congress may have concurrent authority, or in which its distribution is uncertain." In this circumstance, Presidential authority can derive support from "congressional inertia, indifference or quiescence." Finally, "[w]hen the President takes measures incompatible with the expressed or implied will of Congress, his power is at its lowest ebb," and the Court can sustain his actions "only by disabling the Congress from acting upon the subject."

The United States marshals' two principal arguments in favor of the President's authority "to establish binding rules of decision that preempt contrary state law." The Solicitor General first argues that the relevant treaties give the President the authority to implement the *Avena* judgment and that Congress has acquiesced in the exercise of such authority. The United States also relies upon an "independent" international dispute-resolution power wholly apart from the asserted authority based on the pertinent treaties. Medellin adds the additional argument that the President's Memorandum is a valid exercise of his power to take care that the laws be faithfully executed.

The United States maintains that the President's Memorandum is authorized by the Optional Protocol and the U.N. Charter. That is, because the relevant treaties "create an obligation to comply with *Avena*," they "implicitly give the President authority to implement that treaty-based obligation." As a result, the President's Memorandum is well grounded in the first category of the *Youngstown* framework.

We disagree. The President has an array of political and diplomatic means available to enforce international obligations, but unilaterally converting a non-self-executing treaty into a self-executing one is not among them. The responsibility for transforming an international obligation arising from a non-self-executing treaty into domestic law falls to Congress. . . .

The requirement that Congress, rather than the President, implement a non-self-executing treaty derives from the text of the Constitution, which divides the treaty-making power between the President and the Senate. The Constitution vests the President with the authority to "make" a treaty. If the Executive determines that a treaty should have domestic effect of its own force, that determination may be implemented "in mak[ing]" the treaty, by ensuring that it contains language plainly providing for domestic enforceability. If the treaty is to be self-executing in this respect, the Senate must consent to the treaty by the requisite two-thirds vote consistent with all other constitutional restraints.

Once a treaty is ratified without provisions clearly according it domestic effect, however, whether the treaty will ever have such effect is governed by the fundamental constitutional principle that " '[t]he power to make the necessary laws is in Congress; the power to execute in the President.' " *Hamdan v. Rumsfeld*, 548 U.S. 557 (2006). As already noted, the terms of a non-self-executing treaty can become domestic law only in the same way as any other law—through passage of legislation by both Houses of Congress, combined with either the President's signature or a congressional override of a Presidential veto. Indeed, "the President's power to see that the laws are faithfully executed refutes the idea that he is to be a lawmaker." *Youngstown*.

A non-self-executing treaty, by definition, is one that was ratified with the understanding that it is not to have domestic effect of its own force. That understanding precludes the assertion that Congress has implicitly authorized the President—acting on his own—to achieve precisely the same result. We therefore conclude, given the absence of congressional legislation, that the non-self-executing treaties at issue here did not "express[ly] or implied[ly]" vest the President with the unilateral authority to make them self-executing. Accordingly, the President's Memorandum does not fall within the first category of the *Youngstown* framework. . . .

The United States nonetheless maintains that the President's Memorandum should be given effect as domestic law because "this case involves a valid Presidential action in the context of Congressional 'acquiescence'." Under the *Youngstown* tripartite framework, congressional acquiescence is pertinent when the President's action falls within the second category— that is, when he "acts in absence of either a congressional grant or denial of authority." Here, however, as we have explained, the President's effort to accord domestic effect to the *Avena* judgment does not meet that prerequisite. . . .

We thus turn to the United States' claim that—independent of the United States' treaty obligations—the Memorandum is a valid exercise of the President's foreign affairs authority to resolve claims disputes with foreign nations. The United States relies on a series of cases in which this Court has upheld the authority of the President to settle foreign claims pursuant to an executive agreement. . . .

This argument is of a different nature than the one rejected above. Rather than relying on the United States' treaty obligations, the President relies on an independent source of authority in ordering Texas to put aside its procedural bar to successive *habeas* petitions. Nevertheless, we find that our claims-settlement cases [*United States v. Pink*, 315 U.S. 202 (1942); *United States v. Belmont*, 301 U.S. 324 (1937)] do not support the authority that the President asserts in this case. . . .

Medellin argues that the President's Memorandum is a valid exercise of his "Take Care" power. The United States, however, does not rely upon the President's responsibility to "take Care that the Laws be faithfully executed." We think this a wise concession. This authority allows the President to execute the laws, not make them. For the reasons we have stated, the *Avena* judgment is not domestic law; accordingly, the President cannot rely on his Take Care powers here.

☐ *Justice BREYER, with whom Justice SOUTER and Justice GINSBURG join, dissenting.*

The Constitution's Supremacy Clause provides that "all Treaties . . . which shall be made . . . under the Authority of the United States, shall be the supreme Law of the Land; and the Judges in every State shall be bound thereby." The Clause means that the "courts" must regard "a treaty . . . as equivalent to an act of the legislature, whenever it operates of itself without the aid of any legislative provision." *Foster v. Neilson*, 2 Pet. 253 (1829).

In the *Avena* case the International Court of Justice (ICJ) (interpreting and applying the Vienna Convention on Consular Relations) issued a judgment that requires the United States to reexamine certain criminal proceedings in the cases of 51 Mexican nationals. The question here is whether the ICJ's *Avena* judgment is enforceable now as a matter of domestic law, i.e., whether it "operates of itself without the aid" of any further legislation.

The United States has signed and ratified a series of treaties obliging it to comply with ICJ judgments in cases in which it has given its consent to the exercise of the ICJ's adjudicatory authority. Specifically, the United States has agreed to submit, in this kind of case, to the ICJ's "compulsory jurisdiction" for purposes of "compulsory settlement." And it agreed that the ICJ's judgments would have "binding force . . . between the parties and in respect of [a] particular case." United Nations Charter, Art. 59 (1945). President Bush has determined that domestic courts should enforce this particular ICJ judgment. Memorandum to the Attorney General (Feb. 28, 2005) (hereinafter President's Memorandum). And Congress has done nothing to suggest the contrary. Under these circumstances, I believe the treaty obligations, and hence the judgment, resting as it does upon the consent of the United States to the ICJ's jurisdiction, bind the courts no less than would "an act of the [federal] legislature." *Foster.*

To understand the issue before us, the reader must keep in mind three separate ratified United States treaties and one ICJ judgment against the United States. The first treaty, the Vienna Convention, contains two relevant provisions. The first requires the United States and other signatory nations to inform arrested foreign nationals of their separate Convention-given right to contact their nation's consul. The second says that these rights (of an arrested person) "shall be exercised in conformity with the laws and regulations" of the arresting nation, provided that the "laws and regulations . . . enable full effect to be given to the purposes for which" those "rights . . . are intended."

The second treaty, the Optional Protocol, concerns the "compulsory settlement" of Vienna Convention disputes. It provides that for parties that elect to subscribe to the Protocol, "[d]isputes arising out of the interpretation or application of the [Vienna] Convention" shall be submitted to the "compulsory jurisdiction of the International Court of Justice." It authorizes any party that has consented to the ICJ's jurisdiction (by signing the Optional Protocol) to bring another such party before that Court.

The third treaty, the United Nations Charter, says that every signatory Nation "undertakes to comply with the decision of the International Court of Justice in any case to which it is a party." Art. 94(1). In an annex to the Charter, the Statute of the International Court of Justice states that an ICJ judgment has "binding force . . . between the parties and in respect of that particular case." Art. 59.

The critical question here is whether the Supremacy Clause requires Texas to follow, i.e., to enforce, this ICJ judgment. The Court says "no." And it reaches its negative answer by interpreting the labyrinth of treaty provisions as creating a legal obligation that binds the United States internationally, but which, for Supremacy Clause purposes, is not automatically enforceable as domestic law. In the majority's view, the Optional Protocol simply sends the dispute to the ICJ; the ICJ statute says that the ICJ will subsequently reach a judgment; and the U.N. Charter contains no more than a promise to " 'undertak[e] to comply' " with that judgment. Such a promise, the majority says, does not as a domestic law matter (in CHIEF JUSTICE MARSHALL's words) "operat[e] of itself without the aid of any legislative provision." *Foster*. Rather, here (and presumably in any other ICJ judgment rendered pursuant to any of the approximately 70 U.S. treaties in force that contain similar provisions for submitting treaty-based disputes to the ICJ for decisions that bind the parties) Congress must enact specific legislation before ICJ judgments entered pursuant to our consent to compulsory ICJ jurisdiction can become domestic law.

In my view, the President has correctly determined that Congress need not enact additional legislation. The majority places too much weight upon treaty language that says little about the matter. The words "undertak[e] to comply," for example, do not tell us whether an ICJ judgment rendered pursuant to the parties' consent to compulsory ICJ jurisdiction does, or does not, automatically become part of our domestic law. To answer that question we must look instead to our own domestic law, in particular, to the many treaty-related cases interpreting the Supremacy Clause. Those cases, including some written by Justices well aware of the Founders' original intent, lead to the conclusion that the ICJ judgment before us is enforceable as a matter of domestic law without further legislation.

Supreme Court case law stretching back more than 200 years helps explain what, for present purposes, the Founders meant when they wrote that "all Treaties . . . shall be the supreme Law of the Land." Art. VI, cl. 2. . . .

Of particular relevance to the present case, the Court has held that the United States may be obligated by treaty to comply with the judgment of an international tribunal interpreting that treaty, despite the absence of any congressional enactment specifically requiring such compliance. See *Comegys v. Vasse*, 1 Pet. 193 (1828) (holding that decision of tribunal rendered pursuant to a United States-Spain treaty, which obliged the parties to "undertake to make satisfaction" of treaty-based rights, was "conclusive and final" and "not re-examinable" in American courts).

All of these cases make clear that self-executing treaty provisions are not uncommon or peculiar creatures of our domestic law; that they cover a wide range of subjects; that the Supremacy Clause itself answers the self-execution question by applying many, but not all, treaty provisions directly to the States;

and that the Clause answers the self-execution question differently than does the law in many other nations. . . .

I would find the relevant treaty provisions self-executing as applied to the ICJ judgment before us (giving that judgment domestic legal effect) for the following reasons, taken together.

First, the language of the relevant treaties strongly supports direct judicial enforceability, at least of judgments of the kind at issue here. The Optional Protocol bears the title "Compulsory Settlement of Disputes," thereby emphasizing the mandatory and binding nature of the procedures it sets forth. The body of the Protocol says specifically that "any party" that has consented to the ICJ's "compulsory jurisdiction" may bring a "dispute" before the court against any other such party. And the Protocol contrasts proceedings of the compulsory kind with an alternative "conciliation procedure," the recommendations of which a party may decide "not" to "accep[t]." Art. III. Thus, the Optional Protocol's basic objective is not just to provide a forum for settlement but to provide a forum for compulsory settlement.

Moreover, in accepting Article 94(1) of the Charter, "[e]ach Member . . . undertakes to comply with the decision" of the ICJ "in any case to which it is a party." And the ICJ Statute (part of the U.N. Charter) makes clear that, a decision of the ICJ between parties that have consented to the ICJ's compulsory jurisdiction has "binding force . . . between the parties and in respect of that particular case.". . .

I recognize, as the majority emphasizes, that the U.N. Charter uses the words "undertakes to comply," rather than, say, "shall comply" or "must comply." But what is inadequate about the word "undertak[e]"? A leading contemporary dictionary defined it in terms of "lay[ing] oneself under obligation . . . to perform or to execute." *Webster's New International Dictionary* (2d ed. 1939). . . .

And even if I agreed with [concurring] Justice STEVENS that the language is perfectly ambiguous (which I do not), I could not agree that "the best reading . . . is . . . one that contemplates future action by the political branches." The consequence of such a reading is to place the fate of an international promise made by the United States in the hands of a single State. And that is precisely the situation that the Framers sought to prevent by enacting the Supremacy Clause. . . .

The upshot is that treaty language says that an ICJ decision is legally binding, but it leaves the implementation of that binding legal obligation to the domestic law of each signatory nation. In this Nation, the Supremacy Clause, as long and consistently interpreted, indicates that ICJ decisions rendered pursuant to provisions for binding adjudication must be domestically legally binding and enforceable in domestic courts at least sometimes. And for purposes of this argument, that conclusion is all that I need. The remainder of the discussion will explain why, if ICJ judgments sometimes bind domestic courts, then they have that effect here.

Second, the Optional Protocol here applies to a dispute about the meaning of a Vienna Convention provision that is itself self-executing and judicially enforceable. The Convention provision is about an individual's "rights," namely, his right upon being arrested to be informed of his separate right to contact his nation's consul. . . .

Third, logic suggests that a treaty provision providing for "final" and "binding" judgments that "settl[e]" treaty-based disputes is self-executing insofar as the judgment in question concerns the meaning of an underlying treaty provision that is itself self-executing. Imagine that two parties to a contract agree to binding arbitration about whether a contract provision's word "grain" includes rye. They would expect that, if the arbitrator decides that the word "grain" does include rye, the arbitrator will then simply read the relevant provision as if it said "grain including rye." They would also expect the arbitrator to issue a binding award that embodies whatever relief would be appropriate under that circumstance.

Why treat differently the parties' agreement to binding ICJ determination about, e.g., the proper interpretation of the Vienna Convention clauses containing the rights here at issue? Why not simply read the relevant Vienna Convention provisions as if (between the parties and in respect to the 51 individuals at issue) they contain words that encapsulate the ICJ's decision? Why would the ICJ judgment not bind in precisely the same way those words would bind if they appeared in the relevant Vienna Convention provisions—just as the ICJ says, for purposes of this case, that they do?

To put the same point differently: What sense would it make (1) to make a self-executing promise and (2) to promise to accept as final an ICJ judgment interpreting that self-executing promise, yet (3) to insist that the judgment itself is not self-executing (i.e., that Congress must enact specific legislation to enforce it)?

I am not aware of any satisfactory answer to these questions. . . .

Fourth, the majority's very different approach has seriously negative practical implications. The United States has entered into at least 70 treaties that contain provisions for ICJ dispute settlement similar to the Protocol before us. Many of these treaties contain provisions similar to those this Court has previously found self-executing—provisions that involve, for example, property rights, contract and commercial rights, trademarks, civil liability for personal injury, rights of foreign diplomats, taxation, domestic-court jurisdiction, and so forth. If the Optional Protocol here, taken together with the U.N. Charter and its annexed ICJ Statute, is insufficient to warrant enforcement of the ICJ judgment before us, it is difficult to see how one could reach a different conclusion in any of these other instances. And the consequence is to undermine longstanding efforts in those treaties to create an effective international system for interpreting and applying many, often commercial, self-executing treaty provisions. . . .

Fifth, other factors, related to the particular judgment here at issue, make that judgment well suited to direct judicial enforcement. The specific issue before the ICJ concerned " 'review and reconsideration' " of the "possible prejudice" caused in each of the 51 affected cases by an arresting State's failure to provide the defendant with rights guaranteed by the Vienna Convention. This review will call for an understanding of how criminal procedure works, including whether, and how, a notification failure may work prejudice. As the ICJ itself recognized, "it is the judicial process that is suited to this task." Courts frequently work with criminal procedure and related prejudice. Legislatures do not. Judicial standards are readily available for working in this technical area. Legislative standards are not readily available. Judges typically determine such matters, deciding, for example, whether further hearings are necessary, after reviewing a record in an individual case. Congress does not normally legislate in respect to individual cases. Indeed, to repeat what I said above, what kind of special legislation does the majority believe Congress ought to consider?

Sixth, to find the United States' treaty obligations self-executing as applied to the ICJ judgment (and consequently to find that judgment enforceable) does not threaten constitutional conflict with other branches; it does not require us to engage in nonjudicial activity; and it does not require us to create a new cause of action. The only question before us concerns the application of the ICJ judgment as binding law applicable to the parties in a particular criminal proceeding that Texas law creates independently of the treaty. I repeat that the question before us does not involve the creation of a private right of action (and the majority's reliance on authority regarding such a circumstance is misplaced).

Seventh, neither the President nor Congress has expressed concern about direct judicial enforcement of the ICJ decision. To the contrary, the President favors enforcement of this judgment. . . .

For these seven reasons, I would find that the United States' treaty obligation to comply with the ICJ judgment in *Avena* is enforceable in court in this case without further congressional action beyond Senate ratification of the relevant treaties. The majority reaches a different conclusion because it looks for the wrong thing (explicit textual expression about self-execution) using the wrong standard (clarity) in the wrong place (the treaty language). Hunting for what the text cannot contain, it takes a wrong turn. It threatens to deprive individuals, including businesses, property owners, testamentary beneficiaries, consular officials, and others, of the workable dispute resolution procedures that many treaties, including commercially oriented treaties, provide. In a world where commerce, trade, and travel have become ever more international, that is a step in the wrong direction. . . .

In sum, a strong line of precedent, likely reflecting the views of the Founders, indicates that the treaty provisions before us and the judgment of the International Court of Justice address themselves to the Judicial Branch and consequently are self-executing. In reaching a contrary conclusion, the Court has failed to take proper account of that precedent and, as a result, the Nation may well break its word even though the President seeks to live up to that word and Congress has done nothing to suggest the contrary.

For the reasons set forth, I respectfully dissent.

D | *War-Making and Emergency Powers*

In another rebuke to the Bush administration's position on holding "enemy combatants" without judicial review, a bare majority held that even foreign nationals detained in Guantanamo Bay have the constitutional right to apply to federal courts for writs of *habeas corpus* to review the basis for their detention. Writing for the Court, in *Boumediene v. Bush* (2008) (excerpted below), Justice Kennedy observed, "The laws and Constitution are designed to survive, and remain in force, in extraordinary times." Justice Souter, joined by Justices Ginsburg and Breyer, filed a concurring opinion, while Chief Justice Roberts and Justice Scalia each filed dissenting opinions, which were joined by Justices Thomas and Alito.

In a related case, *Munaf v. Geren*, 128 S.Ct. 2207 (2008), handed down on the same day, a unanimous Court held that U.S. citizens held by U.S. forces in Iraq have the right to file *habeas corpus* petitions, but that federal courts do not have the authority to bar their transfer and trial by Iraqi authorities for charges of terrorism-related crimes. Chief Justice Roberts delivered the opinion of the Court, while Justice Souter filed a concurring opinion, joined by Justices Ginsburg and Breyer. In their view, the ruling would not foreclose U.S. courts from preventing the transfer of citizens into foreign custody when "the probability of torture is well documented, even if the Executive fails to acknowledge it."

■ THE DEVELOPMENT OF LAW

The Treatment of "Enemy Combatants"

Following the Court's ruling in *Boumediene v. Bush* (2008) (excerpted in this chapter), which held that foreign nationals detained in Guantanamo Bay, Cuba, have a constitutional right to apply to federal courts for writs of *habeas corpus* to review their detentions, and which struck down a section of the Military Commissions Act (MCA) of 2006 that eliminated federal court jurisdiction over appeals from detainees, Boumediene was released and transferred to France. The MCA was enacted after the Court's decision in *Hamdan v. Rumsfeld* (2006) (excerpted in Vol. 1, Ch. 3), holding that the Detainee Treatment Act of 2005, which also aimed at stripping federal courts of jurisdiction over detainees' appeals, did not apply to Salim Ahmed Hamdan and others whose appeals were pending at the time of the passage of the law. Subsequently, after the Court's decision, in 2008 Hamdan was transferred to Yemen to serve out his military commission sentence and then released.

In the aftermath of the ruling in *Boumediene*, federal courts in New York and Virginia began reviewing other appeals of detainees, leading to conflicting rulings, while a task force appointed by Democratic President Barack Obama reviewed the status of about 240 "enemy combatants" still held in Guantanamo Bay to decide who to repatriate, try in civilian courts or by military commissions, continue to hold, or transfer to prisons in the United States. In a number of cases, the government reached plea agreements with detainees. In the case of Ali Saleh Kahlah al-Marri, an alleged "sleeper agent" of al Qaeda who was held in a naval brig, the Bush administration asserted the power to indefinitely detain "enemy combatants." The Court of Appeals for the Fourth Circuit upheld the Bush administration and al-Marri appealed to the Supreme Court. But after granting review the Court vacated the lower court's decision, in *Al-Marri v. Spagone*, 129 S.Ct. 1545 (2009), and dismissed the case as moot because the Obama administration decided to indict him on conspiracy charges in federal court.

President Obama campaigned in part on closing Guantanamo Bay and ending the Bush administration's trials of detainees by military commissions. Shortly after coming into the White House, he vowed to eliminate the term "enemy combatants," appointed a task force with the aim of closing Guatanamo Bay by January 2010, defined "waterboarding" as torture, and said he would discontinue trials by military commissions. However, in 2009 he announced that the administration would retain military commissions to try some detainees, while moving others to civilian courts or repatriating them. In doing so, President Obama also promised on May 15, 2009, to reform the military process in five ways: "First, statements that have been obtained from detainees using cruel, inhuman and degrading interrogation methods will no longer be admitted as evidence at trial. Second, the use of hearsay will be limited, so that the burden will no longer be on the party who objects to hearsay to disprove its reliability. Third, the accused will have greater latitude in selecting their counsel. Fourth, basic protections will be provided for those who refuse to testify. And, fifth, military commission judges may establish the jurisdiction of their own courts." Subsequently, President Obama explained that some of the then remaining 240 detainees would be transferred to prisons and tried, some might be returned to their countries of national origin, but some might still be held indefinitely without trials—what he termed "prolonged detention" of those deemed to pose national security risks.

Boumediene v. Bush
128 S.Ct. 2229 (2008)

In 2002, Lakhdar Boumediene and several other Algerian nationals were seized by Bosnian police when U.S. intelligence officers suspected them of plotting to attack an embassy. Boumediene and the others were classified as "enemy combatants" and held in the Naval Base in Guantanamo Bay, Cuba. Boumediene filed a petition for *habeas corpus*, claiming violation of due process and various statutes and treaties. A federal district court granted the government's motion to have all claims dismissed on the ground that Boumediene was an alien detained overseas and, hence, had no right to a *habeas* petition. The U.S. Court of Appeals for the District of Columbia Circuit affirmed, but the U.S. Supreme Court reversed in *Rasul v. Bush*, 542 U.S. 466 (2004) (excerpted in Vol. 1 of the casebook), in holding that noncitizen detainees in Guantanamo were entitled to *habeas* relief. In response, Congress passed the Detainee Treatment Act of 2005, which basically stripped the federal courts of jurisdiction over *habeas* petitions from those held in Guantanamo Bay. The detainees, however, argued that the act did not apply to their cases since they were pending before its passage and that they were denied due process. On appeal, the Supreme Court agreed in *Hamdan v. Rumsfeld*, 548 U.S. 557 (2006) (excerpted in Vol. I of the casebook). Congress in turn passed the Military Commissions Act (MCA) of 2006, which eliminated federal courts' jurisdiction over *habeas* petitions filed by Guantanamo Bay detainees who had been designated "enemy combatants" under the procedures established, after the Court's ruling in *Hamdi v. Rumsfeld*, 542 U.S. 507 (2004) (excerpted in Vol. 1 of the casebook), for Combatant Status Review Tribunals (CSRTs) to review the military's designation of "enemy combatant" status. Subsequently, Boumediene and other Guantanamo Bay prisoners challenged their detention, but a federal district court agreed with the government and dismissed their petitions. Shortly thereafter, however, another district court rejected the government's motion to dismiss the petitions of other Guantanamo Bay detainees, in ruling that they are entitled to Fifth Amendment due process rights. A divided panel of the U.S. Court of Appeals for the District of Columbia Circuit then vacated the district court judgments and dismissed the cases for lack of jurisdiction. The majority concluded that the Military Commissions Act of 2006 stripped the federal courts of jurisdiction over *habeas* petitions filed by Guantanamo Bay detainees and rejected their claim that the MCA ran afoul of Article 1, Section 9, of the Constitution that stipulates, "The Privilege of the Writ of *Habeas Corpus* shall not be suspended, unless when in Cases of Rebellion or Invasion the public Safety may require it." Boumediene appealed the appellate court's decision and the Supreme Court granted review.

The appellate court's decision was reversed by a bare majority. Justice Kennedy delivered the opinion for the Court. Justice Souter filed a concurring opinion, which Justices Ginsburg and Breyer joined. Chief Justice Roberts and Justice Scalia each filed dissenting opinions, which were joined by Justices Thomas and Alito.

☐ *Justice KENNEDY delivered the opinion of the Court.*

Petitioners present a question not resolved by our earlier cases relating to the detention of aliens at Guantanamo: whether they have the constitutional privilege of *habeas corpus*, a privilege not to be withdrawn except in conformance with the Suspension Clause, Art. I, Sec. 9, cl. 2. We hold these petitioners do have the *habeas corpus* privilege. Congress has enacted a statute, the Detainee Treatment Act of 2005 (DTA), that provides certain procedures for review of the detainees' status. We hold that those procedures are not an adequate and effective substitute for *habeas corpus*. Therefore Sec. 7 of the Military Commissions Act of 2006 (MCA) operates as an unconstitutional suspension of the writ. We do not address whether the President has authority to detain these petitioners nor do we hold that the writ must issue. These and other questions regarding the legality of the detention are to be resolved in the first instance by the District Court.

Under the Authorization for Use of Military Force (AUMF), the President is authorized "to use all necessary and appropriate force against those nations, organizations, or persons he determines planned, authorized, committed, or aided the terrorist attacks that occurred on September 11, 2001, or harbored such organizations or persons, in order to prevent any future acts of international terrorism against the United States by such nations, organizations or persons."

In *Hamdi v. Rumsfeld*, 542 U.S. 507 (2004), five Members of the Court recognized that detention of individuals who fought against the United States in Afghanistan "for the duration of the particular conflict in which they were captured, is so fundamental and accepted an incident to war as to be an exercise of the 'necessary and appropriate force' Congress has authorized the President to use." After *Hamdi*, the Deputy Secretary of Defense established Combatant Status Review Tribunals (CSRTs) to determine whether individuals detained at Guantanamo were "enemy combatants," as the Department defines that term. A later memorandum established procedures to implement the CSRTs. The Government maintains these procedures were designed to comply with the due process requirements identified by the plurality in *Hamdi*. . . .

The first actions commenced in February 2002. The District Court ordered the cases dismissed for lack of jurisdiction because the naval station is outside the sovereign territory of the United States. The Court of Appeals for the District of Columbia Circuit affirmed. We granted *certiorari* and reversed, holding that 28 U.S. C. Sec. 2241 extended statutory *habeas corpus* jurisdiction to Guantanamo. See *Rasul v. Bush*, 542 U.S. 466 (2004). The constitutional issue presented in the instant cases was not reached in *Rasul*.

As a threshold matter, we must decide whether MCA Section 7 denies the federal courts jurisdiction to hear *habeas corpus* actions pending at the time of its enactment. We hold the statute does deny that jurisdiction, so that, if the statute is valid, petitioners' cases must be dismissed. . . .

We acknowledge, moreover, the litigation history that prompted Congress to enact the MCA. In *Hamdan* the Court found it unnecessary to address the petitioner's Suspension Clause arguments but noted the relevance of the clear statement rule in deciding whether Congress intended to reach pending *habeas corpus* cases. This interpretive rule facilitates a dialogue between Congress and the Court. If the Court invokes a clear statement rule to advise that certain statutory interpretations are favored in order to avoid constitutional difficulties, Congress can make an informed legislative choice either to amend the statute or to retain its existing text. If Congress amends, its intent must be respected even if a difficult constitutional question is presented. The usual presumption is that Members of Congress, in accord with their oath of office, considered the constitutional issue and determined the amended statute to be a lawful one; and the Judiciary, in light of that determination, proceeds to its own independent judgment on the constitutional question when required to do so in a proper case.

If this ongoing dialogue between and among the branches of Government is to be respected, we cannot ignore that the MCA was a direct response to *Hamdan*'s holding that the DTA's jurisdiction-stripping provision had no application to pending cases.

In deciding the constitutional questions now presented we must determine whether petitioners are barred from seeking the writ or invoking the protections of the Suspension Clause either because of their status, i.e., petitioners' designation by the Executive Branch as enemy combatants, or their physical location, i.e., their presence at Guantanamo Bay. The Government contends that noncitizens designated as enemy combatants and detained in territory located outside our Nation's borders have no constitutional rights and no privilege of *habeas corpus*. Petitioners contend they do have cognizable constitutional rights and that Congress, in seeking to eliminate recourse to *habeas corpus* as a means to assert those rights, acted in violation of the Suspension Clause.

We begin with a brief account of the history and origins of the writ. Our account proceeds from two propositions. First, protection for the privilege of *habeas corpus* was one of the few safeguards of liberty specified in a Constitution that, at the outset, had no Bill of Rights. In the system conceived by the Framers the writ had a centrality that must inform proper interpretation of the Suspension Clause. Second, to the extent there were settled precedents or legal commentaries in 1789 regarding the extraterritorial scope of the writ or its application to enemy aliens, those authorities can be instructive for the present cases.

The Framers viewed freedom from unlawful restraint as a fundamental precept of liberty, and they understood the writ of *habeas corpus* as a vital instrument to secure that freedom. Experience taught, however, that the common-law writ all too often had been insufficient to guard against the abuse of monarchial power. That history counseled the necessity for specific language in the Constitution to secure the writ and ensure its place in our legal system.

Magna Carta decreed that no man would be imprisoned contrary to the law of the land.

The development was painstaking, even by the centuries-long measures of English constitutional history. The writ was known and used in some form at least as early as the reign of Edward I. Yet at the outset it was used to protect not the rights of citizens but those of the King and his courts. The early courts were considered agents of the Crown, designed to assist the King in the exercise of his power. Thus the writ, while it would become part of the foundation of liberty for the King's subjects, was in its earliest use a mechanism for securing compliance with the King's laws. . . .

Still, the writ proved to be an imperfect check. Even when the importance of the writ was well understood in England, *habeas* relief often was denied by the courts or suspended by Parliament. Denial or suspension occurred in times of political unrest, to the anguish of the imprisoned and the outrage of those in sympathy with them. . . .

This history was known to the Framers. It no doubt confirmed their view that pendular swings to and away from individual liberty were endemic to undivided, uncontrolled power. The Framers' inherent distrust of governmental power was the driving force behind the constitutional plan that allocated powers among three independent branches. This design serves not only to make Government accountable but also to secure individual liberty. . . .

That the Framers considered the writ a vital instrument for the protection of individual liberty is evident from the care taken to specify the limited grounds for its suspension: "The Privilege of the Writ of *Habeas Corpus* shall not be suspended, unless when in Cases of Rebellion or Invasion the public Safety may require it." Art. I, Sec. 9, cl. 2. The word "privilege" was used, perhaps, to avoid mentioning some rights to the exclusion of others. (Indeed, the only mention of the term "right" in the Constitution, as ratified, is in its clause giving Congress the power to protect the rights of authors and inventors. See Art. I, Sec. 8, cl. 8.)

Surviving accounts of the ratification debates provide additional evidence that the Framers deemed the writ to be an essential mechanism in the separation-of-powers scheme. . . .

Post-1789 *habeas* developments in England, though not bearing upon the Framers' intent, do verify their foresight. Those later events would underscore the need for structural barriers against arbitrary suspensions of the writ. Just as the writ had been vulnerable to executive and parliamentary encroachment on both sides of the Atlantic before the American Revolution, despite the *Habeas Corpus* Act of 1679, the writ was suspended with frequency in England during times of political unrest after 1789. Parliament suspended the writ for much of the period from 1792 to 1801, resulting in rampant arbitrary imprisonment.

In our own system the Suspension Clause is designed to protect against these cyclical abuses. The Clause protects the rights of the detained by a means consistent with the essential design of the Constitution. It ensures that, except during periods of formal suspension, the Judiciary will have a time-tested device, the writ, to maintain the "delicate balance of governance" that is itself the surest safeguard of liberty. The Clause protects the rights of the detained by affirming the duty and authority of the Judiciary to call the jailer to account. The separation-of-powers doctrine, and the history that influenced its design, therefore must inform the reach and purpose of the Suspension Clause.

The broad historical narrative of the writ and its function is central to our analysis, but we seek guidance as well from founding-era authorities addressing the specific question before us: whether foreign nationals, apprehended and detained in distant countries during a time of serious threats to our Nation's security, may assert the privilege of the writ and seek its protection. The Court has been careful not to foreclose the possibility that the protections of the Suspension Clause have expanded along with post-1789 developments that define the present scope of the writ. . . .

We know that at common law a petitioner's status as an alien was not a categorical bar to *habeas corpus* relief. See, e.g., *Sommersett's Case*, 20 How. St. Tr. 1 (1772) (ordering an African slave freed upon finding the custodian's return insufficient). . . .

We find the evidence as to the geographic scope of the writ at common law informative, but, again, not dispositive. Petitioners argue the site of their detention is analogous to two territories outside of England to which the writ did run: the so-called "exempt jurisdictions," like the Channel Islands; and (in former times) India. There are critical differences between these places and Guantanamo, however.

As the Court noted in *Rasul*, common-law courts granted *habeas corpus* relief to prisoners detained in the exempt jurisdictions. But these areas, while not in theory part of the realm of England, were nonetheless under the Crown's control. And there is some indication that these jurisdictions were considered sovereign territory. Because the United States does not maintain formal sovereignty over Guantanamo Bay, the naval station there and the exempt jurisdictions discussed in the English authorities are not similarly situated. . . .

In the end a categorical or formal conception of sovereignty does not provide a comprehensive or altogether satisfactory explanation for the general understanding that prevailed when Lord Mansfield considered issuance of the writ outside England. In 1759 the writ did not run to Scotland but did run to Ireland, even though, at that point, Scotland and England had merged under the rule of a single sovereign, whereas the Crowns of Great Britain and Ireland remained separate (at least in theory). But there was at least one major difference between Scotland's and Ireland's relationship with England during this period that might explain why the writ ran to Ireland but not to Scotland. English law did not generally apply in Scotland (even after the Act of Union) but it did apply in Ireland. . . .

The prudential barriers that may have prevented the English courts from issuing the writ to Scotland and Hanover are not relevant here. We have no reason to believe an order from a federal court would be disobeyed at Guantanamo. No Cuban court has jurisdiction to hear these petitioners' claims, and no law other than the laws of the United States applies at the naval station. The modern-day relations between the United States and Guantanamo thus differ in important respects from the 18th-century relations between

England and the kingdoms of Scotland and Hanover. This is reason enough for us to discount the relevance of the Government's analogy. . . .

Drawing from its position that at common law the writ ran only to territories over which the Crown was sovereign, the Government says the Suspension Clause affords petitioners no rights because the United States does not claim sovereignty over the place of detention.

Guantanamo Bay is not formally part of the United States. And under the terms of the lease between the United States and Cuba, Cuba retains "ultimate sovereignty" over the territory while the United States exercises "complete jurisdiction and control." Under the terms of the 1934 Treaty, however, Cuba effectively has no rights as a sovereign until the parties agree to modification of the 1903 Lease Agreement or the United States abandons the base. . . .

Were we to hold that the present cases turn on the political question doctrine, we would be required first to accept the Government's premise that *de jure* sovereignty is the touchstone of *habeas corpus* jurisdiction. This premise, however, is unfounded. For the reasons indicated above, the history of common-law *habeas corpus* provides scant support for this proposition; and, for the reasons indicated below, that position would be inconsistent with our precedents and contrary to fundamental separation-of-powers principles.

The Court has discussed the issue of the Constitution's extraterritorial application on many occasions. These decisions undermine the Government's argument that, at least as applied to noncitizens, the Constitution necessarily stops where *de jure* sovereignty ends. . . .

Fundamental questions regarding the Constitution's geographic scope first arose at the dawn of the 20th century when the Nation acquired noncontiguous Territories: Puerto Rico, Guam, and the Philippines—ceded to the United States by Spain at the conclusion of the Spanish-American War—and Hawaii—annexed by the United States in 1898. At this point Congress chose to discontinue its previous practice of extending constitutional rights to the territories by statute.

In a series of opinions later known as the *Insular Cases*, the Court addressed whether the Constitution, by its own force, applies in any territory that is not a State. The Court held that the Constitution has independent force in these territories, a force not contingent upon acts of legislative grace. Yet it took note of the difficulties inherent in that position.

Prior to their cession to the United States, the former Spanish colonies operated under a civil-law system, without experience in the various aspects of the Anglo-American legal tradition, for instance the use of grand and petit juries. At least with regard to the Philippines, a complete transformation of the prevailing legal culture would have been not only disruptive but also unnecessary, as the United States intended to grant independence to that Territory. The Court thus was reluctant to risk the uncertainty and instability that could result from a rule that displaced altogether the existing legal systems in these newly acquired Territories.

These considerations resulted in the doctrine of territorial incorporation, under which the Constitution applies in full in incorporated Territories surely destined for statehood but only in part in unincorporated Territories. . . .

Practical considerations weighed heavily as well in *Johnson v. Eisentrager*, 339 U.S. 763 (1950), where the Court addressed whether *habeas corpus* jurisdiction extended to enemy aliens who had been convicted of violating the laws of war. The prisoners were detained at Landsberg Prison in Germany during the Allied Powers' postwar occupation. The Court stressed the difficulties of ordering the Government to produce the prisoners in a *habeas corpus* proceeding. It "would require allocation of shipping space, guarding personnel, billeting and rations" and would damage the prestige of military commanders at a sensitive time. In considering these factors the Court sought to balance the constraints of military occupation with constitutional necessities.

True, the Court in *Eisentrager* denied access to the writ, and it noted the prisoners "at no relevant time were within any territory over which the United States is sovereign, and [that] the scenes of their offense, their capture, their trial and their punishment were all beyond the territorial jurisdiction of any court of the United States." The Government seizes upon this language as proof positive that the *Eisentrager* Court adopted a formalistic, sovereignty-based test for determining the reach of the Suspension Clause. We reject this reading for three reasons.

First, we do not accept the idea that the above-quoted passage from *Eisentrager* is the only authoritative language in the opinion and that all the rest is *dicta*.

Second, because the United States lacked both *de jure* sovereignty and plenary control over Landsberg Prison, it is far from clear that the *Eisentrager* Court used the term sovereignty only in the narrow technical sense and not to connote the degree of control the military asserted over the facility. . . .

Third, if the Government's reading of *Eisentrager* were correct, the opinion would have marked not only a change in, but a complete repudiation of, the *Insular Cases'* functional approach to questions of extraterritoriality. We cannot accept the Government's view. Nothing in *Eisentrager* says that *de jure* sovereignty is or has ever been the only relevant consideration in determining the geographic reach of the Constitution or of *habeas corpus*. Were that the case, there would be considerable tension between *Eisentrager*, on the one hand, and the *Insular Cases*, on the other. Our cases need not be read to conflict in this manner. A constricted reading of *Eisentrager* overlooks what we see as a common thread uniting the *Insular Cases* [and] *Eisentrager*; the idea that questions of extraterritoriality turn on objective factors and practical concerns, not formalism.

The Government's formal sovereignty-based test raises troubling separation-of-powers concerns as well. The political history of Guantanamo illustrates the deficiencies of this approach. The United States has maintained complete and uninterrupted control of the bay for over 100 years. At the close of the Spanish-American War, Spain ceded control over the entire island of Cuba to the United States and specifically "relinquishe[d] all claim[s] of sovereignty . . . and title." See Treaty of Paris, Dec. 10, 1898. From the date the treaty with Spain was signed until the Cuban Republic was established on May 20, 1902, the United States governed the territory "in trust" for the benefit of the Cuban people. And although it recognized, by entering into the 1903 Lease Agreement, that Cuba retained "ultimate sovereignty" over Guantanamo, the United States continued to maintain the same plenary control it had enjoyed since 1898. . . .

The Constitution grants Congress and the President the power to acquire, dispose of, and govern territory, not the power to decide when and where its terms apply. Even when the United States acts outside its borders, its powers are not "absolute and unlimited" but are subject "to such restrictions as are expressed in the Constitution." *Murphy v. Ramsey*, 114 U.S. 15 (1885). . . .

As we recognized in *Rasul*, the outlines of a framework for determining the reach of the Suspension Clause are suggested by the factors the Court relied upon in *Eisentrager*. In addition to the practical concerns discussed above, the *Eisentrager* Court found relevant that each petitioner: "(a) is an enemy alien; (b) has never been or resided in the United States; (c) was captured outside of our territory and there held in military custody as a prisoner of war; (d) was tried and convicted by a Military Commission sitting outside the United States; (e) for offenses against laws of war committed outside the United States; (f) and is at all times imprisoned outside the United States." Based on this language from *Eisentrager*, and the reasoning in our other extra-territoriality opinions, we conclude that at least three factors are relevant in determining the reach of the Suspension Clause: (1) the citizenship and status of the detainee and the adequacy of the process through which that status determination was made; (2) the nature of the sites where apprehension and then detention took place; and (3) the practical obstacles inherent in resolving the prisoner's entitlement to the writ.

Applying this framework, we note at the onset that the status of these detainees is a matter of dispute. The petitioners, like those in *Eisentrager*, are not American citizens. But the petitioners in *Eisentrager* did not contest, it seems, the Court's assertion that they were "enemy alien[s]." In the instant cases, by contrast, the detainees deny they are enemy combatants. They have been afforded some process in CSRT proceedings to determine their status; but, unlike in *Eisentrager*, there has been no trial by military commission for violations of the laws of war. The difference is not trivial. The records from the *Eisentrager* trials suggest that, well before the petitioners brought their case to this Court, there had been a rigorous adversarial process to test the legality of their detention. The *Eisentrager* petitioners were charged by a bill of particulars that made detailed factual allegations against them. To rebut the accusations, they were entitled to representation by counsel, allowed to introduce evidence on their own behalf, and permitted to cross-examine the prosecution's witnesses.

In comparison the procedural protections afforded to the detainees in the CSRT hearings are far more limited, and, we conclude, fall well short of the procedures and adversarial mechanisms that would eliminate the need for *habeas corpus* review. Although the detainee is assigned a "Personal Representative" to assist him during CSRT proceedings, the Secretary of the Navy's memorandum makes clear that person is not the detainee's lawyer or even his "advocate." The Government's evidence is accorded a presumption of validity. The detainee is allowed to present "reasonably available" evidence, but his ability to rebut the Government's evidence against him is limited by the circumstances of his confinement and his lack of counsel at this stage. And although the detainee can seek review of his status determination in the Court of Appeals, that review process cannot cure all defects in the earlier proceedings.

As to the second factor relevant to this analysis, the detainees here are similarly situated to the *Eisentrager* petitioners in that the sites of their apprehension and detention are technically outside the sovereign territory of the United States. . . .

As to the third factor, we recognize, as the Court did in *Eisentrager*, that there are costs to holding the Suspension Clause applicable in a case of military detention abroad. *Habeas corpus* proceedings may require expenditure of funds by the Government and may divert the attention of military personnel from other pressing tasks. While we are sensitive to these concerns, we do not find them dispositive. Compliance with any judicial process requires some incremental expenditure of resources. Yet civilian courts and the Armed Forces have functioned alongside each other at various points in our history. . . .

We hold that Art. I, Sec. 9, cl. 2, of the Constitution has full effect at Guantanamo Bay. If the privilege of *habeas corpus* is to be denied to the detainees now before us, Congress must act in accordance with the requirements of the Suspension Clause. The MCA does not purport to be a formal suspension of the writ; and the Government, in its submissions to us, has not argued that it is. Petitioners, therefore, are entitled to the privilege of *habeas corpus* to challenge the legality of their detention.

In light of this holding the question becomes whether the statute stripping jurisdiction to issue the writ avoids the Suspension Clause mandate because Congress has provided adequate substitute procedures for *habeas corpus*. The Government submits there has been compliance with the Suspension Clause because the DTA review process in the Court of Appeals provides an adequate substitute. Congress has granted that court jurisdiction to consider "(i) whether the status determination of the [CSRT] . . . was consistent with the standards and procedures specified by the Secretary of Defense . . . and (ii) to the extent the Constitution and laws of the United States are applicable, whether the use of such standards and procedures to make the determination is consistent with the Constitution and laws of the United States." . . .

Our case law does not contain extensive discussion of standards defining suspension of the writ or of circumstances under which suspension has occurred. This simply confirms the care Congress has taken throughout our Nation's history to preserve the writ and its function. Indeed, most of the major legislative enactments pertaining to *habeas corpus* have acted not to contract the writ's protection but to expand it or to hasten resolution of prisoners' claims.

We do not endeavor to offer a comprehensive summary of the requisites for an adequate substitute for *habeas corpus*. We do consider it uncontroversial, however, that the privilege of *habeas corpus* entitles the prisoner to a meaningful opportunity to demonstrate that he is being held pursuant to "the erroneous application or interpretation" of relevant law. And the *habeas* court must have the power to order the conditional release of an individual unlawfully detained—though release need not be the exclusive remedy and is not the appropriate one in every case in which the writ is granted. . . .

[W]here relief is sought from a sentence that resulted from the judgment of a court of record, as was the case in *Watkins* and indeed in most federal *habeas* cases, considerable deference is owed to the court that ordered confinement. . . .

Where a person is detained by executive order, rather than, say, after being tried and convicted in a court, the need for collateral review is most pressing. A criminal conviction in the usual course occurs after a judicial hearing before a tribunal disinterested in the outcome and committed to procedures designed to ensure its own independence. These dynamics are not inherent in executive detention orders or executive review procedures. In this context the need for *habeas corpus* is more urgent. The intended duration of the detention and the reasons for it bear upon the precise scope of the inquiry. *Habeas corpus* proceedings need not resemble a criminal trial, even when the detention is by executive order. But the writ must be effective. The *habeas* court must have sufficient authority to conduct a meaningful review of both the cause for detention and the Executive's power to detain.

To determine the necessary scope of *habeas corpus* review, therefore, we must assess the CSRT process, the mechanism through which petitioners' designation as enemy combatants became final. Whether one characterizes the CSRT process as direct review of the Executive's battlefield determination

that the detainee is an enemy combatant—as the parties have and as we do—
or as the first step in the collateral review of a battlefield determination
makes no difference in a proper analysis of whether the procedures Congress
put in place are an adequate substitute for *habeas corpus*. What matters is the
sum total of procedural protections afforded to the detainee at all stages, direct
and collateral. Petitioners identify what they see as myriad deficiencies in the
CSRTs. The most relevant for our purposes are the constraints upon the
detainee's ability to rebut the factual basis for the Government's assertion that
he is an enemy combatant. As already noted, at the CSRT stage the detainee
has limited means to find or present evidence to challenge the Government's
case against him. He does not have the assistance of counsel and may not be
aware of the most critical allegations that the Government relied upon to
order his detention. The detainee can confront witnesses that testify during
the CSRT proceedings. But given that there are in effect no limits on the
admission of hearsay evidence—the only requirement is that the tribunal
deem the evidence "relevant and helpful"—the detainee's opportunity to
question witnesses is likely to be more theoretical than real. . . .

Even if we were to assume that the CSRTs satisfy due process standards,
it would not end our inquiry. *Habeas corpus* is a collateral process that exists, in
Justice HOLMES' words, to "cu[t] through all forms and g[o] to the very tissue
of the structure. It comes in from the outside, not in subordination to the proceedings, and although every form may have been preserved opens the inquiry
whether they have been more than an empty shell." *Frank v. Mangum*, 237 U.S.
309 (1915). Even when the procedures authorizing detention are structurally
sound, the Suspension Clause remains applicable and the writ relevant. . . .

Although we make no judgment as to whether the CSRTs, as currently
constituted, satisfy due process standards, we agree with petitioners that, even
when all the parties involved in this process act with diligence and in good
faith, there is considerable risk of error in the tribunal's findings of fact. And
given that the consequence of error may be detention of persons for the
duration of hostilities that may last a generation or more, this is a risk too
significant to ignore.

For the writ of *habeas corpus*, or its substitute, to function as an effective
and proper remedy in this context, the court that conducts the *habeas* proceeding must have the means to correct errors that occurred during the CSRT
proceedings. This includes some authority to assess the sufficiency of the
Government's evidence against the detainee. It also must have the authority
to admit and consider relevant exculpatory evidence that was not introduced
during the earlier proceeding. Federal *habeas* petitioners long have had the
means to supplement the record on review, even in the post conviction *habeas*
setting. Here that opportunity is constitutionally required.

Consistent with the historic function and province of the writ, *habeas
corpus* review may be more circumscribed if the underlying detention proceedings are more thorough than they were here. In two *habeas* cases involving enemy aliens tried for war crimes, *In re Yamashita*, 327 U.S. 1 (1946), and
Ex parte Quirin, 317 U.S. 1 (1942), for example, this Court limited its review
to determining whether the Executive had legal authority to try the petitioners by military commission. We need not revisit these cases, however. For
on their own terms, the proceedings in *Yamashita* and *Quirin*, like those in
Eisentrager, had an adversarial structure that is lacking here.

The extent of the showing required of the Government in these cases is
a matter to be determined. We need not explore it further at this stage. We

do hold that when the judicial power to issue *habeas corpus* properly is invoked the judicial officer must have adequate authority to make a determination in light of the relevant law and facts and to formulate and issue appropriate orders for relief, including, if necessary, an order directing the prisoner's release.

We now consider whether the DTA allows the Court of Appeals to conduct a proceeding meeting these standards. . . .

The DTA does not explicitly empower the Court of Appeals to order the applicant in a DTA review proceeding released should the court find that the standards and procedures used at his CSRT hearing were insufficient to justify detention. This is troubling. Yet, for present purposes, we can assume congressional silence permits a constitutionally required remedy. In that case it would be possible to hold that a remedy of release is impliedly provided for. . . .

The absence of a release remedy and specific language allowing AUMF challenges are not the only constitutional infirmities from which the statute potentially suffers, however. The more difficult question is whether the DTA permits the Court of Appeals to make requisite findings of fact. The DTA enables petitioners to request "review" of their CSRT determination in the Court of Appeals, but the "Scope of Review" provision confines the Court of Appeals' role to reviewing whether the CSRT followed the "standards and procedures" issued by the Department of Defense and assessing whether those "standards and procedures" are lawful. Among these standards is "the requirement that the conclusion of the Tribunal be supported by a preponderance of the evidence . . . allowing a rebuttable presumption in favor of the Government's evidence."

Assuming the DTA can be construed to allow the Court of Appeals to review or correct the CSRT's factual determinations, as opposed to merely certifying that the tribunal applied the correct standard of proof, we see no way to construe the statute to allow what is also constitutionally required in this context: an opportunity for the detainee to present relevant exculpatory evidence that was not made part of the record in the earlier proceedings.

On its face the statute allows the Court of Appeals to consider no evidence outside the CSRT record. In the parallel litigation, however, the Court of Appeals determined that the DTA allows it to order the production of all "'reasonably available information in the possession of the U.S. Government bearing on the issue of whether the detainee meets the criteria to be designated as an enemy combatant,'" regardless of whether this evidence was put before the CSRT. For present purposes, we can assume that the Court of Appeals was correct that the DTA allows introduction and consideration of relevant exculpatory evidence that was "reasonably available" to the Government at the time of the CSRT but not made part of the record. Even so, the DTA review proceeding falls short of being a constitutionally adequate substitute, for the detainee still would have no opportunity to present evidence discovered after the CSRT proceedings concluded.

Under the DTA the Court of Appeals has the power to review CSRT determinations by assessing the legality of standards and procedures. This implies the power to inquire into what happened at the CSRT hearing and, perhaps, to remedy certain deficiencies in that proceeding. But should the Court of Appeals determine that the CSRT followed appropriate and lawful standards and procedures, it will have reached the limits of its jurisdiction. There is no language in the DTA that can be construed to allow the Court of Appeals to admit and consider newly discovered evidence that could not have been made part of the CSRT record because it was unavailable to either the Government or the detainee when the CSRT made its findings. This evidence, however, may be critical to the detainee's argument that he is not an enemy combatant and there is no cause to detain him. . . .

By foreclosing consideration of evidence not presented or reasonably available to the detainee at the CSRT proceedings, the DTA disadvantages the detainee by limiting the scope of collateral review to a record that may not be accurate or complete. In other contexts, e.g., in post-trial *habeas* cases where the prisoner already has had a full and fair opportunity to develop the factual predicate of his claims, similar limitations on the scope of *habeas* review may be appropriate. In this context, however, where the underlying detention proceedings lack the necessary adversarial character, the detainee cannot be held responsible for all deficiencies in the record. . . .

We do not imply DTA review would be a constitutionally sufficient replacement for *habeas corpus* but for these limitations on the detainee's ability to present exculpatory evidence. For even if it were possible, as a textual matter, to read into the statute each of the necessary procedures we have identified, we could not overlook the cumulative effect of our doing so. To hold that the detainees at Guantanamo may, under the DTA, challenge the President's legal authority to detain them, contest the CSRT's findings of fact, supplement the record on review with exculpatory evidence, and request an order of release would come close to reinstating the *habeas corpus* process Congress sought to deny them. The language of the statute, read in light of Congress' reasons for enacting it, cannot bear this interpretation. Petitioners have met their burden of establishing that the DTA review process is, on its face, an inadequate substitute for *habeas corpus*. . . .

Although we hold that the DTA is not an adequate and effective substitute for *habeas corpus*, it does not follow that a *habeas corpus* court may disregard the dangers the detention in these cases was intended to prevent. [T]he Suspension Clause does not resist innovation in the field of *habeas corpus*. Certain accommodations can be made to reduce the burden *habeas corpus* proceedings will place on the military without impermissibly diluting the protections of the writ. . . .

In considering both the procedural and substantive standards used to impose detention to prevent acts of terrorism, proper deference must be accorded to the political branches. See *United States v. Curtiss-Wright Export Corp.*, 299 U.S. 304 (1936). Unlike the President and some designated Members of Congress, neither the Members of this Court nor most federal judges begin the day with briefings that may describe new and serious threats to our Nation and its people. The law must accord the Executive substantial authority to apprehend and detain those who pose a real danger to our security. . . .

It bears repeating that our opinion does not address the content of the law that governs petitioners' detention. That is a matter yet to be determined. We hold that petitioners may invoke the fundamental procedural protections of *habeas corpus*. The laws and Constitution are designed to survive, and remain in force, in extraordinary times. Liberty and security can be reconciled; and in our system they are reconciled within the framework of the law. The Framers decided that *habeas corpus*, a right of first importance, must be a part of that framework, a part of that law.

The determination by the Court of Appeals that the Suspension Clause and its protections are inapplicable to petitioners was in error. The judgment of the Court of Appeals is reversed. The cases are remanded to the Court of

Appeals with instructions that it remand the cases to the District Court for proceedings consistent with this opinion. It is so ordered.

☐ *Justice SOUTER, with whom Justice GINSBURG and Justice BREYER join, concurring.*

Four years ago, this Court in *Rasul v. Bush*, 542 U.S. 466 (2004) held that statutory *habeas* jurisdiction extended to claims of foreign nationals imprisoned by the United States at Guantanamo Bay, "to determine the legality of the Executive's potentially indefinite detention" of them. Subsequent legislation eliminated the statutory *habeas* jurisdiction over these claims, so that now there must be constitutionally based jurisdiction or none at all. Justice SCALIA is thus correct that here, for the first time, this Court holds there is (he says "confers") constitutional *habeas* jurisdiction over aliens imprisoned by the military outside an area of *de jure* national sovereignty. But no one who reads the Court's opinion in *Rasul* could seriously doubt that the jurisdictional question must be answered the same way in purely constitutional cases, given the Court's reliance on the historical background of *habeas* generally in answering the statutory question.

Indeed, the Court in *Rasul* directly answered the very historical question that Justice SCALIA says is dispositive; it wrote that "[a]pplication of the *habeas* statute to persons detained at [Guantanamo] is consistent with the historical reach of the writ of *habeas corpus.*" Justice SCALIA dismisses the statement as *dictum*, but if *dictum* it was, it was *dictum* well considered, and it stated the view of five Members of this Court on the historical scope of the writ. Of course, it takes more than a quotation from *Rasul*, however much on point, to resolve the constitutional issue before us here, which the majority opinion has explored afresh in the detail it deserves. But whether one agrees or disagrees with today's decision, it is no bolt out of the blue.

A second fact insufficiently appreciated by the dissents is the length of the disputed imprisonments, some of the prisoners represented here today having been locked up for six years. Hence the hollow ring when the dissenters suggest that the Court is somehow precipitating the judiciary into reviewing claims that the military (subject to appeal to the Court of Appeals for the District of Columbia Circuit) could handle within some reasonable period of time. . . .

It is in fact the very lapse of four years from the time *Rasul* put everyone on notice that *habeas* process was available to Guantanamo prisoners, and the lapse of six years since some of these prisoners were captured and incarcerated, that stand at odds with the repeated suggestions of the dissenters that these cases should be seen as a judicial victory in a contest for power between the Court and the political branches. The several answers to the charge of triumphalism might start with a basic fact of Anglo-American constitutional history: that the power, first of the Crown and now of the Executive Branch of the United States, is necessarily limited by *habeas corpus* jurisdiction to enquire into the legality of executive detention. And one could explain that in this Court's exercise of responsibility to preserve *habeas corpus* something much more significant is involved than pulling and hauling between the judicial and political branches. Instead, though, it is enough to repeat that some of these petitioners have spent six years behind bars. After six years of sustained executive detentions in Guantanamo, subject to *habeas* jurisdiction but without any actual *habeas* scrutiny, today's decision is no judicial victory, but an act of perseverance in trying to make *habeas* review, and the obligation of the courts to provide it, mean something of value both to prisoners and to the Nation.

☐ *Justice SCALIA, with whom THE CHIEF JUSTICE, Justice THOMAS, and Justice ALITO join, dissenting.*

Today, for the first time in our Nation's history, the Court confers a constitutional right to *habeas corpus* on alien enemies detained abroad by our military forces in the course of an ongoing war. THE CHIEF JUSTICE's dissent, which I join, shows that the procedures prescribed by Congress in the Detainee Treatment Act provide the essential protections that *habeas corpus* guarantees; there has thus been no suspension of the writ, and no basis exists for judicial intervention beyond what the Act allows. My problem with today's opinion is more fundamental still: The writ of *habeas corpus* does not, and never has, run in favor of aliens abroad; the Suspension Clause thus has no application, and the Court's intervention in this military matter is entirely *ultra vires*.

I shall devote most of what will be a lengthy opinion to the legal errors contained in the opinion of the Court. Contrary to my usual practice, however, I think it appropriate to begin with a description of the disastrous consequences of what the Court has done today.

America is at war with radical Islamists. The enemy began by killing Americans and American allies abroad: 241 at the Marine barracks in Lebanon, 19 at the Khobar Towers in Dhahran, 224 at our embassies in Dar es Salaam and Nairobi, and 17 on the USS Cole in Yemen. On September 11, 2001, the enemy brought the battle to American soil, killing 2,749 at the Twin Towers in New York City, 184 at the Pentagon in Washington, D. C., and 40 in Pennsylvania. It has threatened further attacks against our homeland; one need only walk about buttressed and barricaded Washington, or board a plane anywhere in the country, to know that the threat is a serious one. Our Armed Forces are now in the field against the enemy, in Afghanistan and Iraq.

The game of bait-and-switch that today's opinion plays upon the Nation's Commander in Chief will make the war harder on us. It will almost certainly cause more Americans to be killed. That consequence would be tolerable if necessary to preserve a time-honored legal principle vital to our constitutional Republic. But it is this Court's blatant abandonment of such a principle that produces the decision today. . . .

In the long term, then, the Court's decision today accomplishes little, except perhaps to reduce the well-being of enemy combatants that the Court ostensibly seeks to protect. In the short term, however, the decision is devastating. At least 30 of those prisoners hitherto released from Guantanamo Bay have returned to the battlefield. But others have succeeded in carrying on their atrocities against innocent civilians. In one case, a detainee released from Guantanamo Bay masterminded the kidnapping of two Chinese dam workers, one of whom was later shot to death when used as a human shield against Pakistani commandoes.

These, mind you, were detainees whom the military had concluded were not enemy combatants. Their return to the kill illustrates the incredible difficulty of assessing who is and who is not an enemy combatant in a foreign theater of operations where the environment does not lend itself to rigorous evidence collection. Astoundingly, the Court today raises the bar, requiring military officials to appear before civilian courts and defend their decisions under procedural and evidentiary rules that go beyond what Congress has specified. . . .

And today it is not just the military that the Court elbows aside. A mere two Terms ago in *Hamdan v. Rumsfeld*, 548 U.S. 557 (2006), when the Court held (quite amazingly) that the Detainee Treatment Act of 2005 had not stripped *habeas* jurisdiction over Guantanamo petitioners' claims, four Members of today's five-Justice majority joined an opinion saying the following: "Nothing prevents the President from returning to Congress to seek the authority [for trial by military commission] he believes necessary." . . .

The Suspension Clause of the Constitution provides: "The Privilege of the Writ of *Habeas Corpus* shall not be suspended, unless when in Cases of Rebellion or Invasion the public Safety may require it." Art. I, Sec. 9, cl. 2. As a court of law operating under a written Constitution, our role is to determine whether there is a conflict between that Clause and the Military Commissions Act. A conflict arises only if the Suspension Clause preserves the privilege of the writ for aliens held by the United States military as enemy combatants at the base in Guantanamo Bay, located within the sovereign territory of Cuba.

We have frequently stated that we owe great deference to Congress's view that a law it has passed is constitutional. Indeed, we accord great deference even when the President acts alone in this area.

In light of those principles of deference, the Court's conclusion that "the common law [does not] yiel[d] a definite answer to the questions before us," leaves it no choice but to affirm the Court of Appeals. The writ as preserved in the Constitution could not possibly extend farther than the common law provided when that Clause was written. The Court admits that it cannot determine whether the writ historically extended to aliens held abroad, and it concedes (necessarily) that Guantanamo Bay lies outside the sovereign territory of the United States. Together, these two concessions establish that it is (in the Court's view) perfectly ambiguous whether the common-law writ would have provided a remedy for these petitioners. If that is so, the Court has no basis to strike down the Military Commissions Act, and must leave undisturbed the considered judgment of the coequal branches.

How, then, does the Court weave a clear constitutional prohibition out of pure interpretive equipoise? The Court resorts to "fundamental separation-of-powers principles" to interpret the Suspension Clause. According to the Court, because "the writ of *habeas corpus* is itself an indispensable mechanism for monitoring the separation of powers," the test of its extraterritorial reach "must not be subject to manipulation by those whose power it is designed to restrain."

That approach distorts the nature of the separation of powers and its role in the constitutional structure. The "fundamental separation-of-powers principles" that the Constitution embodies are to be derived not from some judicially imagined matrix, but from the sum total of the individual separation-of-powers provisions that the Constitution sets forth. Only by considering them one-by-one does the full shape of the Constitution's separation-of-powers principles emerge. It is nonsensical to interpret those provisions themselves in light of some general "separation-of-powers principles" dreamed up by the Court. Rather, they must be interpreted to mean what they were understood to mean when the people ratified them. And if the understood scope of the writ of *habeas corpus* was "designed to restrain" (as the Court says) the actions of the Executive, the understood limits upon that scope were (as the Court seems not to grasp) just as much "designed to restrain" the incursions of the Third Branch. "Manipulation" of the territorial reach of the writ by the Judiciary poses just as much a threat to the proper separation of powers as "manipulation" by the Executive. . . .

The Court purports to derive from our precedents a "functional" test for the extraterritorial reach of the writ, which shows that the Military Commissions Act unconstitutionally restricts the scope of *habeas*. That is remarkable because the most pertinent of those precedents, *Johnson v. Eisentrager*, conclusively establishes the opposite. There we were confronted with the claims of 21 Germans held at Landsberg Prison, an American military facility located in the American Zone of occupation in postwar Germany. They had been captured in China, and an American military commission sitting there had convicted them of war crimes—collaborating with the Japanese after Germany's surrender. Like the petitioners here, the Germans claimed that their detentions violated the Constitution and international law, and sought a writ of *habeas corpus*. Writing for the Court, Justice JACKSON held that American courts lacked *habeas* jurisdiction: "We are cited to [sic] no instance where a court, in this or any other country where the writ is known, has issued it on behalf of an alien enemy who, at no relevant time and in no stage of his captivity, has been within its territorial jurisdiction. Nothing in the text of the Constitution extends such a right, nor does anything in our statutes." Justice JACKSON then elaborated on the historical scope of the writ: "The alien, to whom the United States has been traditionally hospitable, has been accorded a generous and ascending scale of rights as he increases his identity with our society. . . . But, in extending constitutional protections beyond the citizenry, the Court has been at pains to point out that it was the alien's presence within its territorial jurisdiction that gave the Judiciary power to act." . . .

Eisentrager thus held—held beyond any doubt—that the Constitution does not ensure habeas for aliens held by the United States in areas over which our Government is not sovereign.

The Court would have us believe that *Eisentrager* rested on "[p]ractical considerations," such as the "difficulties of ordering the Government to produce the prisoners in a *habeas corpus* proceeding." Formal sovereignty, says the Court, is merely one consideration "that bears upon which constitutional guarantees apply" in a given location. This is a sheer rewriting of the case. *Eisentrager* mentioned practical concerns, to be sure—but not for the purpose of determining under what circumstances American courts could issue writs of *habeas corpus* for aliens abroad. It cited them to support its holding that the Constitution does not empower courts to issue writs of *habeas corpus* to aliens abroad in any circumstances. As Justice BLACK accurately said in dissent, "the Court's opinion inescapably denies courts power to afford the least bit of protection for any alien who is subject to our occupation government abroad, even if he is neither enemy nor belligerent and even after peace is officially declared." . . .

What drives today's decision is neither the meaning of the Suspension Clause, nor the principles of our precedents, but rather an inflated notion of judicial supremacy. The Court says that if the extraterritorial applicability of the Suspension Clause turned on formal notions of sovereignty, "it would be possible for the political branches to govern without legal constraint" in areas beyond the sovereign territory of the United States. That cannot be, the Court says, because it is the duty of this Court to say what the law is. . . . Our power "to say what the law is" is circumscribed by the limits of our statutorily and constitutionally conferred jurisdiction. And that is precisely the question in these cases: whether the Constitution confers *habeas* jurisdiction on federal courts to decide petitioners' claims. It is both irrational and arrogant to say that the answer must be yes, because otherwise we would not be supreme.

But so long as there are some places to which *habeas* does not run—so long as the Court's new "functional" test will not be satisfied in every case—

then there will be circumstances in which "it would be possible for the political branches to govern without legal constraint." Or, to put it more impartially, areas in which the legal determinations of the other branches will be (shudder!) supreme. In other words, judicial supremacy is not really assured by the constitutional rule that the Court creates. The gap between rationale and rule leads me to conclude that the Court's ultimate, unexpressed goal is to preserve the power to review the confinement of enemy prisoners held by the Executive anywhere in the world. The "functional" test usefully evades the precedential landmine of *Eisentrager* but is so inherently subjective that it clears a wide path for the Court to traverse in the years to come.

Putting aside the conclusive precedent of *Eisentrager*, it is clear that the original understanding of the Suspension Clause was that *habeas corpus* was not available to aliens abroad.

The Suspension Clause reads: "The Privilege of the Writ of *Habeas Corpus* shall not be suspended, unless when in Cases of Rebellion or Invasion the public Safety may require it." The proper course of constitutional interpretation is to give the text the meaning it was understood to have at the time of its adoption by the people. That course is especially demanded when (as here) the Constitution limits the power of Congress to infringe upon a pre-existing common-law right. The nature of the writ of *habeas corpus* that cannot be suspended must be defined by the common-law writ that was available at the time of the founding.

It is entirely clear that, at English common law, the writ of *habeas corpus* did not extend beyond the sovereign territory of the Crown. To be sure, the writ had an "extraordinary territorial ambit," because it was a so-called "prerogative writ," which, unlike other writs, could extend beyond the realm of England to other places where the Crown was sovereign.

But prerogative writs could not issue to foreign countries, even for British subjects; they were confined to the King's dominions—those areas over which the Crown was sovereign. Thus, the writ has never extended to Scotland, which, although united to England when James I succeeded to the English throne in 1603, was considered a foreign dominion under a different Crown—that of the King of Scotland.

The common-law writ was codified by the *Habeas Corpus* Act of 1679, which "stood alongside Magna Charta and the English Bill of Rights of 1689 as a towering common law lighthouse of liberty—a beacon by which framing lawyers in America consciously steered their course." The writ was established in the Colonies beginning in the 1690's and at least one colony adopted the 1679 Act almost verbatim. Section XI of the Act stated where the writ could run. It "may be directed and run into any county palatine, the cinque-ports, or other privileged places within the kingdom of England, dominion of Wales, or town of Berwick upon Tweed, and the islands of Jersey or Guernsey."

The Act did not extend the writ elsewhere, even though the existence of other places to which British prisoners could be sent was recognized by the Act. . . .

In sum, all available historical evidence points to the conclusion that the writ would not have been available at common law for aliens captured and held outside the sovereign territory of the Crown. . . .

Today the Court warps our Constitution in a way that goes beyond the narrow issue of the reach of the Suspension Clause, invoking judicially brainstormed separation-of-powers principles to establish a manipulable "functional" test for the extraterritorial reach of *habeas corpus* (and, no doubt, for the extraterritorial reach of other constitutional protections as well). It blatantly misdescribes important precedents, most conspicuously Justice JACKSON's opinion for the Court in *Johnson v. Eisentrager*. It breaks a chain of precedent as old as the common law that prohibits judicial inquiry into detentions of aliens abroad absent statutory authorization. And, most tragically, it sets our military commanders the impossible task of proving to a civilian court, under whatever standards this Court devises in the future, that evidence supports the confinement of each and every enemy prisoner.

The Nation will live to regret what the Court has done today. I dissent.

☐ *CHIEF JUSTICE ROBERTS, with whom Justice SCALIA, Justice THOMAS, and Justice ALITO join, dissenting.*

Today the Court strikes down as inadequate the most generous set of procedural protections ever afforded aliens detained by this country as enemy combatants. The political branches crafted these procedures amidst an ongoing military conflict, after much careful investigation and thorough debate. The Court rejects them today out of hand, without bothering to say what due process rights the detainees possess, without explaining how the statute fails to vindicate those rights, and before a single petitioner has even attempted to avail himself of the law's operation. And to what effect? The majority merely replaces a review system designed by the people's representatives with a set of shapeless procedures to be defined by federal courts at some future date. One cannot help but think, after surveying the modest practical results of the majority's ambitious opinion, that this decision is not really about the detainees at all, but about control of federal policy regarding enemy combatants.

The majority is adamant that the Guantanamo detainees are entitled to the protections of *habeas corpus*—its opinion begins by deciding that question. I regard the issue as a difficult one, primarily because of the unique and unusual jurisdictional status of Guantanamo Bay. I nonetheless agree with Justice SCALIA's analysis of our precedents and the pertinent history of the writ, and accordingly join his dissent. The important point for me, however, is that the Court should have resolved these cases on other grounds. *Habeas* is most fundamentally a procedural right, a mechanism for contesting the legality of executive detention. The critical threshold question in these cases, prior to any inquiry about the writ's scope, is whether the system the political branches designed protects whatever rights the detainees may possess. If so, there is no need for any additional process, whether called "*habeas*" or something else. . . .

I believe the system the political branches constructed adequately protects any constitutional rights aliens captured abroad and detained as enemy combatants may enjoy. I therefore would dismiss these cases on that ground. With all respect for the contrary views of the majority, I must dissent. . . .

■ In Comparative Perspective

The Supreme Court of Canada's 2008 Ruling on the Rights of Detainees

In 2007, the Supreme Court of Canada struck down a law authorizing the government to detain foreign-born terrorist suspects indefinitely in *R. v. Hape*, [2007] 2 S.C.R. 292, 2007 S.C.C. 26. Subsequently, in 2008 the Court held that the U.S. "regime" for detaining and interrogating a teenage Canadian in Guantanamo Bay since 2002 amounted to "a clear violation of fundamental human rights protected by international law," in *Canada v. Khadr*, 2008 SCC 28. The Court also ordered Canadian officials to disclose the records of interrogation of Omar Ahmed Khadr for the defense lawyers' use in defending him against war crimes charges made by the U.S. military. Khadr was captured in Afghanistan when he was fifteen years old and subsequently held in Guantanamo Bay.

The decision's conclusion that the detention and questioning of Khadr was illegal rested on the rulings of the U.S. Supreme Court in *Rasul v. Bush*, 542 U.S. 466 (2004) (excerpted in Vol. 1, Ch. 3) and *Hamdan v. Rumsfeld*, 126 S.Ct. 2749 (2006) (excerpted in Vol. 1, Ch. 3). The court did not mention the developments following *Hamdan*, and Congress's passage of the Military Commissions Act of 2006. In the Court's words, "The process in place at the time Canadian officials interviewed Mr. Khadr and passed the fruits of the interviews on to U.S. officials has been found by the United States Supreme Court to violate U.S. domestic law and international human rights obligations to which Canada is a party." Because of that, the Canadian security agents who interrogated Khadr violated the Canadian Charter of Rights and Freedoms. Hence, it ordered the disclosure to defense counsel of all documents in Canadian government hands bearing on the war crimes charges that Khadr faces before a U.S. military commission. The remedy under the Charter, however, the court ruled, does not require that Khadr have access to completely unedited versions of the documents and interrogations. Unredacted copies of those materials, the court noted, had already been turned over to a Canadian judge. And that judge should now review the material and "decide which documents fall within the scope of the disclosure obligation." In doing so, the court stressed that what was ultimately disclosed depended on a "balancing of national security and other considerations" under Canada's laws of evidence.

■ THE DEVELOPMENT OF LAW

Electronic Surveillance and the Foreign Intelligence Surveillance Court

In 2008, Congress revised the Foreign Intelligence Surveillance Act, which was created to issue warrants for domestic spying cases related to espionage and terrorism. (See the related boxes in Vol. 1, Ch.3, and Vol. 2, Ch. 7.) It did so because of controversies over the Bush administration's bypassing the court and conducting warrantless searches of electronic communications. The major provisions of the law, which will expire in 2012, provide the following:

1. Telecommunication companies that assisted the government in warrantless surveillance on the Internet after the September 11, 2001, terrorist attacks are shielded from lawsuits for invasion of privacy.
2. Procedures for monitoring telephone calls and e-mails of foreigners must be approved by the Foreign Intelligence Surveillance Court and the government's surveillance on U.S. citizens, including those abroad, require that court's approval of individual warrants.
3. The government is prohibited from targeting a foreigner in order to secretly eavesdrop on a U.S. citizen's telephone calls and e-mails without court approval.
4. The government may conduct emergency eavesdropping without a court-approved warrant but must seek approval within one week.

4

THE PRESIDENT AS
CHIEF EXECUTIVE IN
DOMESTIC AFFAIRS

B | *Appointment and Removal Powers*

In its 2009–2010 term, the Roberts Court considered whether Congress unconstitutionally delegated to the executive branch by creating the Public Company Accounting Oversight Board (PCAOB) and delegated powers of appointment and removal of its members to the Securities and Exchange Commission (SEC), in *Free Enterprise Fund v. Public Company Accounting Oversight Board* (No. 08-861). Congress enacted the Sarbanes-Oxley Act of 2002 in response to highly publicized accounting scandals. The law established a five-member PCAOB and gave it the power to regulate audits of public companies. PCAOB members are appointed by the SEC and are only removable by the SEC for cause. The Free Enterprise Fund (FEF) sought a declaratory judgment that the provisions of the law were unconstitutional in violating the separation of powers, the Appointments Clause, and the nondelegation doctrine. A federal district court upheld the law because PCAOB members are inferior officers and Congress provided intelligible standards for the agency to follow. The district noted that the Appointments Clause would be satisfied if PCAOB members were selected by the SEC chairman alone, but held the FEF lacked standing to sue on that issue. The court denied the FEF's petition for a rehearing and the FEF appealed to the Supreme Court, which granted review.

While not overturning the Sarbanes-Oxley Act, passed in response to the accounting scandals of Enron and Worldcom, a bare majority ruled that the provision for removing members of the Public Company Accounting Oversight Board (PCAOB), which oversees firms that audit publicly traded companies, violated the separation of powers by giving executive branch responsibility to officials beyond the president's control to members of the Securities and Exchange Commission (SEC), an independent commission whose members may not be removed by the president except for "good cause" or "inefficiency, neglect of duty, or malfeasance in office," relying on *Humphrey's Executor v. United States*, 295 U.S. 602 (1935) (excerpted in Vol. I, Ch. 4). Writing for the majority in *Free Enterprise Fund v. Public Company Accounting Oversight Board*, 130 S.Ct. 3138 (2010), Chief Justice Roberts distinguished prior decisions limiting the president's power of removal of subordinates by focusing on the fact that members of the PCAOB could be removed for "good cause" by the SEC but the SEC's members could not be removed by the president. In the majority's view that provision violated Article II's vesting of the executive power in the president. Justices Stevens, Ginsburg, Breyer, and Sotomayor dissented.

D | *Accountability and Immunities*

In its 2008–2009 term, the Court considered the matter of qualified immunity from lawsuits against members of the president's cabinet and other high federal officials for alleged constitutional violations. The case, *Ashcroft v. Iqbal*, 129 S.Ct. 1937 (2009) stems from a suit against former Attorney General John D. Ashcroft and current Federal Bureau of Investigation (FBI) director Robert Mueller, among others, based on federal actions during the roundup and detention of men of Arab descent or identified with the Muslim faith, in the aftermath of the terrorists' attacks on September 11, 2001. Javiad Iqbal and others were detained by the FBI and held in a maximum-security facility, where he alleged that his constitutional rights were violated based on unlawful racial and religious discrimination. A federal district granted most of the defendants' motions to dismiss the suit based on their claims of qualified immunity. That decision was for the most part affirmed by the Court of Appeals for the Second Circuit, which reasoned that government officials are entitled to qualified immunity if they didn't clearly violate the law, or if they objectively and reasonably believed their actions did not violate the law. Subsequently, Iqbal was cleared of any alleged involvement in terrorism, but pled guilty to Social Security fraud and, after a year in prison, was deported to Pakistan. On appeal the Supreme Court split five to four in holding that high government officials cannot be held responsible for actions of subordinates and are liable for only their own personal misconduct. Writing for the majority, Justice Kennedy in this case determined personal liability for alleged torture had not been established. Justices Souter and Breyer filed dissenting opinions, which Justices Stevens and Ginsburg joined.

7

THE STATES AND
AMERICAN FEDERALISM

A | States' Power over Commerce and Regulation

■ THE DEVELOPMENT OF LAW

Other Rulings on State Regulatory Powers in Alleged Conflict with Federal Legislation

CASE	VOTE	RULING
Rowe v. New Hampshire Motor Transportation Association, 128 S.Ct. 989 (2008)	9:0	Writing for the Court, Justice Breyer held that provisions of the Federal Aviation Administration Authorization Act (FAAAA) pre-

empted Maine's law requiring tobacco shippers to verify that the buyer was of legal age and prohibiting unlicensed tobacco shipments from out of state. Several other states have similar laws aimed at cutting down on the delivery of cigarettes bought over the Internet.

Wyeth v. Levine, 129 S.Ct.   6:3   Writing for the Court, Justice
1187 (2009)   Stevens held that the Food, Drug,
and Cosmetic Act (FDCA) label-
ing requirements for drugs do not preempt state court tort claims against
drug manufacturers for failure to fully warn about potential harms of the
usage of a drug. Chief Justice Roberts and Justices Scalia and Alito dissented.

Cuomo v. Clearing House   5:4   Writing for the Court, Justice
Association, 129 S.Ct. 2710   Scalia held that under the 1864
(2009)   National Bank Act, "visitorial"
powers preempt a state attorney
from issuing executive subpoenas in order to enforce state-free lending laws
against national banks, though not the state's power of law enforcement. Justice Thomas issued a separate opinion, in part concurring and dissenting, which
was joined by Chief Justice Roberts and Justices Kennedy and Alito.

Preston v. Ferrer, 128 S.Ct.   8:1   Writing for the Court, Justice
978 (2008)   Ginsburg held that the Federal
Arbitration Act preempts a state
law that would refer a dispute to an administrative agency. Justice Thomas
dissented.

Riegel v. Medtronic, 128 S.Ct.   8:1   Writing for the Court, Chief
999 (2008)   Justice Roberts held that the
Medical Device Amendments
preemption clause overrides state common law claims against producers of
medical devices that were approved by the Food and Drug Administration.
Justice Ginsburg dissented.

Chamber of Commerce of the   7:2   The majority held that the
United States of America v.   National Labor Relations Act as
Brown, 128 S.Ct. 2408 (2008)   amended by the Taft-Hartley Act
of 1947 preempted a California
law that prohibited employers who receive state grants of more than $10,000
per year from using the money "to assist, promote, or deter union organiz-
ing." Writing for the Court, Justice Stevens held that federal law demonstrated a "congressional intent to encourage free debate on issues dividing
labor and management." Justices Ginsburg and Breyer dissented.

Altria Group, Inc. v. Good,   5:4   Writing for a bare majority, Jus-
129 S.Ct. 538 (2008)   tice Stevens held that the Federal
Cigarette Labeling and Advertis-
ing Act, which prohibits states from placing "smoking and health" requirements on cigarette advertisements, does not preempt suits against tobacco
manufacturers for deceptive advertising. The Altria Group was sued under
Maine's Unfair Trade Practices Act for fraudulently advertising that their
"light" cigarettes delivered less tar and nicotine than regular brands. Justice
Stevens emphasized that such suits are "predicated on the duty not to deceive"
and thus are separate from the federal government's regulation of warnings
on cigarette packs. Chief Justice Roberts and Justices Scalia and Alito joined
Justice Thomas' dissent.

■ THE DEVELOPMENT OF LAW

Other Rulings on State Regulation of Commerce in the Absence of Federal Legislation

CASE	VOTE	RULING
Department of Revenue of Kentucky v. Davis, 128 S.Ct. 1801 (2008)	7:2	The Court upheld Kentucky's law exempting interest on bonds issued by the state from taxation, while permitting the taxing of

interest on out-of-state bonds. Writing for the Court, Justice Souter held that while the dormant commerce clause bars "economic protectionism," regulations that benefit in-state economic interests by burdening out-of-state competitors, here the state's interests in financing its own civic responsibilities and state autonomy, outweighed the claim of economic protectionism. Justice Stevens and Thomas filed concurring opinions, while Justices Kennedy and Alito dissented, and Chief Justice Roberts and Justice Scalia filed separate opinions concurring in part.

B | *The Tenth and Eleventh Amendments and the States*

In its 2010–2011 term, the Court will consider whether an individual may sue a state or state official in his or her official capacity for damages for violations of the Religious Land Use and Institutionalized Persons Act, in *Sossamon v. Texas* (No. 08-1438). Harvey Sossamon alleged that the state denied the use of a prison chapel and access to all worship services while on cell restriction when he was a state inmate in Texas. Subsequently, Sossaman filed suit pursuant to the Religious Land Use and Institutionalized Persons Act (RLUIPA), seeking both injunctive relief and damages against the state officers in their official capacity. Texas admitted that no one had permission to use the prison chapel for worship, and admitted to denying Sossaman access to worship services during cell restriction. A federal district court granted summary judgment to Texas, in holding that the Eleventh Amendment barred Sossaman's claim for damages against the state officials. The Court of Appeals for the Fifth Circuit affirmed, reasoning that the spending clause did not abrogate the Eleventh Amendment immunity, since the state officials were not parties to the contract for services.

8

REPRESENTATIVE
GOVERNMENT,
VOTING RIGHTS, AND
ELECTORAL POLITICS

A | *Representative Government and the Franchise*

■ THE DEVELOPMENT OF LAW

Other Rulings Interpreting the Voting Rights Act

CASE	VOTE	RULING
Northwest Austin Municipal Utility District No. 1 v. Holder, 129 S.Ct. 2504 (2009)	8:1	Although declining to declare unconstitutional the 2006 extension of Section 5 of the voting Rights Act of 1965, which re-

quires Department of Justice preclearance of changes in election procedures in southern states and some counties in Alaska, California, Florida, Michigan, and elsewhere that once discriminated against minority voters, the Court held that a Texas utility district, which does not register voters, could apply

---

for a "bailout" under Section 4 of the law from the required Section 5 pre-clearance review if they could demonstrate that they had not recently engaged in voter discrimination, but also invited further constitutional challenges to law. Writing for the Court, Chief Justice Roberts observed: "more than forty years ago, this Court concluded that 'exceptional conditions' prevailing in certain parts of the country justified extraordinary legislation otherwise un-familiar to our federal system. In part due to the success of that legislation, we are now a very different Nation. Whether conditions continue to justify such legislation is a difficult constitutional question we do not answer today." When extending the Voting Rights Act in 2006, Congress relied on evidence of voter discrimination that was decades old and offered no evidence of the persistence of such discrimination. Dissenting, Justice Clarence Thomas would have struck down Section 5 as unconstitutional, observing:

> The extensive pattern of discrimination that led the Court to pre-viously uphold Section 5 as enforcing the Fifteenth Amendment no longer exists. Covered jurisdictions are not now engaged in a sys-tematic campaign to deny black citizens access to the ballot through intimidation and violence. . . . Punishment for long past sins is not a legitimate basis for imposing a forward-looking preventative mea-sure that has already served its purpose. Those supporting Section 5's reenactment argue that without it these jurisdictions would re-turn to the racially discriminatory practices of thirty and forty years ago. But there is no evidence that public officials stand ready, if given the chance, to again engage in concerted acts of violence, terror, and subterfuge in order to keep minorities from voting. . . . Admitting that a prophylactic law as broad as Section 5 is no longer consti-tutionally justified based on current evidence of discrimination is not a sign of defeat. It is an acknowledgement of victory.

B | *Voting Rights and the Reapportionment Revolution*

In the 2008–2009 term, the Court handed down an important decision interpreting the application of the Voting Rights Act to racial redistrict-ing. In *Bartlett v. Strickland* (2009) (summarized in the box that follows), the Court held that Section 2 of the Voting Rights Act does not require states to redraw voting district lines to allow racial minorities from other districts to cross over in order to vote in a district when the minority group in that district constitutes less than 50 percent of the population.

■ THE DEVELOPMENT OF LAW

Other Post–Shaw v. Reno Rulings on Racial Gerrymandering

CASE	VOTE	RULING
Bartlett v. Strtickland, 129 S.Ct. 1231 (2009)	5:4	Writing for a plurality, Justice Kennedy held that Section 2 of the Voting Rights Act does not

require states to redraw voting district lines to allow racial minorities from other districts to cross over in order to vote in a district when the minority group in that district constitutes less than 50 percent of the population. In spite of North Carolina's constitutional "whole county" provision prohibiting the general assembly from dividing counties when redrawing legislative districts, in 1991 the legislature redrew House District 18 to include portions of four counties, including Pender County, which at the time was a geographically compact majority-minority voting district. However, when that district was to be redrawn in 2003, the African American population had fallen below 50 percent, and instead of redrawing Pender County whole, the legislature split the district and crossed over portions of other districts. As a result, District 18 African American voting age population was 39.36 percent, whereas if Pender County's district had remained whole it would have had an African American voting age population of 35.33 percent. The rationale was that splitting Pender County gave African American voters the potential to elect a minority group's candidate, while leaving Pender County whole would have violated Section 2 of the Voting Rights Act. Justice Kennedy's words were, "There is an underlying principle of fundamental importance: We must be most cautious before interpreting a statute to require courts to make inquiries based on racial classifications and race-based predictions," though he added that "Racial discrimination and racially polarized voting are not ancient history. . . . Much remains to be done to ensure that citizens of all races have equal opportunity to share and participate in our democratic processes and traditions." By contrast, concurring Justice Thomas, joined by Justice Scalia, contended that the Voting Rights Act does not authorize any claim by minority voters; their influence is diluted in redistricting, no matter the size of the minority. Justices Stevens, Souter, Ginsburg, and Breyer dissented.

C | Campaigns and Elections

In its 2008–2009 term, the Court held that an Idaho law prohibiting pay-roll deductions for "political activities" does not violate the First Amendment by restricting speech in nonpublic forums in *Ysursa v. Pocatello Educational Association*, 129 S.Ct. 1093 (2009) (see The Development of Law box in this section). The Pocatello Educational Association sued the state of Idaho over the Voluntary Contribution Act, arguing that it burdened First Amendment protected "political speech." The term "political activities" in law includes virtually all types of electioneering and spending in support of or against candidates, ballot measures, and political parties. In the district court, the state conceded that all of the challenged provisions were unconstitutional, except for the one that prohibits payroll deductions for "political activities." The district court held that that provision was constitutional as applied to state employees but unconstitutional as applied to private and local government employees. The Court of Appeals for the Ninth Circuit held that the provision as applied to local government employees violated the First Amendment, but the Supreme Court reversed it by a six-to-three vote.

By five-to-four vote in *Davis v. Federal Election Commission*, 128 S.Ct. 2759 (2008), the Court invalidated Section 319, the so-called Millionaires' Amendment to the Bipartisan Campaign Reform Act of 2002 (BCRA), for violating the First and Fifth Amendments. The Millionaires' Amendment provided equalizing advantages to a candidate relying primarily on contributed funds who campaigns against a self-financed candidate. House of Representatives candidate Jack Davis challenged the law in federal district court in anticipation that his personal expenditures would exceed the statutory limitation in an upcoming election. Davis claims that the provision violated his First and Fifth Amendment rights through its disclosure requirements and contribution limitations. Under the law, a candidate for the House who spent more than $350,000 of his or her own money triggered additional reporting requirements and permitted the candidate's opponents to solicit three times the normal limit of $2,300 per contributor and granted greater spending by the opponent's party in behalf of the candidate. Writing for the majority, Justice Alito held that the provisions forced self-financed candidates "to choose between the right to engage in unfettered political speech and subjection to discriminatory fund raising levels," and that "the resulting drag on First Amendment right" was unconstitutional. Justices Stevens and Ginsburg issued separate opinions, in part concurring and dissenting, which Justices Souter and Breyer joined. The decision invites further challenges to state laws, such as Arizona's, North Carolina's, and Maine's, that penalize private funding of elections and promote public funding of campaigns.

In its 2007–2008 term, another sharply fragmented Court, however, upheld by a six-to-three vote Indiana's law requiring voters to produce a photo identification before casting a ballot in an election. Writing for a plurality and delivering the opinion for the Court in *Crawford v. Marion County Election Board* (excerpted below), Justice Stevens rejected a Fourteenth Amendment and Voting Rights Act challenge to the law, based on its discriminatory effect on the poor, the elderly, and the disabled. Justice Scalia, joined by Justices Thomas and Alito, filed a concurring opinion. Justices Souter and Breyer filed separate dissenting opinions; Justice Ginsburg joined the former's dissent.

In its 2008–2009 term, the Roberts Court declined to decide but instead chose to carry over to its 2009–2010 term *Citizens United v. Federal Election Commission* for reargument. The case involved a challenge to the applilcation of the so-called McCain-Feingold campaign finance reform act, the Bipartisan Campaign Reform Act of 2002 (BCRA). That law was challenged in *McConnell v. Federal Election Commission*, 540 U.S. 93 (2003) (excerpted in Vol. 1, Ch. 3) and sharply divided the Rehnquist Court. At issue in *Citizens United* was whether a conservative group's distribution of a ninety-minute political film called *Hillary: The Movie*, attacking Senator Hillary Clinton's bid for the presidency in 2008, ran afoul of the BCRA or is protected by the First Amendment. A bare majority of the Roberts Court overturned two precedents, including a portion of *McConnell*, in a major ruling holding that the First Amendment protects corporations' direct expenditures for candidates for federal office, in *Citizens United v. Federal Election Commission* (2010) (excerpted below).

In its 2009–2010 term, the Roberts Court also held, in *Doe v. Reed*, 130 S.Ct. 486 (2010), that the First Amendment does not necessarily bar the required disclosure of the names of those who sign petitions for state referendums. In 2009, a new state law expanded the rights of same-sex partners, and some Washington citizens decided to file a referendum to repeal the law. The Washington Public Records Act required the public release of names of those who signed the petition. Signatories of the referendum petition, afraid of reprisal, sought to enjoin the release of their identities and contended that their release violated the First Amendment. A federal district court held that the First Amendment granted a right to anonymity, but the Court of Appeals for the Ninth Circuit reversed, holding that there was no absolute right to anonymity under the First Amendment. Although the Court agreed with the appellate court, writing for the majority, Chief Justice Roberts ruled that there might be in this case an exception, since disclosure might lead to harassment of signatories, and therefore the First Amendment might grant protection. Thus, the case was remanded for consideration on narrower First Amendment analysis. Justice Thomas dissented.

Crawford v. Marion County Election Board
128 S.Ct. 1610 (2008)

The Roberts Court weighed into the controversy between Republicans and Democrats over requiring government-issued photo identification as a precondition for voting in elections. In 2005 the Republican-controlled legislature in Indiana enacted a law requiring voters to provide a photo identification before casting a ballot on the ground that it counters voter fraud and political corruption. Besides Indiana, six other states—Florida, Georgia, Hawaii, Louisiana, Michigan, and South Dakota—have similar laws, and two dozen other states were considering such legislation. Democrats immediately challenged the law for disadvantaging the poor, the elderly, and the disabled, on the ground that it violated the Fourteenth Amendment and the Voting Rights Act. A federal district court upheld the statute and its decision was affirmed by the Court of Appeals for the Seventh Circuit. That decision was appealed and the Supreme Court granted review.

The appellate court's decision was affirmed by a six-to-three vote. Justice Stevens delivered the opinion for the Court, which commanded only the votes of Chief Justice Roberts and Justice Kennedy. Justice Scalia filed a concurring opinion, which Justices Thomas and Alito joined. Justices Breyer and Souter filed dissenting opinions, and Justice Ginsburg joined the latter's dissent.

☐ *Justice STEVENS announced the judgment of the Court and delivered an opinion in which THE CHIEF JUSTICE and Justice KENNEDY join.*

At issue in these cases is the constitutionality of an Indiana statute requiring citizens voting in person on election day, or casting a ballot in person at the office of the circuit court clerk prior to election day, to present photo identification issued by the government.

Referred to as either the "Voter ID Law" or "SEA 483," the statute applies to in-person voting at both primary and general elections. The requirement does not apply to absentee ballots submitted by mail, and the statute contains an exception for persons living and voting in a state-licensed facility such as a nursing home. A voter who is indigent or has a religious objection to being photographed may cast a provisional ballot that will be counted only if she executes an appropriate affidavit before the circuit court clerk within 10 days following the election. A voter who has photo identification but is unable to present that identification on election day may file a provisional ballot that will be counted if she brings her photo identification to the circuit county clerk's office within 10 days. No photo identification is required in order to register to vote, and the State offers free photo identification to qualified voters able to establish their residence and identity. . . .

In *Harper v. Virginia Bd. of Elections,* 383 U.S. 663 (1966), the Court held that Virginia could not condition the right to vote in a state election on the payment of a poll tax of $1.50. We rejected the dissenters' argument that the interest in promoting civic responsibility by weeding out those voters who did not care enough about public affairs to pay a small sum for the privilege of voting provided a rational basis for the tax. Applying a stricter standard, we concluded that a State "violates the Equal Protection Clause of the Fourteenth Amendment whenever it makes the affluence of the voter or payment of any fee an electoral standard." We used the term "invidiously discriminate" to describe conduct prohibited under that standard, noting that we had previously held that while a State may obviously impose "reasonable residence restrictions on the availability of the ballot," it "may not deny the opportunity to vote to a bona fide resident merely because he is a member of the armed services."

Although the State's justification for the tax was rational, it was invidious because it was irrelevant to the voter's qualifications.

Thus, under the standard applied in *Harper*, even rational restrictions on the right to vote are invidious if they are unrelated to voter qualifications. In *Anderson v. Celebrezze*, 460 U.S. 780 (1983), however, we confirmed the general rule that "evenhanded restrictions that protect the integrity and reliability of the electoral process itself" are not invidious and satisfy the standard set forth in *Harper*. Rather than applying any "litmus test" that would neatly separate valid from invalid restrictions, we concluded that a court must identify and evaluate the interests put forward by the State as justifications for the burden imposed by its rule, and then make the "hard judgment" that our adversary system demands.

In later election cases we have followed *Anderson*'s balancing approach. Thus, in *Norman v. Reed*, 502 U.S. 279 (1992), after identifying the burden Illinois imposed on a political party's access to the ballot, we "called for the demonstration of a corresponding interest sufficiently weighty to justify the limitation," and concluded that the "severe restriction" was not justified by a narrowly drawn state interest of compelling importance. Later, in *Burdick v. Takushi*, 504 U.S. 428 (1992), we applied *Anderson*'s standard for "'reasonable, nondiscriminatory restrictions,'" and upheld Hawaii's prohibition on write-in voting despite the fact that it prevented a significant number of "voters from participating in Hawaii elections in a meaningful manner." We reaffirmed Anderson's requirement that a court evaluating a constitutional challenge to an election regulation weigh the asserted injury to the right to vote against the "'precise interests put forward by the State as justifications for the burden imposed by its rule.'"

In neither *Norman* nor *Burdick* did we identify any litmus test for measuring the severity of a burden that a state law imposes on a political party, an individual voter, or a discrete class of voters. However slight that burden may appear, as *Harper* demonstrates, it must be justified by relevant and legitimate state interests "sufficiently weighty to justify the limitation." We therefore begin our analysis of the constitutionality of Indiana's statute by focusing on those interests.

The State has identified several state interests that arguably justify the burdens that SEA 483 imposes on voters and potential voters. While petitioners argue that the statute was actually motivated by partisan concerns and dispute both the significance of the State's interests and the magnitude of any real threat to those interests, they do not question the legitimacy of the interests the State has identified. Each is unquestionably relevant to the State's interest in protecting the integrity and reliability of the electoral process.

The first is the interest in deterring and detecting voter fraud. The State has a valid interest in participating in a nationwide effort to improve and modernize election procedures that have been criticized as antiquated and inefficient.... In the National Voter Registration Act of 1993 (NVRA) Congress established procedures that would both increase the number of registered voters and protect the integrity of the electoral process. The statute requires state motor vehicle driver's license applications to serve as voter registration applications. While that requirement has increased the number of registered voters, the statute also contains a provision restricting States' ability to remove names from the lists of registered voters. These protections have been partly responsible for inflated lists of registered voters....

The only kind of voter fraud that SEA 483 addresses is in-person voter impersonation at polling places. The record contains no evidence of any such fraud actually occurring in Indiana at any time in its history. Moreover, petitioners argue that provisions of the Indiana Criminal Code punishing such conduct as a felony provide adequate protection against the risk that such conduct will occur in the future. It remains true, however, that flagrant examples of such fraud in other parts of the country have been documented throughout this Nation's history by respected historians and journalists, that occasional examples have surfaced in recent years, and that Indiana's own experience with fraudulent voting in the 2003 Democratic primary for East Chicago Mayor—though perpetrated using absentee ballots and not in-person fraud—demonstrate that not only is the risk of voter fraud real but that it could affect the outcome of a close election.

There is no question about the legitimacy or importance of the State's interest in counting only the votes of eligible voters. Moreover, the interest in orderly administration and accurate recordkeeping provides a sufficient justification for carefully identifying all voters participating in the election process. While the most effective method of preventing election fraud may well be debatable, the propriety of doing so is perfectly clear. . . .

Finally, the State contends that it has an interest in protecting public confidence "in the integrity and legitimacy of representative government." While that interest is closely related to the State's interest in preventing voter fraud, public confidence in the integrity of the electoral process has independent significance, because it encourages citizen participation in the democratic process. States employ different methods of identifying eligible voters at the polls. Some merely check off the names of registered voters who identify themselves; others require voters to present registration cards or other documentation before they can vote; some require voters to sign their names so their signatures can be compared with those on file; and in recent years an increasing number of States have relied primarily on photo identification. A photo identification requirement imposes some burdens on voters that other methods of identification do not share. For example, a voter may lose his photo identification, may have his wallet stolen on the way to the polls, or may not resemble the photo in the identification because he recently grew a beard. Burdens of that sort arising from life's vagaries, however, are neither so serious nor so frequent as to raise any question about the constitutionality of SEA 483; the availability of the right to cast a provisional ballot provides an adequate remedy for problems of that character.

The burdens that are relevant to the issue before us are those imposed on persons who are eligible to vote but do not possess a current photo identification that complies with the requirements of SEA 483. The fact that most voters already possess a valid driver's license, or some other form of acceptable identification, would not save the statute under our reasoning in *Harper*, if the State required voters to pay a tax or a fee to obtain a new photo identification. But just as other States provide free voter registration cards, the photo identification cards issued by Indiana's BMV are also free. For most voters who need them, the inconvenience of making a trip to the BMV, gathering the required documents, and posing for a photograph surely does not qualify as a substantial burden on the right to vote, or even represent a significant increase over the usual burdens of voting.

Both evidence in the record and facts of which we may take judicial notice, however, indicate that a somewhat heavier burden may be placed on a limited number of persons. They include elderly persons born out-of-state, who may have difficulty obtaining a birth certificate; persons who because of economic or other personal limitations may find it difficult either to secure a copy of their birth certificate or to assemble the other required documentation to obtain a state-issued identification; homeless persons; and persons with a religious objection to being photographed. If we assume, as the evidence suggests, that some members of these classes were registered voters when SEA 483 was enacted, the new identification requirement may have imposed a special burden on their right to vote.

The severity of that burden is, of course, mitigated by the fact that, if eligible, voters without photo identification may cast provisional ballots that will ultimately be counted. To do so, however, they must travel to the circuit court clerk's office within 10 days to execute the required affidavit. It is unlikely that such a requirement would pose a constitutional problem unless it is wholly unjustified. And even assuming that the burden may not be justified as to a few voters, that conclusion is by no means sufficient to establish petitioners' right to the relief they seek in this litigation....

[If] a nondiscriminatory law is supported by valid neutral justifications, those justifications should not be disregarded simply because partisan interests may have provided one motivation for the votes of individual legislators. The state interests identified as justifications for SEA 483 are both neutral and sufficiently strong to require us to reject petitioners' facial attack on the statute. The application of the statute to the vast majority of Indiana voters is amply justified by the valid interest in protecting "the integrity and reliability of the electoral process." *Anderson.*

☐ *Justice SCALIA, with whom Justice THOMAS and Justice ALITO join, concurring in the judgment.*

The lead opinion assumes petitioners' premise that the voter-identification law "may have imposed a special burden on" some voters, but holds that petitioners have not assembled evidence to show that the special burden is severe enough to warrant strict scrutiny. That is true enough, but for the sake of clarity and finality (as well as adherence to precedent), I prefer to decide these cases on the grounds that petitioners' premise is irrelevant and that the burden at issue is minimal and justified.

To evaluate a law respecting the right to vote—whether it governs voter qualifications, candidate selection, or the voting process—we use the approach set out in *Burdick v. Takushi*, 504 U.S. 428 (1992). This calls for application of a deferential "important regulatory interests" standard for nonsevere, nondiscriminatory restrictions, reserving strict scrutiny for laws that severely restrict the right to vote. The lead opinion resists the import of *Burdick* by characterizing it as simply adopting "the balancing approach" of *Anderson v. Celebrezze*, 460 U.S. 780 (1983). Although *Burdick* liberally quoted *Anderson*, *Burdick* forged *Anderson*'s amorphous "flexible standard" into something resembling an administrable rule.

Since *Burdick*, we have repeatedly reaffirmed the primacy of its two-track approach. Of course, we have to identify a burden before we can weigh it. The Indiana law affects different voters differently, but what petitioners view as the law's several light and heavy burdens are no more than the different impacts of the single burden that the law uniformly imposes on all voters. To vote in person in Indiana, everyone must have and present a photo identification that can be obtained for free. The State draws no classifications, let alone discriminatory ones, except to establish optional absentee and provisional balloting for certain poor, elderly, and institutionalized voters and for religious objectors. Nor are voters who already have photo identifications exempted from the burden, since those voters must maintain the accuracy of the information displayed on the identifications, renew them before they expire, and replace them if they are lost.

The Indiana photo-identification law is a generally applicable, nondiscriminatory voting regulation, and our precedents refute the view that individual impacts are relevant to determining the severity of the burden it imposes. . . .

Not all of our decisions predating *Burdick* addressed whether a challenged voting regulation severely burdened the right to vote, but when we began to grapple with the magnitude of burdens, we did so categorically and did not consider the peculiar circumstances of individual voters or candidates.

Insofar as our election-regulation cases rest upon the requirements of the Fourteenth Amendment, weighing the burden of a nondiscriminatory voting law upon each voter and concomitantly requiring exceptions for vulnerable voters would effectively turn back decades of equal-protection jurisprudence. A voter complaining about such a law's effect on him has no valid equal-protection claim because, without proof of discriminatory intent, a generally applicable law with disparate impact is not unconstitutional.

Even if I thought that *stare decisis* did not foreclose adopting an individual-focused approach, I would reject it as an original matter. This is an area where the dos and don'ts need to be known in advance of the election, and voter-by-voter examination of the burdens of voting regulations would prove especially disruptive. . . .

[D]etailed judicial supervision of the election process would flout the Constitution's express commitment of the task to the States. It is for state legislatures to weigh the costs and benefits of possible changes to their election codes, and their judgment must prevail unless it imposes a severe and unjustified overall burden upon the right to vote, or is intended to disadvantage a particular class. Judicial review of their handiwork must apply an objective, uniform standard that will enable them to determine whether the burden they impose is too severe.

The lead opinion's record-based resolution of these cases, which neither rejects nor embraces the rule of our precedents, provides no certainty, and will embolden litigants who surmise that our precedents have been abandoned. There is no good reason to prefer that course. The universally applicable requirements of Indiana's voter-identification law are eminently reasonable. The burden of acquiring, possessing, and showing a free photo identification is simply not severe, because it does not "even represent a significant increase over the usual burdens of voting." And the State's interests are sufficient to sustain that minimal burden. That should end the matter. . . .

☐ *Justice BREYER, dissenting.*

Indiana's statute requires registered voters to present photo identification at the polls. It imposes a burden upon some voters, but it does so in order to prevent fraud, to build confidence in the voting system, and thereby to maintain the integrity of the voting process. In determining whether this statute violates the Federal Constitution, I would balance the voting-related interests that the statute affects, asking "whether the statute burdens any one such interest in a manner out of proportion to the statute's salutary effects upon the others (perhaps, but not necessarily, because of the existence of a clearly superior, less restrictive alternative)." *Nixon v. Shrink Missouri Government PAC*, 528 U.S. 377 (2000) (BREYER, J., concurring). Applying this standard, I believe the statute is unconstitutional because it imposes a disproportionate burden upon those eligible voters who lack a driver's license or other statutorily valid form of photo ID.

Like Justice STEVENS, I give weight to the fact that a national commission, chaired by former President Jimmy Carter and former Secretary of State James Baker, studied the issue and recommended that States should require voter photo IDs. (Carter-Baker Report). Because the record does not discredit the Carter-Baker Report or suggest that Indiana is exceptional, I see nothing to prevent Indiana's Legislature (or a federal court considering the constitutionality of the statute) from taking account of the legislatively relevant facts the report sets forth and paying attention to its expert conclusions. Thus, I share the general view of the lead opinion insofar as it holds that the Constitution does not automatically forbid Indiana from enacting a photo ID requirement. Were I also to believe, as Justice STEVENS believes, that the burden imposed by the Indiana statute on eligible voters who lack photo IDs is indeterminate "on the basis of the record that has been made in this litigation," or were I to believe, as Justice SCALIA believes, that the burden the statute imposes is "minimal" or "justified," then I too would reject the petitioners' facial attack, primarily for the reasons set forth in . . . the lead opinion.

I cannot agree, however, with Justice STEVENS' or Justice SCALIA's assessment of the burdens imposed by the statute. The Carter-Baker Commission conditioned its recommendation upon the States' willingness to ensure that the requisite photo IDs "be easily available and issued free of charge" and that the requirement be "phased in" over two federal election cycles, to ease the transition. . . . Indiana's law fails to satisfy these aspects of the Commission's recommendation.

For one thing, an Indiana nondriver, most likely to be poor, elderly, or disabled, will find it difficult and expensive to travel to the Bureau of Motor Vehicles, particularly if he or she resides in one of the many Indiana counties lacking a public transportation system. For another, many of these individuals may be uncertain about how to obtain the underlying documentation, usually a passport or a birth certificate, upon which the statute insists. And some may find the costs associated with these documents unduly burdensome (up to $12 for a copy of a birth certificate; up to $100 for a passport). By way of comparison, this Court previously found unconstitutionally burdensome a poll tax of $1.50 (less than $10 today, inflation-adjusted). See *Harper v. Virginia Bd. of Elections*, 383 U.S. 663 (1966). Further, Indiana's exception for voters who cannot afford this cost imposes its own burden: a postelection trip to the county clerk or county election board to sign an indigency affidavit after each election.

By way of contrast, two other States—Florida and Georgia—have put into practice photo ID requirements significantly less restrictive than Indiana's. Under the Florida law, the range of permissible forms of photo ID is substantially greater than in Indiana (including employee badge or ID, a debit or credit card, a student ID, a retirement center ID, a neighborhood association ID, and a public assistance ID). Moreover, a Florida voter who lacks photo ID may cast a provisional ballot at the polling place that will be counted if the State determines that his signature matches the one on his voter registration form.

Georgia restricts voters to a more limited list of acceptable photo IDs than does Florida, but accepts in addition to proof of voter registration a broader range of underlying documentation than does Indiana. . . .

For these reasons, I dissent.

☐ *Justice SOUTER, with whom Justice GINSBURG joins, dissenting.*

Indiana's "Voter ID Law"delete threatens to impose nontrivial burdens on the voting right of tens of thousands of the State's citizens, and a significant percentage of those individuals are likely to be deterred from voting. The statute is unconstitutional under the balancing standard of *Burdick v. Takushi,* 504 U.S. 428 (1992): a State may not burden the right to vote merely by invoking abstract interests, be they legitimate or even compelling, but must make a particular, factual showing that threats to its interests outweigh the particular impediments it has imposed. The State has made no such justification here, and as to some aspects of its law, it has hardly even tried. I therefore respectfully dissent from the Court's judgment sustaining the statute.

Voting-rights cases raise two competing interests, the one side being the fundamental right to vote. As against the unfettered right, however, lies the "[c]ommon sense, as well as constitutional law . . . that government must play an active role in structuring elections; 'as a practical matter, there must be a substantial regulation of elections if they are to be fair and honest and if some sort of order, rather than chaos, is to accompany the democratic processes.' " *Burdick.*

Given the legitimacy of interests on both sides, we have avoided pre-set levels of scrutiny in favor of a sliding-scale balancing analysis: the scrutiny varies with the effect of the regulation at issue. And whatever the claim, the Court has long made a careful, ground-level appraisal both of the practical burdens on the right to vote and of the State's reasons for imposing those precise burdens. Thus, in *Burdick*: "A court considering [such] a challenge . . . must weigh 'the character and magnitude of the asserted injury to the rights protected by the First and Fourteenth Amendments that the plaintiff seeks to vindicate' against 'the precise interests put forward by the State as justifications for the burden imposed by its rule,' taking into consideration 'the extent to which those interests make it necessary to burden the plaintiff's rights.' " But I think it does not insist enough on the hard facts that our standard of review demands. . . .

The first set of burdens shown in these cases is the travel costs and fees necessary to get one of the limited variety of federal or state photo identifications needed to cast a regular ballot under the Voter ID Law. The travel is required for the personal visit to a license branch of the Indiana Bureau of Motor Vehicles (BMV), which is demanded of anyone applying for a driver's license or nondriver photo identification. . . .

Although making voters travel farther than what is convenient for most and possible for some does not amount to a "severe" burden under *Burdick,* that is no reason to ignore the burden altogether. It translates into an obvious economic cost (whether in work time lost, or getting and paying for transportation) that an Indiana voter must bear to obtain an ID. For those voters who can afford the roundtrip, a second financial hurdle appears: in order to get photo identification for the first time, they need to present " 'a birth certificate, a certificate of naturalization, U.S. veterans photo identification, U.S. military photo identification, or a U.S. passport.' " As the lead opinion says, the two most common of these documents come at a price: Indiana counties charge anywhere from $3 to $12 for a birth certificate (and in some other States the fee is significantly higher), and that same price must usually be paid for a first-time passport, since a birth certificate is required to prove U.S. citizenship by birth. The total fees for a passport, moreover, are up to about $100. So most voters must pay at least one fee to get the ID necessary to cast a regular ballot. As with the travel costs, these fees are far from shocking on their face, but in the *Burdick* analysis it matters that both the travel costs and the fees are disproportionately heavy for, and thus disproportionately likely to deter, the poor, the old, and the immobile.

To be sure, Indiana has a provisional-ballot exception to the ID requirement for individuals the State considers "indigent" as well as those with religious objections to being photographed. . . .

[The] provisional ballots do not obviate the burdens of getting photo identification. And even if that were not so, the provisional-ballot option would be inadequate for a further reason: the indigency exception by definition offers no relief to those voters who do not consider themselves (or would not be considered) indigent but as a practical matter would find it hard, for nonfinancial reasons, to get the required ID (most obviously the disabled).

Indiana's Voter ID Law thus threatens to impose serious burdens on the voting right, even if not "severe" ones, and the next question under *Burdick* is whether the number of individuals likely to be affected is significant as well. Record evidence and facts open to judicial notice answer yes. Although the District Court found that petitioners failed to offer any reliable empirical study of numbers of voters affected, we may accept that court's rough calculation that 43,000 voting-age residents lack the kind of identification card required by Indiana's law. The District Court made that estimate by comparing BMV records reproduced in petitioners' statistician's report with U.S. Census Bureau figures for Indiana's voting-age population in 2004, and the State does not argue that these raw data are unreliable. . . .

The upshot is this. Tens of thousands of voting-age residents lack the necessary photo identification. A large proportion of them are likely to be in bad shape economically. The Voter ID Law places hurdles in the way of either getting an ID or of voting provisionally, and they translate into nontrivial economic costs. There is accordingly no reason to doubt that a significant number of state residents will be discouraged or disabled from voting. . . .

There is no denying the abstract importance, the compelling nature, of combating voter fraud. But it takes several steps to get beyond the level of abstraction here. To begin with, requiring a voter to show photo identification before casting a regular ballot addresses only one form of voter fraud: in-person voter impersonation. The photo ID requirement leaves untouched the problems of absentee-ballot fraud, which (unlike in-person voter impersonation) is a documented problem in Indiana; of registered voters voting more than once (but maintaining their own identities) in different counties or in different States; of felons and other disqualified individuals voting in their own names; of vote buying; or, for that matter, of ballot-stuffing, ballot miscounting, voter intimidation, or any other type of corruption on the part of officials administering elections. And even the State's interest in deterring a voter from showing up at the polls and claiming to be someone he is not must, in turn, be discounted for the fact that the State has not come across a single instance of in-person voter impersonation fraud in all of Indiana's history. . . .

In sum, fraud by individuals acting alone, however difficult to detect, is unlikely. And while there may be greater incentives for organized groups to engage in broad-gauged in-person voter impersonation fraud, it is also far more difficult to conceal larger enterprises of this sort. The State's argument about the difficulty of detecting the fraud lacks real force. . . .

The State's asserted interests in modernizing elections and combating fraud are decidedly modest; at best, they fail to offset the clear inference that thousands of Indiana citizens will be discouraged from voting. The two remaining justifications, meanwhile, actually weaken the State's case.

The lead opinion agrees with the State that "the inflation of its voter rolls is further support for its enactment of" the Voter ID Law. This is a puzzling conclusion, given the fact, which the lead opinion notes, that the National Government filed a complaint against Indiana, containing this allegation: "Indiana has failed to conduct a general program that makes a reasonable effort to identify and remove ineligible voters from the State's registration list; has failed to remove such ineligible voters; and has failed to engage in oversight actions sufficient to ensure that local election jurisdictions identify and remove such ineligible voters." The Federal Government and the State agreed to settle the case, and a consent decree and order have been entered, requiring Indiana to fulfill its list-maintenance obligations under Sec. 8 of the National Voter Registration Act of 1993.

How any of this can justify restrictions on the right to vote is difficult to say. The State is simply trying to take advantage of its own wrong: if it is true that the State's fear of in-person voter impersonation fraud arises from its bloated voter checklist, the answer to the problem is in the State's own hands. The claim that the State has an interest in addressing a symptom of the problem (alleged impersonation) rather than the problem itself (the negligently maintained bloated rolls) is thus self-defeating; it shows that the State has no justifiable need to burden the right to vote as it does, and it suggests that the State is not as serious about combating fraud as it claims to be.

The State's final justification, its interest in safeguarding voter confidence, similarly collapses. The problem with claiming this interest lies in its connection to the bloated voter rolls; the State has come up with nothing to suggest that its citizens doubt the integrity of the State's electoral process, except its own failure to maintain its rolls. The answer to this problem is not to burden the right to vote, but to end the official negligence.

It should go without saying that none of this is to deny States' legitimate interest in safeguarding public confidence. The Court has, for example, recognized that fighting perceptions of political corruption stemming from large political contributions is a legitimate and substantial state interest, underlying not only campaign finance laws, but bribery and anti-gratuity statutes as well. But the force of the interest depends on the facts (or plausibility of the assumptions) said to justify invoking it. . . . Without a shred of evidence that in-person voter impersonation is a problem in the State, much less a crisis, Indiana has adopted one of the most restrictive photo identification requirements in the country. The State recognizes that tens of thousands of qualified voters lack the necessary federally issued or state-issued identification, but it insists on implementing the requirement immediately, without allowing a transition period for targeted efforts to distribute the required identification to individuals who need it.

The State hardly even tries to explain its decision to force indigents or religious objectors to travel all the way to their county seats every time they wish to vote, and if there is any waning of confidence in the administration of elections it probably owes more to the State's violation of federal election law than to any imposters at the polling places. It is impossible to say, on this

record, that the State's interest in adopting its signally inhibiting photo identification requirement has been shown to outweigh the serious burdens it
imposes on the right to vote. . . .

The Indiana Voter ID Law is thus unconstitutional: the state interests fail
to justify the practical limitations placed on the right to vote, and the law
imposes an unreasonable and irrelevant burden on voters who are poor and
old. I would vacate the judgment of the Seventh Circuit, and remand for
further proceedings.

Citizens United v. Federal Election Commission
130 S.Ct. 876 (2010)

Citizens United, a nonprofit corporation, released a film entitled *Hillary:
The Movie.* The ninety-minute documentary was about then-Senator Hillary
Clinton, who was a candidate in the Democratic Party's 2008 presidential
primary elections. The film mentioned Senator Clinton by name and
featured interviews with political commentators and other persons, most
of them quite critical of Senator Clinton. The film was released in theaters
and on DVD, but Citizens United wanted to increase distribution by
making it available through video-on-demand. Video-on-demand allows
digital cable subscribers to select programming from various menus, including movies, television shows, sports, news, and music. In December
2007, a cable company offered, for a payment of $1.2 million, to make
Hillary available on a video-on-demand channel called "Elections '08."

Before and after the Bipartisan Campaign Reform Act of 2002
(BCRA), federal law prohibited corporations and unions from using general funds to make direct contributions to candidates or independent
expenditures that expressly advocate the election or defeat of a candidate,
through any form of media, in connection with certain federal elections.
The Federal Election Commission's (FEC) regulations further defined
an electioneering communication as a communication that is "publicly
distributed." Corporations and unions were barred from using their general funds for express advocacy or electioneering communications. They
could establish, however, a "separate segregated fund" (known as a political action committee, or PAC) for these purposes. Citizens United wanted
to make *Hillary* available through video-on-demand within thirty days
of the 2008 primary elections. It feared, however, that both the film and
the ads would be covered by Section 441b's ban on corporate-funded
independent expenditures, thus subjecting the corporation to civil and
criminal penalties under Section 437g. In December 2007, Citizens
United sought declaratory and injunctive relief against the FEC. It argued
that (1) Section 441b was unconstitutional as applied to *Hillary*; and
(2) BCRA's disclaimer and disclosure requirements, BCRA Sections

201 and 311, were unconstitutional as applied to *Hillary* and to the three ads for the movie.

A federal district court denied Citizens United's motion for a preliminary injunction and then granted the FEC's motion for summary judgment. The court held that Section 441b was facially constitutional under *McConnell v. Federal Election Commission*, 540 U.S. 93 (2003) (excerpted in Vol. 1, Ch. 8) and that Section 441b was constitutional as applied to *Hillary* because it was "susceptible of no other interpretation than to inform the electorate that Senator Clinton is unfit for office, that the United States would be a dangerous place in a President Hillary Clinton world, and that viewers should vote against her." The court also rejected Citizens United's challenge to BCRA's disclaimer and disclosure requirements.

The district court's decision was reversed in part and affirmed in part. Justice Kennedy delivered the opinion for the Court. Chief Justice Roberts and Justice Scalia filed concurring opinions. Justice Stevens and Thomas each filed opinions concurring and dissenting in part. Justices Ginsburg, Breyer, and Sotomayor joined Justice Stevens' opinion.

☐ *Justice KENNEDY delivered the opinion of the Court.*

Limits on electioneering communications were upheld in *McConnell v. Federal Election Comm'n*, 540 U.S. 93 (2003). The holding of *McConnell* rested to a large extent on an earlier case, *Austin v. Michigan Chamber of Commerce*, 494 U. S. 652 (1990). *Austin* had held that political speech may be banned based on the speaker's corporate identity.

In this case we are asked to reconsider *Austin* and, in effect, *McConnell*. It has been noted that "*Austin* was a significant departure from ancient First Amendment principles," *Federal Election Comm'n v. Wisconsin Right to Life, Inc.*, 551 U. S. 449(2007) (*WRTL*) (SCALIA, J., concurring). We agree with that conclusion and hold that *stare decisis* does not compel the continued acceptance of *Austin*. The Government may regulate corporate political speech through disclaimer and disclosure requirements, but it may not suppress that speech altogether. . . .

As the District Court found, there is no reasonable interpretation of *Hillary* other than as an appeal to vote against Senator Clinton. Under the standard stated in *McConnell* and further elaborated in *WRTL*, the film qualifies as the functional equivalent of express advocacy. . . .

When the statute now at issue came before the Court in *McConnell*, both the majority and the dissenting opinions considered the question of its facial validity. The holding and validity of *Austin* were essential to the reasoning of the *McConnell* majority opinion, which upheld BCRA's extension of Sec. 441b. *McConnell* permitted federal felony punishment for speech by all corporations, including nonprofit ones, that speak on prohibited subjects shortly before federal elections. . . .

The First Amendment provides that "Congress shall make no law . . . abridging the freedom of speech." . . .

The law before us is an outright ban, backed by criminal sanctions. Section 441b makes it a felony for all corporations—including nonprofit advocacy corporations—either to expressly advocate the election or defeat of candidates or to broadcast electioneering communications within 30 days of a primary election and 60 days of a general election. Thus, the following acts would all be felonies under Sec. 441b: The Sierra Club runs an ad, within the crucial phase of 60 days before the general election, that exhorts the public to disapprove of a Congressman who favors logging in national forests; the National Rifle Association publishes a book urging the public to vote for the challenger because the incumbent U.S. Senator supports a handgun ban; and the American Civil Liberties Union creates a Web site telling the public to vote for a Presidential candidate in light of that candidate's defense of free speech. These prohibitions are classic examples of censorship.

Section 441b is a ban on corporate speech notwithstanding the fact that a PAC created by a corporation can still speak. A PAC is a separate association from the corporation. So the PAC exemption from Sec. 441b's expenditure ban does not allow corporations to speak. Even if a PAC could somehow allow a corporation to speak—and it does not—the option to form PACs does not alleviate the First Amendment problems with Sec. 441b.

Section 441b's prohibition on corporate independent expenditures is thus a ban on speech. As a "restriction on the amount of money a person or group can spend on political communication during a campaign," that statute "necessarily reduces the quantity of expression by restricting the number of issues discussed, the depth of their exploration, and the size of the audience reached." *Buckley v. Valeo*, 424 U. S. 1 (1976) (*per curiam*). Were the Court to uphold these restrictions, the Government could repress speech by silencing certain voices at any of the various points in the speech process. . . .

Speech is an essential mechanism of democracy, for it is the means to hold officials accountable to the people. The right of citizens to inquire, to hear, to speak, and to use information to reach consensus is a precondition to enlightened self-government and a necessary means to protect it.

For these reasons, political speech must prevail against laws that would suppress it, whether by design or inadvertence. Laws that burden political speech are "subject to strict scrutiny," which requires the Government to prove that the restriction "furthers a compelling interest and is narrowly tailored to achieve that interest." . . .

We find no basis for the proposition that, in the context of political speech, the Government may impose restrictions on certain disfavored speakers. Both history and logic lead us to this conclusion.

At least since the latter part of the 19th century, the laws of some States and of the United States imposed a ban on corporate direct contributions to candidates. Yet not until 1947 did Congress first prohibit independent expenditures by corporations and labor unions in Sec. 304 of the Labor Management Relations Act 1947.

For almost three decades thereafter, the Court did not reach the question whether restrictions on corporate and union expenditures are constitutional.

In *Buckley*, the Court addressed various challenges to the Federal Election Campaign Act of 1971 (FECA) as amended in 1974. These amendments created 18 U.S.C. Sec. 608(e), an independent expenditure ban separate from Sec. 610 that applied to individuals as well as corporations and labor unions.

Before addressing the constitutionality of Sec. 608(e)'s independent expenditure ban, *Buckley* first upheld Sec. 608(b), FECA's limits on direct contributions to candidates. The *Buckley* Court recognized a "sufficiently important" governmental interest in "the prevention of corruption and the appearance of corruption." This followed from the Court's concern that large contributions could be given "to secure a political *quid pro quo*." . . .

Buckley did not consider Sec. 610's separate ban on corporate and union independent expenditures. . . .

Less than two years after *Buckley*, *Bellotti* reaffirmed the First Amendment principle that the Government cannot restrict political speech based on the speaker's corporate identity. *Bellotti* could not have been clearer when it struck down a state-law prohibition on corporate independent expenditures related to referenda issues. . . .

Bellotti did not address the constitutionality of the State's ban on corporate independent expenditures to support candidates. In our view, however, that restriction would have been unconstitutional under *Bellotti*'s central principle: that the First Amendment does not allow political speech restrictions based on a speaker's corporate identity.

Thus the law stood until *Austin*. *Austin* "uph[eld] a direct restriction on the independent expenditure of funds for political speech for the first time in [this Court's] history." (KENNEDY, J., dissenting). There, the Michigan Chamber of Commerce sought to use general treasury funds to run a newspaper ad supporting a specific candidate. Michigan law, however, prohibited corporate independent expenditures that supported or opposed any candidate for state office. A violation of the law was punishable as a felony. The Court sustained the speech prohibition.

To bypass *Buckley* and *Bellotti*, the *Austin* Court identified a new governmental interest in limiting political speech: an antidistortion interest. *Austin* found a compelling governmental interest in preventing "the corrosive and distorting effects of immense aggregations of wealth that are accumulated with the help of the corporate form and that have little or no correlation to the public's support for the corporation's political ideas."

The Court is thus confronted with conflicting lines of precedent: a pre-*Austin* line that forbids restrictions on political speech based on the speaker's corporate identity and a post-*Austin* line that permits them. No case before *Austin* had held that Congress could prohibit independent expenditures for political speech based on the speaker's corporate identity. Before *Austin* Congress had enacted legislation for this purpose, and the Government urged the same proposition before this Court.

In its defense of the corporate-speech restrictions in Sec. 441b, the Government notes the antidistortion rationale on which *Austin* and its progeny rest in part, yet it all but abandons reliance upon it. It argues instead that two other compelling interests support *Austin*'s holding that corporate expenditure restrictions are constitutional: an anticorruption interest. We consider the three points in turn.

As for *Austin*'s antidistortion rationale, the Government does little to defend it. And with good reason, for the rationale cannot support Sec. 441b.

If the First Amendment has any force, it prohibits Congress from fining or jailing citizens, or associations of citizens, for simply engaging in political speech. If the antidistortion rationale were to be accepted, however, it would permit Government to ban political speech simply because the speaker is an association that has taken on the corporate form. . . .

The Court reaffirmed these conclusions when it invalidated the BCRA [Bipartisan Campaign Reform Act] provision that increased the cap on contributions to one candidate if the opponent made certain expenditures from personal funds. The rule that political speech cannot be limited based on a speaker's wealth is a necessary consequence of the premise that the First Amendment generally prohibits the suppression of political speech based on the speaker's identity. . . .

There is simply no support for the view that the First Amendment, as originally understood, would permit the suppression of political speech by media corporations. The Framers may not have anticipated modern business and media corporations. Yet television networks and major newspapers owned by media corporations have become the most important means of mass communication in modern times. The First Amendment was certainly not understood to condone the suppression of political speech in society's most salient media. . . .

The purpose and effect of this law is to prevent corporations, including small and nonprofit corporations, from presenting both facts and opinions to the public. This makes *Austin's* antidistortion rationale all the more an aberration. . . .

Even if Sec. 441b's expenditure ban were constitutional, wealthy corporations could still lobby elected officials, although smaller corporations may not have the resources to do so. And wealthy individuals and unincorporated associations can spend unlimited amounts on independent expenditures. . . .

What we have said also shows the invalidity of other arguments made by the Government. For the most part relinquishing the antidistortion rationale, the Government falls back on the argument that corporate political speech can be banned in order to prevent corruption or its appearance. In *Buckley*, the Court found this interest "sufficiently important" to allow limits on contributions but did not extend that reasoning to expenditure limits. When *Buckley* examined an expenditure ban, it found "that the governmental interest in preventing corruption and the appearance of corruption [was] inadequate to justify [the ban] on independent expenditures." . . .

When *Buckley* identified a sufficiently important governmental interest in preventing corruption or the appearance of corruption, that interest was limited to *quid pro quo* corruption. The fact that speakers may have influence over or access to elected officials does not mean that these officials are corrupt. . . .

The Government contends further that corporate independent expenditures can be limited because of its interest in protecting dissenting shareholders from being compelled to fund corporate political speech. This asserted interest, like *Austin's* antidistortion rationale, would allow the Government to ban the political speech even of media corporations. . . .

Those reasons are sufficient to reject this shareholder-protection interest; and, moreover, the statute is both underinclusive and overinclusive. As to the first, if Congress had been seeking to protect dissenting shareholders, it would not have banned corporate speech in only certain media within 30 or 60 days before an election. A dissenting shareholder's interests would be implicated by speech in any media at any time. As to the second, the statute is overinclusive because it covers all corporations, including nonprofit corporations and for-profit corporations with only single shareholders. As to other corporations, the remedy is not to restrict speech but to consider and explore other regulatory mechanisms. The regulatory mechanism here, based on speech, contravenes the First Amendment. . . .

Rapid changes in technology—and the creative dynamic inherent in the concept of free expression—counsel against upholding a law that restricts political speech in certain media or by certain speakers. Today, 30-second television ads may be the most effective way to convey a political message. Soon, however, it may be that Internet sources, such as blogs and social networking

Web sites, will provide citizens with significant information about political candidates and issues. Yet, Sec. 441b would seem to ban a blog post expressly advocating the election or defeat of a candidate if that blog were created with corporate funds. The First Amendment does not permit Congress to make these categorical distinctions based on the corporate identity of the speaker and the content of the political speech. . . .

Austin is overruled, so it provides no basis for allowing the Government to limit corporate independent expenditures. . . .

Given our conclusion we are further required to overrule the part of *McConnell* that upheld BCRA Sec. 203's extension of Sec. 441b's restrictions on corporate independent expenditures. The *McConnell* Court relied on the antidistortion interest recognized in *Austin* to uphold a greater restriction on speech than the restriction upheld in *Austin*, and we have found this interest unconvincing and insufficient. This part of *McConnell* is now overruled.

Citizens United next challenges BCRA's disclaimer and disclosure provisions as applied to *Hillary* and the three advertisements for the movie. Under BCRA Sec. 311, televised electioneering communications funded by anyone other than a candidate must include a disclaimer that "'is responsible for the content of this advertising.'" The required statement must be made in a "clearly spoken manner," and displayed on the screen in a "clearly readable manner" for at least four seconds. It must state that the communication "is not authorized by any candidate or candidate's committee"; it must also display the name and address (or Web site address) of the person or group that funded the advertisement. . . .

Disclaimer and disclosure requirements may burden the ability to speak, but they "impose no ceiling on campaign-related activities," *Buckley*. The Court has subjected these requirements to "exacting scrutiny," which requires a "substantial relation" between the disclosure requirement and a "sufficiently important" governmental interest. . . .

The judgment of the District Court is reversed with respect to the constitutionality of 2 U.S.C. Sec. 441b's restrictions on corporate independent expenditures. The judgment is affirmed with respect to BCRA's disclaimer and disclosure requirements. The case is remanded for further proceedings consistent with this opinion.

☐ *Justice SCALIA, with whom Justice ALITO joins, and with whom Justice THOMAS joins in part, concurring.*

I write separately to address Justice STEVENS' discussion of "Original Understandings." This section of the dissent purports to show that today's decision is not supported by the original understanding of the First Amendment. The dissent attempts this demonstration, however, in splendid isolation from the text of the First Amendment. It never shows why "the freedom of speech" that was the right of Englishmen did not include the freedom to speak in association with other individuals, including association in the corporate form. To be sure, in 1791 (as now) corporations could pursue only the objectives set forth in their charters; but the dissent provides no evidence that their speech in the pursuit of those objectives could be censored.

Instead of taking this straightforward approach to determining the Amendment's meaning, the dissent embarks on a detailed exploration of the Framers' views about the "role of corporations in society." The Framers didn't like corporations, the dissent concludes, and therefore it follows (as night the day) that corporations had no rights of free speech. Of course the Framers' personal affection or disaffection for corporations is relevant only insofar as it can be thought to be reflected in the understood meaning of the text they enacted— not, as the dissent suggests, as a freestanding substitute for that text. But the dissent's distortion of proper analysis is even worse than that. Though faced with a constitutional text that makes no distinction between types of speakers, the dissent feels no necessity to provide even an isolated statement from the founding era to the effect that corporations are not covered, but places the burden on petitioners to bring forward statements showing that they are ("there is not a scintilla of evidence to support the notion that anyone believed [the First Amendment] would preclude regulatory distinctions based on the corporate form").

Despite the corporation-hating quotations the dissent has dredged up, it is far from clear that by the end of the 18th century corporations were despised. If so, how came there to be so many of them? The dissent's statement that there were few business corporations during the eighteenth century— "only a few hundred during all of the 18th century"—is misleading. There were approximately 335 charters issued to business corporations in the United States by the end of the 18th century. This was a "considerable extension of corporate enterprise in the field of business," and represented "unprecedented growth." Moreover, what seems like a small number by today's standards surely does not indicate the relative importance of corporations when the Nation was considerably smaller. . . .

The lack of a textual exception for speech by corporations cannot be explained on the ground that such organizations did not exist or did not speak. To the contrary, colleges, towns and cities, religious institutions, and guilds had long been organized as corporations at common law and under the King's charter, and as I have discussed, the practice of incorporation only expanded in the United States. Both corporations and voluntary associations actively petitioned the Government and expressed their views in newspapers and pamphlets. . . .

But to return to, and summarize, my principal point, which is the conformity of today's opinion with the original meaning of the First Amendment. The Amendment is written in terms of "speech," not speakers. Its text offers no foothold for excluding any category of speaker, from single individuals to partnerships of individuals, to unincorporated associations of individuals, to incorporated associations of individuals—and the dissent offers no evidence about the original meaning of the text to support any such exclusion. We are therefore simply left with the question whether the speech at issue in this case is "speech" covered by the First Amendment. No one says otherwise. A documentary film critical of a potential Presidential candidate is core political speech, and its nature as such does not change simply because it was funded by a corporation. Nor does the character of that funding produce any reduction whatever in the "inherent worth of the speech" and "its capacity for informing the public," *First Nat. Bank of Boston v. Bellotti.* Indeed, to exclude or impede corporate speech is to muzzle the principal agents of the modern free economy. We should celebrate rather than condemn the addition of this speech to the public debate.

☐ *CHIEF JUSTICE ROBERTS, with whom Justice ALITO joins, concurring.*

The Government urges us in this case to uphold a direct prohibition on political speech. It asks us to embrace a theory of the First Amendment that would allow censorship not only of television and radio broadcasts, but of pamphlets, posters, the Internet, and virtually any other medium that corporations and unions might find useful in expressing their views on matters of public concern. Its theory, if accepted, would empower the Government to prohibit newspapers from running editorials or opinion pieces supporting or opposing candidates for office, so long as the newspapers were owned by corporations—as the major ones are. First Amendment rights could be confined to individuals, subverting the vibrant public discourse that is at the foundation of our democracy.

The Court properly rejects that theory, and I join its opinion in full. The First Amendment protects more than just the individual on a soapbox and the lonely pamphleteer. . . .

☐ *Justice THOMAS, concurring in part and dissenting in part.*

Political speech is entitled to robust protection under the First Amendment. Section 203 of the Bipartisan Campaign Reform Act of 2002 (BCRA) has never been reconcilable with that protection. By striking down Sec. 203, the Court takes an important first step toward restoring full constitutional protection to speech that is "indispensable to the effective and intelligent use of the processes of popular government." *McConnell v. Federal Election Comm'n*, (THOMAS, J., concurring in part, and dissenting in part). I dissent from Part IV of the Court's opinion, however, because the Court's constitutional analysis does not go far enough. The disclosure, disclaimer, and reporting requirements in BCRA Secs. 201 and 311 are also unconstitutional.

Congress may not abridge the "right to anonymous speech" based on the "'simple interest in providing voters with additional relevant information.'" In continuing to hold otherwise, the Court misapprehends the import of "recent events" that some *amici* describe "in which donors to certain causes were blacklisted, threatened, or otherwise targeted for retaliation." The Court properly recognizes these events as "cause for concern," but fails to acknowledge their constitutional significance. In my view, *amici's* submissions show why the Court's insistence on upholding Secs. 201 and 311 will ultimately prove as misguided (and ill fated) as was its prior approval of Sec. 203. . . .

☐ *Justice STEVENS, with whom Justice GINSBURG, Justice BREYER, and Justice SOTOMAYOR join, concurring in part and dissenting in part.*

The basic premise underlying the Court's ruling is its iteration, and constant reiteration, of the proposition that the First Amendment bars regulatory distinctions based on a speaker's identity, including its "identity" as a corporation. While that glittering generality has rhetorical appeal, it is not a correct statement of the law. Nor does it tell us when a corporation may engage in electioneering that some of its shareholders oppose. It does not even resolve the specific question whether Citizens United may be required to finance some of its messages with the money in its PAC. The conceit that corporations must be treated identically to natural persons in the political sphere is not only inaccurate but also inadequate to justify the Court's disposition of this case.

In the context of election to public office, the distinction between corporate and human speakers is significant. Although they make enormous contributions to our society, corporations are not actually members of it. They cannot vote or run for office. Because they may be managed and controlled by nonresidents, their interests may conflict in fundamental respects with the interests of eligible voters. The financial resources, legal structure, and instrumental orientation of corporations raise legitimate concerns about their role in the electoral process. Our lawmakers have a compelling constitutional basis, if not also a democratic duty, to take measures designed to guard against the potentially deleterious effects of corporate spending in local and national races.

The majority's approach to corporate electioneering marks a dramatic break from our past. Congress has placed special limitations on campaign spending by corporations ever since the passage of the Tillman Act in 1907. We have unanimously concluded that this "reflects a permissible assessment of the dangers posed by those entities to the electoral process," *FEC v. National Right to Work Comm.*, 459 U.S. 197 (1982) (*NRWC*), and have accepted the "legislative judgment that the special characteristics of the corporate structure require particularly careful regulation." The Court today rejects a century of history when it treats the distinction between corporate and individual campaign spending as an invidious novelty born of *Austin v. Michigan Chamber of Commerce*, 494 U.S. 652 (1990). Relying largely on individual dissenting opinions, the majority blazes through our precedents, overruling or disavowing a body of case law including *FEC v. Wisconsin Right to Life, Inc.*, 551 U.S. 449 (2007) (*WRTL*), *McConnell v. FEC*, 540 U.S. 93 (2003), *FEC v. Beaumont*, 539 U.S. 146 (2003), *FEC v. Massachusetts Citizens for Life, Inc.*, 479 U.S. 238 (1986) (*MCFL*), *NRWC*, and *California Medical Assn. v. FEC*, 453 U.S. 182 (1981)....

Although I concur in the Court's decision to sustain BCRA's disclosure provisions and join Part IV of its opinion, I emphatically dissent from its principal holding....

The ruling rests on several premises. First, the Court claims that *Austin* and *McConnell* have "banned" corporate speech. Second, it claims that the First Amendment precludes regulatory distinctions based on speaker identity, including the speaker's identity as a corporation. Third, it claims that *Austin* and *McConnell* were radical outliers in our First Amendment tradition and our campaign finance jurisprudence. Each of these claims is wrong.

Pervading the Court's analysis is the ominous image of a "categorical ba[n]" on corporate speech. Indeed, the majority invokes the specter of a "ban" on nearly every page of its opinion. This characterization is highly misleading, and needs to be corrected....

Our cases have repeatedly pointed out that, "[c]ontrary to the [majority's] critical assumptions," the statutes upheld in *Austin* and *McConnell* do "not impose an absolute ban on all forms of corporate political spending." For starters, both statutes provide exemptions for PACs, separate segregated funds established by a corporation for political purposes. "The ability to form and administer separate segregated funds," we observed in *McConnell*, "has provided corporations and unions with a constitutionally sufficient opportunity to engage in express advocacy. That has been this Court's unanimous view."

Under BCRA, any corporation's "stockholders and their families and its executive or administrative personnel and their families" can pool their resources to finance electioneering communications. A significant and growing number of corporations avail themselves of this option; during the most recent election cycle, corporate and union PACs raised nearly a billion dollars....

At the time Citizens United brought this lawsuit, the only types of speech that could be regulated under Sec. 203 were: (1) broadcast, cable, or satellite communications; (2) capable of reaching at least 50,000 persons in the relevant electorate; (3) made within 30 days of a primary or 60 days of a general federal election; (4) by a labor union or a non-MCFL, nonmedia corporation; (5) paid for with general treasury funds; and (6) "susceptible of no reasonable interpretation other than as an appeal to vote for or against a specific candidate." The category of communications meeting all of these criteria is not trivial, but the notion that corporate political speech has been "suppress[ed] . . . altogether," that corporations have been "exclu[ded] . . . from the general public dialogue," or that a work of fiction such as *Mr. Smith Goes to Washington* might be covered, is nonsense. Even the plaintiffs in *McConnell*, who had every incentive to depict BCRA as negatively as possible, declined to argue that Sec. 203's prohibition on certain uses of general treasury funds amounts to a complete ban.

In many ways, then, Sec. 203 functions as a source restriction or a time, place, and manner restriction. . . .

The second pillar of the Court's opinion is its assertion that "the Government cannot restrict political speech based on the speaker's . . . identity." The case on which it relies for this proposition is *First Nat. Bank of Boston v. Bellotti*, 435 U.S. 765 (1978). As I shall explain, the holding in that case was far narrower than the Court implies.

"Our jurisprudence over the past 216 years has rejected an absolutist interpretation" of the First Amendment. *WRTL*. The First Amendment provides that "Congress shall make no law . . . abridging the freedom of speech, or of the press." Apart perhaps from measures designed to protect the press, that text might seem to permit no distinctions of any kind. Yet in a variety of contexts, we have held that speech can be regulated differentially on account of the speaker's identity, when identity is understood in categorical or institutional terms. The Government routinely places special restrictions on the speech rights of students, prisoners, members of the Armed Forces, foreigners, and its own employees. When such restrictions are justified by a legitimate governmental interest, they do not necessarily raise constitutional problems. In contrast to the blanket rule that the majority espouses, our cases recognize that the Government's interests may be more or less compelling with respect to different classes of speakers.

In short, the Court dramatically overstates its critique of identity-based distinctions, without ever explaining why corporate identity demands the same treatment as individual identity. Only the most wooden approach to the First Amendment could justify the unprecedented line it seeks to draw.

A third fulcrum of the Court's opinion is the idea that *Austin* and *McConnell* are radical outliers, "aberration[s]," in our First Amendment tradition. The Court has it exactly backwards. It is today's holding that is the radical departure from what had been settled First Amendment law. To see why, it is useful to take a long view.

Let us start from the beginning. The Court invokes "ancient First Amendment principles," and original understandings, to defend today's ruling, yet it makes only a perfunctory attempt to ground its analysis in the principles or understandings of those who drafted and ratified the Amendment. Perhaps this is because there is not a scintilla of evidence to support the notion that anyone believed it would preclude regulatory distinctions based on the corporate form. To the extent that the Framers' views are discernible and relevant to the disposition of this case, they would appear to cut strongly against the majority's position. . . .

Although Justice SCALIA makes a perfectly sensible argument that an individual's right to speak entails a right to speak with others for a common cause, he does not explain why those two rights must be precisely identical, or why that principle applies to electioneering by corporations that serve no "common cause." Nothing in his account dislodges my basic point that members of the founding generation held a cautious view of corporate power and a narrow view of corporate rights (not that they "despised" corporations), and that they conceptualized speech in individualistic terms. If no prominent Framer bothered to articulate that corporate speech would have lesser status than individual speech, that may well be because the contrary proposition—if not also the very notion of "corporate speech"—was inconceivable. . . .

Today's decision is backwards in many senses. It elevates the majority's agenda over the litigants' submissions, facial attacks over as-applied claims, broad constitutional theories over narrow statutory grounds, individual dissenting opinions over precedential holdings, assertion over tradition, absolutism over empiricism, rhetoric over reality. Our colleagues have arrived at the conclusion that *Austin* must be overruled and that Sec. 203 is facially unconstitutional only after mischaracterizing both the reach and rationale of those authorities, and after bypassing or ignoring rules of judicial restraint used to cabin the Court's lawmaking power. Their conclusion that the societal interest in avoiding corruption and the appearance of corruption does not provide an adequate justification for regulating corporate expenditures on candidate elections relies on an incorrect description of that interest, along with a failure to acknowledge the relevance of established facts and the considered judgments of state and federal legislatures over many decades.

In a democratic society, the longstanding consensus on the need to limit corporate campaign spending should outweigh the wooden application of judge-made rules. The majority's rejection of this principle "elevate[s] corporations to a level of deference which has not been seen at least since the days when substantive due process was regularly used to invalidate regulatory legislation thought to unfairly impinge upon established economic interests." *Bellotti* (WHITE, J., dissenting). At bottom, the Court's opinion is thus a rejection of the common sense of the American people, who have recognized a need to prevent corporations from undermining self-government since the founding, and who have fought against the distinctive corrupting potential of corporate electioneering since the days of Theodore Roosevelt. It is a strange time to repudiate that common sense. While American democracy is imperfect, few outside the majority of this Court would have thought its flaws included a dearth of corporate money in politics.

■ The Development of Law

Other Rulings on Campaigns and Elections

CASE	VOTE	RULING
New York State Board of Elections v. Lopez Torres, 128 S.Ct. 791 (2008)	9:0	Writing for the Court, Justice Scalia upheld New York's process for selecting its supreme court justices through party conventions.

tions. Under the state law, each political party selects one candidate to run in the general election. That law was challenged as a violation of the First

Amendment freedom of association for discriminating against challengers to party-selected candidates. But the Court held that political parties have First Amendment protection to determine their own selection process and rejected the claims of candidates who do not have party leadership support.

Washington State Grange v. Washington State Republican Party, 128 S.Ct. 1194 (2008) 　　7:2　　Writing for the Court, Justice Thomas upheld Washington State's law requiring candidates for elective office to be identified on the ballot by their self-designated "party preference." The majority held that the requirement did not unduly burden political parties' freedom of association under the First Amendment. Justices Scalia and Kennedy dissented.

Ysursa v. Pocatello Education Association, 129 S.Ct. 1093 (2009) 　　6:3　　Writing for the Court, Chief Justice Roberts held that states may order local governments to forbid payroll deductions for union political activities and rejected the union's claim that that violated the First Amendment. In his words: "The First Amendment prohibits government from 'abridging the freedom of speech'; it does not confer an affirmative right to use government payroll mechanisms for the purpose of obtaining funds for expression."

Caperton v. A. T. Massey Coal Co., 129 S.Ct. 2252 (2009) 　　5:4　　By a five-to-four vote, the Court held that it is unconstitutional for a state supreme court justice to sit on a case involving the financial interests of a major donor to the justices election campaign. Writing for the majority, Justice Kennedy held that West Virginia Supreme Court Chief Justice Brent Benjamin should have recused himself from a case that overturned a $50-million verdict against a company headed by a man who contributed $3 million to the justice's election. The failure to do so ran afoul of the Due Process Clause, which incorporates the common-law rule requiring recusal when a judge has "a direct, personal, substantial, pecuniary interest" in a case. According to the Court's precedents, recusal is required where "the probability of actual bias on the part of the judge or decisionmaker is too high to be constitutionally tolerable." In Justice Kennedy's words: "Not every campaign contribution by a litigant or attorney creates a probability of bias that requires a judge's recusal, but this is an exceptional case." By contrast, dissenting Chief Justice Roberts, joined by Justices Scalia, Thomas, and Alito, countered that the ruling "requires state and federal judges simultaneously to act as political scientists (why did candidate X win the election?), economists (was the financial support disproportionate?), and psychologists (is there likely to be a debt of gratitude?)."

9

ECONOMIC RIGHTS AND
AMERICAN CAPITALISM

C | *The "Takings Clause" and Just Compensation*

In its 2009–2010 term, the Court reconsidered constitutional limits on states' power to restore storm-eroded beaches along the ocean and lakeshores, when such action infringes on private property lines, in *Stop the Beach Renourishment v. Florida* 130 S.Ct. 2592 (2010). Florida's legislature enacted the Shore Preservation Act to establish procedures to restore eroded shorelines damaged by hurricanes. Stop the Beach Renourishment (STBR), a nonprofit association of owners of beachfront property, challenged the constitutionality of the beach restoration project. STBR claimed that a provision of the law pertaining to the shoreline boundary unconstitutionally deprived waterfront property owners of upland property rights without just compensation. A state appellate court held that the takings required eminent domain proceedings, but subsequently certified the question as having public importance since beach erosion posed a serious problem for the economy and general welfare of the public. The state supreme court reversed, ruling that the law fixing shoreline boundaries did not unconstitutionally deprive upland owners of their rights without just compensation.

Writing for the Court in *Stop the Beach Renourishment*, Justice Scalia affirmed the state supreme court's ruling rejecting the claim that beach restoration of submerged land constituted a taking under the Fifth Amendment, reaffirming the previous ruling in *Lucas v. South Carolina Coastal Council*, 505 U.S. 1003 (1992) (excerpted in Vols. 1 and 2). Justice Thomas dissented.

SUPREME COURT WATCH 2010
VOLUME TWO

4

The Nationalization

of the

Bill of Rights

A | *The Selective Nationalization of Guarantees of the Bill of Rights plus Other Fundamental Rights*

In a landmark ruling in *McDonald v. City of Chicago* (2010) (excerpted below), a bare majority incorporated the Second Amendment right to keep and bear arms into the Due Process Clause of the Fourteenth Amendment and extended its protection against state and local firearm regulations.

■ The Development of Law

The Supreme Court Rules on the Second Amendment Right to Keep and Bear Arms

In a historic ruling in *District of Columbia v. Heller*, 128 S.Ct. 2783(2008), the Court struck down two key provisions of the District of Columbia's 1976 ban on handguns, the strictest in the nation: (1) a flat ban on possessing a handgun in one's home; and (2) a requirement that any gun, except one kept at a business, must be unloaded and disassembled or have a trigger lock in place. The Court left intact other provisions, such as the requirement that guns must be registered and licensed. Not since *United States v. Miller*, 307 U.S. 174 (1939), had the Court addressed the amendment (see the Constitutional History box on the Second and Third Amendments in Vol. 2, Ch. 4). For the first time, the Court held that the Second Amendment (providing that "A well regulated Militia, being necessary to the security of a free State, the right of the people to keep and bear Arms, shall not be infringed") guarantees individuals the right to possess handguns in their homes.

Writing for a bare majority, Justice Scalia advanced several arguments—textualist, intratextualist, and based on the original understanding of the amendment—for invalidating the ban on handguns. First, he separated the prefatory and operative clauses of the amendment, observing that "The Second Amendment is naturally divided into two parts: its prefatory clause [A well regulated Militia] and its operative clause [the right of the people to keep and bear Arms] . . . [A] prefatory clause does not limit or expand the scope of the operative clause. . . . The prefatory clause does not suggest that preserving the militia was the only reason Americans valued the ancient right; most undoubtedly thought it even more important for self-defense and hunting." Turning to the operative clause—"to keep and bear Arms"—he added: "Although the phrase implies that the carrying of the weapon is for the purpose of 'offensive or defensive action,' it in no way connotes participation in a structured military organization. . . . [T]he most natural reading of 'keep Arms' in the Second Amendment is to have weapons." After separating those clauses, he focused on "the right of the people" and offered an intratextualist analysis, emphasizing that "in all six other provisions of the Constitution that mention 'the people,' the term unambiguously refers to all members of the political community, not an unspecified subset. . . . Putting all of these textual elements together, we find that they guarantee the individual right to possess and carry

weapons in case of confrontation." Finally, Justice Scalia drew on the "original understanding" of the amendment, which he asserted applied "to weapons
that were not specifically designed for military use and were not employed
in a military capacity." "In sum," he concluded, "the District's ban on handgun possession in the home violates the Second Amendment, as does its prohibition against rendering any lawful firearm in the home operable for the
purpose of immediate self-defense. Assuming that Heller is not disqualified
from the exercise of Second Amendment rights, the District must permit him
to register his handgun and must issue him a license to carry it in the home."

Justice Scalia's opinion for the Court, joined by Chief Justice Roberts
and Justices Kennedy, Thomas, and Alito, however, emphasized that "the right
secured by the Second Amendment is not unlimited." More specifically, Justice Scalia expressly emphasized that the amendment applies only to federal
regulations and does not apply to the states under the Fourteenth Amendment. In underscoring that the decision applied only to the possession of
handguns in one's home for purpose of self-defense, he noted that "we do
not read the Second Amendment to protect the right of citizens to carry
arms for any sort of confrontation, just as we do not read the First Amendment to protect the right of citizens to speak for any purpose." Justice Scalia
also noted that the decision did not apply to other long-standing restrictions,
such as prohibitions on the possession of firearms by felons and the mentally
ill, the carrying of concealed weapons, as well as to bans on the carrying of
firearms into schools and government buildings, and to conditions imposed
on the commercial sale of firearms. In addition, he emphasized the narrow-
ness of the ruling as applying only to "the sorts of weapons protected . . . 'in
common use at the time'" of the ratification of the amendment; thus, leaving
open the regulation of semi-automatic, assault and other weapons.

Subsequently, without mentioning the Second Amendment or the ruling in *Heller*, the Court upheld a federal statute, as amended in 1996, banning
the possession of firearms by individuals convicted of felonies or of "a misdemeanor of domestic violence." Justice Ginsburg wrote for the Court in
United States v. Hayes, 129 S.Ct. 1079 (2009), and Chief Justice Roberts and
Justice Scalia dissented. But after the ruling in *Heller*, the Court inexorably
confronted the issue of whether the Second Amendment applies to the states
and limits their powers over gun control regulations. The Court took up that
issue in *McDonald v. City of Chicago* (2010) (excerpted in this chapter) and a bare
majority held that the amendment was incorporated into the Fourteenth
Amendment's Due Process Clause and applies to state and local government
regulations.

McDonald v. City of Chicago
130 S.Ct. 1037 (2010)

In 1983, the city of Chicago enacted, in response to a number of killings, an ordinance banning the possession of unregistered firearms. Under the ordinance, gun owners had to register with police their possession of firearms, and annually re-register their ownership and/or sale of the arms. A first violation of the regulation is punishable by a fine of $300 to $500, incarceration for ten to ninety days, or both. In light of the Supreme Court's ruling in *District of Columbia v. Heller*, 128 S.Ct. 2783 (2008), striking down the District of Columbia's firearm regulations, four residents challenged Chicago's regulation. A three-judge panel of the Court Appeals for the Seventh Circuit upheld Chicago's ordinances.

The appellate court's decision was reversed by a five to four vote. Justice Alito delivered the opinion of the Court for a plurality. Justices Scalia and Thomas each filed concurring opinions. Justices Stevens and Breyer each filed dissenting opinions. Justices Ginsburg and Sotomayor joined the latter's dissent.

☐ *Justice ALITO announced the judgment of the Court and delivered the opinion of the Court with respect to Parts I, II–A, II–B, II–D, III–A, and III–B, in which THE CHIEF JUSTICE, Justice SCALIA, Justice KENNEDY, and Justice THOMAS join, and an opinion with respect to Parts II–C, IV, and V, in which THE CHIEF JUSTICE, Justice SCALIA, and Justice KENNEDY join.*

Two years ago, in *District of Columbia v. Heller* (2008), we held that the Second Amendment protects the right to keep and bear arms for the purpose of self-defense, and we struck down a District of Columbia law that banned the possession of handguns in the home. The city of Chicago (City) and the village of Oak Park, a Chicago suburb, have laws that are similar to the District of Columbia's, but Chicago and Oak Park argue that their laws are constitutional because the Second Amendment has no application to the States. We have previously held that most of the provisions of the Bill of Rights apply with full force to both the Federal Government and the States. Applying the standard that is well established in our case law, we hold that the Second Amendment right is fully applicable to the States. . . .

■ II–A

Petitioners argue that the Chicago and Oak Park laws violate the right to keep and bear arms for two reasons. Petitioners' primary submission is that this right is among the "privileges or immunities of citizens of the United States" and that the narrow interpretation of the Privileges or Immunities Clause adopted in the *Slaughter-House Cases*, 6 Wall. 86 (1873), should now be rejected. As a secondary argument, petitioners contend that the Fourteenth Amendment's Due Process Clause "incorporates" the Second Amendment right. . . .

■ II–B

The Bill of Rights, including the Second Amendment, originally applied only to the Federal Government.

The constitutional Amendments adopted in the aftermath of the Civil War fundamentally altered our country's federal system. The provision at issue in this case, Section 1 of the Fourteenth Amendment, provides, among other things, that a State may not abridge "the privileges or immunities of citizens of the United States" or deprive "any person of life, liberty, or property, without due process of law."

Four years after the adoption of the Fourteenth Amendment, this Court was asked to interpret the Amendment's reference to "the privileges or immunities of citizens of the United States." The *Slaughter-House Cases* involved challenges to a Louisiana law permitting the creation of a state-sanctioned monopoly on the butchering of animals within the city of New Orleans. Justice SAMUEL MILLER's opinion for the Court concluded that the Privileges or Immunities Clause protects only those rights "which owe their existence to the Federal government, its National character, its Constitution, or its laws." The Court held that other fundamental rights—rights that predated the creation of the Federal Government and that "the State governments were created to establish and secure"—were not protected by the Clause.

In drawing a sharp distinction between the rights of federal and state citizenship, the Court relied on two principal arguments. First, the Court emphasized that the Fourteenth Amendment's Privileges or Immunities Clause spoke of "the privileges or immunities of citizens of the United States," and the Court contrasted this phrasing with the wording in the first sentence of the Fourteenth Amendment and in the Privileges and Immunities Clause of Article IV, both of which refer to state citizenship. Second, the Court stated that a contrary reading would "radically chang[e] the whole theory of the relations of the State and Federal governments to each other and of both these governments to the people," and the Court refused to conclude that such a change had been made "in the absence of language which expresses such a purpose too clearly to admit of doubt." Finding the phrase "privileges or immunities of citizens of the United States" lacking by this high standard, the Court reasoned that the phrase must mean something more limited.

Under the Court's narrow reading, the Privileges or Immunities Clause protects such things as the right "to come to the seat of government to assert any claim [a citizen] may have upon that government, to transact any business he may have with it, to seek its protection, to share its offices, to engage in administering its functions . . . [and to] become a citizen of any State of the Union by a bonfide residence therein, with the same rights as other citizens of that State." . . .

Today, many legal scholars dispute the correctness of the narrow *Slaughter-House* interpretation.

Three years after the decision in the *Slaughter-House Cases*, the Court decided *Cruikshank* [92 U.S. 542 (1876)], the first of the three 19th-century cases on which the Seventh Circuit relied. In that case, the Court reviewed convictions stemming from the infamous Colfax Massacre in Louisiana on Easter Sunday 1873. Dozens of blacks, many unarmed, were slaughtered by a rival band of armed white men. Cruikshank himself allegedly marched unarmed African-American prisoners through the streets and then had them summarily executed. Ninety-seven men were indicted for participating in the massacre, but only nine went to trial. Six of the nine were acquitted of all charges; the remaining three were acquitted of murder but convicted under the Enforcement Act of 1870, for banding and conspiring together to deprive their victims of various constitutional rights, including the right to bear arms.

The Court reversed all of the convictions, including those relating to the deprivation of the victims' right to bear arms. The Court wrote that the right of bearing arms for a lawful purpose "is not a right granted by the Constitution" and is not "in any manner dependent upon that instrument for its existence." "The second amendment," the Court continued, "declares that it shall not be infringed; but this . . . means no more than that it shall not be infringed by Congress." "Our later decisions in *Presser v. Illinois*, 116 U.S. 252 (1886), and *Miller v. Texas*, 153 U.S. 535 (1894), reaffirmed that the Second Amendment applies only to the Federal Government."

■ II–C

As previously noted, the Seventh Circuit concluded that *Cruikshank, Presser,* and *Miller* doomed petitioners' claims at the Court of Appeals level. Petitioners argue, however, that we should overrule those decisions and hold that the right to keep and bear arms is one of the "privileges or immunities of citizens of the United States." In petitioners' view, the Privileges or Immunities Clause protects all of the rights set out in the Bill of Rights, as well as some others, but petitioners are unable to identify the Clause's full scope. Nor is there any consensus on that question among the scholars who agree that the *Slaughter-House Cases'* interpretation is flawed.

We see no need to reconsider that interpretation here. For many decades, the question of the rights protected by the Fourteenth Amendment against state infringement has been analyzed under the Due Process Clause of that Amendment and not under the Privileges or Immunities Clause. We therefore decline to disturb the *Slaughter-House* holding.

At the same time, however, this Court's decisions in *Cruikshank, Presser,* and *Miller* do not preclude us from considering whether the Due Process Clause of the Fourteenth Amendment makes the Second Amendment right binding on the States. . . .

■ II–D

In the late 19th century, the Court began to consider whether the Due Process Clause prohibits the States from infringing rights set out in the Bill of Rights. See *Hurtado v. California*, 110 U.S. 516 (1884) (due process does not require grand jury indictment); *Chicago, B. & Q. R. Co. v. Chicago*, 166 U.S. 226 (1897) (due process prohibits States from taking of private property for public use without just compensation). Five features of the approach taken during the ensuing era should be noted.

First, the Court viewed the due process question as entirely separate from the question whether a right was a privilege or immunity of national citizenship.

Second, the Court explained that the only rights protected against state infringement by the Due Process Clause were those rights "of such a nature that they are included in the conception of due process of law."

Third, in some cases decided during this era the Court "can be seen as having asked, when inquiring into whether some particular procedural safeguard was required of a State, if a civilized system could be imagined that would not accord the particular protection." *Duncan v. Louisiana*, 391 U.S. 145 (1968). Thus, in holding that due process prohibits a State from taking private property without just compensation, the Court described the right as "a principle of natural equity, recognized by all temperate and civilized governments, from a deep and universal sense of its justice." Similarly, the Court found that due process did not provide a right against compelled incrimination in part because this right "has no place in the jurisprudence of civilized and free countries outside the domain of the common law."

Fourth, the Court during this era was not hesitant to hold that a right set out in the Bill of Rights failed to meet the test for inclusion within the protection of the Due Process Clause. The Court found that some such rights qualified. See, e.g., *Gitlow v. New York*, 268 U.S. 652 (1925) (freedom of speech and press); *Near v. Minnesota ex rel. Olson*, 283 U.S. 697 (1931)(same); *Powell* (assistance of counsel in capital cases); *De Jonge* (freedom of assembly); *Cantwell v. Connecticut*, 310 U.S. 296 (1940) (free exercise of religion). But others did not. See, e.g., *Hurtado* (grand jury indictment requirement); *Twining* (privilege against self-incrimination).

Finally, even when a right set out in the Bill of Rights was held to fall within the conception of due process, the protection or remedies afforded against state infringement sometimes differed from the protection or remedies provided against abridgment by the Federal Government. To give one example, in *Betts* the Court held that, although the Sixth Amendment required the appointment of counsel in all federal criminal cases in which the defendant was unable to retain an attorney, the Due Process Clause required appointment of counsel in state criminal proceedings only where "want of counsel in [the] particular case ... result[ed] in a conviction lacking in ... fundamental fairness."

An alternative theory regarding the relationship between the Bill of Rights and Section 1 of the Fourteenth Amendment was championed by Justice BLACK. This theory held that Section 1 of the Fourteenth Amendment totally incorporated all of the provisions of the Bill of Rights. As Justice BLACK noted, the chief congressional proponents of the Fourteenth Amendment espoused the view that the Amendment made the Bill of Rights applicable to the States and, in so doing, overruled this Court's decision in *Barron*. Nonetheless, the Court never has embraced Justice BLACK's "total incorporation" theory.

While Justice BLACK's theory was never adopted, the Court eventually moved in that direction by initiating what has been called a process of "selective incorporation," i.e., the Court began to hold that the Due Process Clause fully incorporates particular rights contained in the first eight Amendments.

The decisions during this time abandoned three of the previously noted characteristics of the earlier period. The Court made it clear that the governing standard is not whether any "civilized system [can] be imagined that would not accord the particular protection." Instead, the Court inquired whether a particular Bill of Rights guarantee is fundamental to our scheme of ordered liberty and system of justice.

The Court also shed any reluctance to hold that rights guaranteed by the Bill of Rights met the requirements for protection under the Due Process Clause. The Court eventually incorporated almost all of the provisions of the Bill of Rights. Only a handful of the Bill of Rights protections remain unincorporated.

Finally, the Court abandoned "the notion that the Fourteenth Amendment applies to the States only a watered-down, subjective version of the individual guarantees of the Bill of Rights," stating that it would be "incongruous" to apply different standards "depending on whether the claim was asserted in a state or federal court." Instead, the Court decisively held that incorporated Bill of Rights protections "are all to be enforced against the States under the Fourteenth Amendment according to the same standards that protect those personal rights against federal encroachment."

Employing this approach, the Court overruled earlier decisions in which it had held that particular Bill of Rights guarantees or remedies did not apply to the States.

■ **III**

With this framework in mind, we now turn directly to the question whether the Second Amendment right to keep and bear arms is incorporated in the concept of due process. In answering that question, as just explained, we must decide whether the right to keep and bear arms is fundamental to our scheme of ordered liberty, or as we have said in a related context, whether this right is "deeply rooted in this Nation's history and tradition."

III–A

Our decision in *Heller* points unmistakably to the answer. Self-defense is a basic right, recognized by many legal systems from ancient times to the present day, and in *Heller*, we held that individual self-defense is "the central component" of the Second Amendment right. Explaining that "the need for defense of self, family, and property is most acute" in the home, we found that this right applies to handguns because they are "the most preferred firearm in the nation to 'keep' and use for protection of one's home and family."

Heller makes it clear that this right is "deeply rooted in this Nation's history and tradition." *Heller* explored the right's origins, noting that the 1689 English Bill of Rights explicitly protected a right to keep arms for self-defense, and that by 1765, Blackstone was able to assert that the right to keep and bear arms was "one of the fundamental rights of Englishmen."

Blackstone's assessment was shared by the American colonists. As we noted in *Heller*, King George III's attempt to disarm the colonists in the 1760's and 1770's "provoked polemical reactions by Americans invoking their rights as Englishmen to keep arms."

The right to keep and bear arms was considered no less fundamental by those who drafted and ratified the Bill of Rights. "During the 1788 ratification debates, the fear that the federal government would disarm the people in order to impose rule through a standing army or select militia was pervasive in Antifederalist rhetoric." *Heller.*

This understanding persisted in the years immediately following the ratification of the Bill of Rights. In addition to the four States that had adopted Second Amendment analogues before ratification, nine more States adopted state constitutional provisions protecting an individual right to keep and bear arms between 1789 and 1820. Founding-era legal commentators confirmed the importance of the right to early Americans. St. George Tucker, for example, described the right to keep and bear arms as "the true palladium of liberty" and explained that prohibitions on the right would place liberty "on the brink of destruction."

III–B

By the 1850's, the perceived threat that had prompted the inclusion of the Second Amendment in the Bill of Rights—the fear that the National Government would disarm the universal militia—had largely faded as a popular concern, but the right to keep and bear arms was highly valued for purposes of self-defense. And when attempts were made to disarm "Free-Soilers" in "Bloody Kansas," Senator Charles Sumner, who later played a leading role in the adoption of the Fourteenth Amendment, proclaimed that "[n]ever was [the rifle] more needed in just self-defense than now in Kansas." Indeed, the 1856 Republican Party Platform protested that in Kansas the constitutional rights of the people had been "fraudulently and violently taken from them" and the "right of the people to keep and bear arms" had been "infringed."

After the Civil War, many of the over 180,000 African Americans who served in the Union Army returned to the States of the old Confederacy, where systematic efforts were made to disarm them and other blacks. The laws of some States formally prohibited African Americans from possessing firearms. For example, a Mississippi law provided that "no freedman, free negro or mulatto, not in the military service of the United States government, and not licensed so to do by the board of police of his or her county, shall keep or carry fire-arms of any kind, or any ammunition, dirk or bowie knife." . . .

Union Army commanders took steps to secure the right of all citizens to keep and bear arms, but the 39th Congress concluded that legislative action was necessary. Its efforts to safeguard the right to keep and bear arms demonstrate that the right was still recognized to be fundamental.

The most explicit evidence of Congress' aim appears in Section 14 of the Freedmen's Bureau Act of 1866, which provided that "the right . . . to have full and equal benefit of all laws and proceedings concerning personal liberty, personal security, and the acquisition, enjoyment, and disposition of estate, real and personal, including the constitutional right to bear arms, shall be secured to and enjoyed by all the citizens. . . without respect to race or color, or previous condition of slavery." Section 14 thus explicitly guaranteed that "all the citizens," black and white, would have "the constitutional right to bear arms."

The Civil Rights Act of 1866, which was considered at the same time as the Freedmen's Bureau Act, similarly sought to protect the right of all citizens to keep and bear arms. Section 1 of the Civil Rights Act guaranteed the "full and equal benefit of all laws and proceedings for the security of person and property, as is enjoyed by white citizens."

Congress, however, ultimately deemed these legislative remedies insufficient. Southern resistance, Presidential vetoes, and this Court's pre-Civil-War precedent persuaded Congress that a constitutional amendment was necessary to provide full protection for the rights of blacks. Today, it is generally accepted that the Fourteenth Amendment was understood to provide a constitutional basis for protecting the rights set out in the Civil Rights Act of 1866.

In debating the Fourteenth Amendment, the 39th Congress referred to the right to keep and bear arms as a fundamental right deserving of protection. Senator Samuel Pomeroy described three "indispensable" "safeguards of liberty under our form of Government." One of these, he said, was the right to keep and bear arms: "Every man . . . should have the right to bear arms for the defense of himself and family and his homestead. And if the cabin door of the freedman is broken open and the intruder enters for purposes as vile as were known to slavery, then should a well-loaded musket be in the hand of the occupant to send the polluted wretch to another world, where his wretchedness will forever remain complete."

Evidence from the period immediately following the ratification of the Fourteenth Amendment only confirms that the right to keep and bear arms was considered fundamental. In an 1868 speech addressing the disarmament of freedmen, Representative Stevens emphasized the necessity of the right: "Disarm a community and you rob them of the means of defending life. Take away their weapons of defense and you take away the inalienable right of defending liberty." . . .

The right to keep and bear arms was also widely protected by state constitutions at the time when the Fourteenth Amendment was ratified. . . .

In sum, it is clear that the Framers and ratifiers of the Fourteenth Amendment counted the right to keep and bear arms among those fundamental rights necessary to our system of ordered liberty. . . .

▪ IV

Municipal respondents' remaining arguments are at war with our central holding in *Heller*: that the Second Amendment protects a personal right to keep and bear arms for lawful purposes, most notably for self-defense within the home. Municipal respondents, in effect, ask us to treat the right recognized in *Heller* as a second-class right, subject to an entirely different body of rules than the other Bill of Rights guarantees that we have held to be incorporated into the Due Process Clause.

Municipal respondents' main argument is nothing less than a plea to disregard 50 years of incorporation precedent and return (presumably for this case only) to a bygone era. Municipal respondents submit that the Due Process Clause protects only those rights "'recognized by all temperate and civilized governments, from a deep and universal sense of [their] justice.'" According to municipal respondents, if it is possible to imagine any civilized legal system that does not recognize a particular right, then the Due Process Clause does not make that right binding on the States. Therefore, the municipal respondents continue, because such countries as England, Canada, Australia, Japan, Denmark, Finland, Luxembourg, and New Zealand either ban or severely limit handgun ownership, it must follow that no right to possess such weapons is protected by the Fourteenth Amendment.

This line of argument is, of course, inconsistent with the long-established standard we apply in incorporation cases. And the present-day implications of municipal respondents' argument are stunning. For example, many of the rights that our Bill of Rights provides for persons accused of criminal offenses are virtually unique to this country. If our understanding of the right to a jury trial, the right against self-incrimination, and the right to counsel were necessary attributes of any civilized country, it would follow that the United States is the only civilized Nation in the world.

Municipal respondents attempt to salvage their position by suggesting that their argument applies only to substantive as opposed to procedural rights. But even in this trimmed form, municipal respondents' argument flies in the face of more than a half-century of precedent. For example, in *Everson v. Board of Ed. of Ewing*, 330 U.S. 1 (1947), the Court held that the Fourteenth Amendment incorporates the Establishment Clause of the First Amendment. Yet several of the countries that municipal respondents recognize as civilized have established state churches. If we were to adopt municipal respondents' theory, all of this Court's Establishment Clause precedents involving actions taken by state and local governments would go by the boards.

Municipal respondents maintain that the Second Amendment differs from all of the other provisions of the Bill of Rights because it concerns the right to possess a deadly implement and thus has implications for public safety. And they note that there is intense disagreement on the question whether the private possession of guns in the home increases or decreases gun deaths and injuries.

The right to keep and bear arms, however, is not the only constitutional right that has controversial public safety implications. . . . Municipal respondents cite no case in which we have refrained from holding that a provision of the Bill of Rights is binding on the States on the ground that the right at issue has disputed public safety implications.

We likewise reject municipal respondents' argument that we should depart from our established incorporation methodology on the ground that making the Second Amendment binding on the States and their subdivisions is inconsistent with principles of federalism and will stifle experimentation. Municipal respondents point out—quite correctly—that conditions and problems differ from locality to locality and that citizens in different jurisdictions have divergent views on the issue of gun control. Municipal respondents therefore urge us to allow state and local governments to enact any gun control law that they deem to be reasonable, including a complete ban on the possession of handguns in the home for self-defense.

There is nothing new in the argument that, in order to respect federalism and allow useful state experimentation, a federal constitutional right should not be fully binding on the States. This argument was made repeatedly and eloquently by Members of this Court who rejected the concept of incorporation and urged retention of the two-track approach to incorporation. Throughout the era of "selective incorporation," Justice HARLAN in particular, invoking the values of federalism and state experimentation, fought a determined rearguard action to preserve the two-track approach.

Time and again, however, those pleas failed. Unless we turn back the clock or adopt a special incorporation test applicable only to the Second Amendment, municipal respondents' argument must be rejected. Under our precedents, if a Bill of Rights guarantee is fundamental from an American perspective, then, unless *stare decisis* counsels otherwise, that guarantee is fully binding on the States and thus limits (but by no means eliminates) their ability to devise solutions to social problems that suit local needs and values. As noted by the 38 States that have appeared in this case as *amici* supporting petitioners, "[s]tate and local experimentation with reasonable firearms regulations will continue under the Second Amendment."

Municipal respondents and their *amici* complain that incorporation of the Second Amendment right will lead to extensive and costly litigation, but this argument applies with even greater force to constitutional rights and remedies that have already been held to be binding on the States. . . .

Municipal respondents argue, finally, that the right to keep and bear arms is unique among the rights set out in the first eight Amendments "because the reason for codifying the Second Amendment (to protect the militia) differs from the purpose (primarily, to use firearms to engage in self-defense) that is claimed to make the right implicit in the concept of ordered liberty." Municipal respondents suggest that the Second Amendment right differs from the rights heretofore incorporated because the latter were "valued for [their] own sake." But we have never previously suggested that incorporation of a right turns on whether it has intrinsic as opposed to instrumental value, and quite a few of the rights previously held to be incorporated—for example the right to counsel and the right to confront and subpoena witnesses—are clearly instrumental by any measure. Moreover, this contention repackages one of the chief arguments that we rejected in *Heller*, i.e., that the scope of the Second Amendment right is defined by the immediate threat that led to the inclusion of that right in the Bill of Rights. In *Heller*, we recognized that the codification of this right was prompted by fear that the Federal Government would disarm and thus disable the militias, but we rejected the suggestion that the right was valued only as a means of preserving the militias. On the contrary, we stressed that the right was also valued because the possession of firearms was thought to be essential for self-defense. As we put it, self-defense was "the central component of the right itself."

■ **V–A**

We turn, finally, to the two dissenting opinions. Justice STEVENS' eloquent opinion covers ground already addressed, and therefore little need be added in response. Justice STEVENS would "'ground the prohibitions against state action squarely on due process, without intermediate reliance on any of the first eight Amendments.'" The question presented in this case, in his view, "is whether the particular right asserted by petitioners applies to the States because of the Fourteenth Amendment itself, standing on its own bottom." He would hold that "[t]he rights protected against state infringement by the Fourteenth Amendment's Due Process Clause need not be identical in shape or scope to the rights protected against Federal Government infringement by the various provisions of the Bill of Rights."

As we have explained, the Court, for the past half-century, has moved away from the two-track approach. If we were now to accept Justice STEVENS' theory across the board, decades of decisions would be undermined. We assume that this is not what is proposed. What is urged instead, it appears, is that this theory be revived solely for the individual right that *Heller* recognized, over vigorous dissents. . . .

V–B

Justice BREYER's dissent makes several points to which we briefly respond. To begin, while there is certainly room for disagreement about *Heller*'s analysis of the history of the right to keep and bear arms, nothing written since *Heller* persuades us to reopen the question there decided. Few other questions of original meaning have been as thoroughly explored.

Justice BREYER's conclusion that the Fourteenth Amendment does not incorporate the right to keep and bear arms appears to rest primarily on four factors: First, "there is no popular consensus" that the right is fundamental; second, the right does not protect minorities or persons neglected by those holding political power; third, incorporation of the Second Amendment right would "amount to a significant incursion on a traditional and important area of state concern, altering the constitutional relationship between the States and the Federal Government" and preventing local variations; and fourth, determining the scope of the Second Amendment right in cases involving state and local laws will force judges to answer difficult empirical questions regarding matters that are outside their area of expertise. Even if we believed that these factors were relevant to the incorporation inquiry, none of these factors undermines the case for incorporation of the right to keep and bear arms for self-defense. . . .

In *Heller*, we held that the Second Amendment protects the right to possess a handgun in the home for the purpose of self-defense. Unless considerations of *stare decisis* counsel otherwise, a provision of the Bill of Rights that protects a right that is fundamental from an American perspective applies equally to the Federal Government and the States. We therefore hold that the Due Process Clause of the Fourteenth Amendment incorporates the Second Amendment right recognized in *Heller*. The judgment of the Court of Appeals is reversed, and the case is remanded for further proceedings.

☐ *Justice SCALIA, concurring.*

I join the Court's opinion. Despite my misgivings about Substantive Due Process as an original matter, I have acquiesced in the Court's incorporation of certain guarantees in the Bill of Rights "because it is both long established and narrowly limited." This case does not require me to reconsider that view, since straightforward application of settled doctrine suffices to decide it.

I write separately only to respond to some aspects of Justice STEVENS' dissent. Not that aspect which disagrees with the majority's application of our precedents to this case, which is fully covered by the Court's opinion. But much of what Justice STEVENS writes is a broad condemnation of the theory of interpretation which underlies the Court's opinion, a theory that makes the traditions of our people paramount. He proposes a different theory, which he claims is more "cautiou[s]" and respectful of proper limits on the judicial role. It is that claim I wish to address.

After stressing the substantive dimension of what he has renamed the "liberty clause," Justice STEVENS proceeds to urge readoption of the theory of incorporation articulated in *Palko v. Connecticut*, 302 U.S. 319 (1937). But in fact he does not favor application of that theory at all. For whether *Palko* requires only that "a fair and enlightened system of justice would be impossible without" the right sought to be incorporated, or requires in addition that the right be rooted in the "traditions and conscience of our people," many of the rights Justice STEVENS thinks are incorporated could not pass muster under either test: abortion; homosexual sodomy; the right to have excluded from criminal trials evidence obtained in violation of the Fourth Amendment; and the right to teach one's children foreign languages, among others.

That Justice STEVENS is not applying any version of *Palko* is clear from comparing, on the one hand, the rights he believes are covered, with, on the other hand, his conclusion that the right to keep and bear arms is not covered. Rights that pass his test include not just those "relating to marriage, procreation, contraception, family relationships, and child rearing and education," but also rights against "[g]overnment action that shocks the conscience, pointlessly infringes settled expectations, trespasses into sensitive private realms or life choices without adequate justification, [or] perpetrates gross injustice." Not all such rights are in, however, since only "some fundamental aspects of personhood, dignity, and the like" are protected. Exactly what is covered is not clear. But whatever else is in, he knows that the right to keep and bear arms is out, despite its being as "deeply rooted in this Nation's history and tradition," *Washington v. Glucksberg*, 521 U.S. 702 (1997) as a right can be. I can find no other explanation for such certitude except that Justice STEVENS, despite his forswearing of "personal and private notions," deeply believes it should be out.

The subjective nature of Justice STEVENS' standard is also apparent from his claim that it is the courts' prerogative—indeed their duty—to update the Due Process Clause so that it encompasses new freedoms the Framers were too narrow-minded to imagine. . . .

If Justice STEVENS' account of the constraints of his approach did not demonstrate that they do not exist, his application of that approach to the case before us leaves no doubt. He offers several reasons for concluding that the Second Amendment right to keep and bear arms is not fundamental enough to be applied against the States. None is persuasive, but more pertinent to my purpose, each is either intrinsically indeterminate, would preclude incorporation of rights we have already held incorporated, or both. His approach therefore does nothing to stop a judge from arriving at any conclusion he sets out to reach.

Justice STEVENS begins with the odd assertion that "firearms have a fundamentally ambivalent relationship to liberty," since sometimes they are used to cause (or sometimes accidentally produce) injury to others. The source of the rule that only nonambivalent liberties deserve Due Process protection is never explained—proof that judges applying Justice STEVENS' approach can add new elements to the test as they see fit. The criterion, moreover, is inherently manipulable. Surely Justice STEVENS does not mean that the Clause covers only rights that have zero harmful effect on anyone. Otherwise even the First Amendment is out. Maybe what he means is that the right to keep and bear arms imposes too great a risk to others' physical well-being. But as the plurality explains, other rights we have already held incorporated pose similarly substantial risks to public safety. In all events, Justice STEVENS supplies neither a standard for how severe the impairment on others' liberty must be for a right to be disqualified, nor (of course) any method of measuring the severity.

Justice STEVENS next suggests that the Second Amendment right is not fundamental because it is "different in kind" from other rights we have recognized. In one respect, of course, the right to keep and bear arms is different from some other rights we have held the Clause protects and he would recognize: It is deeply grounded in our nation's history and tradition. But Justice STEVENS has a different distinction in mind: Even though he does "not doubt for a moment that many Americans . . . see [firearms] as critical to their way of life as well as to their security," he pronounces that owning a handgun is not "critical to leading a life of autonomy, dignity, or political equality." Who says? Deciding what is essential to an enlightened, liberty-filled life is an inherently political, moral judgment—the antithesis of an objective approach that reaches conclusions by applying neutral rules to verifiable evidence. . . .

Justice STEVENS also argues that since the right to keep and bear arms was codified for the purpose of "prevent[ing] elimination of the militia," it should be viewed as "'a federalism provision'" logically incapable of incorporation. This criterion, too, evidently applies only when judges want it to. . . .

Justice STEVENS next argues that even if the right to keep and bear arms is "deeply rooted in some important senses," the roots of States' efforts to regulate guns run just as deep. But this too is true of other rights we have held incorporated. No fundamental right—not even the First Amendment —is absolute. The traditional restrictions go to show the scope of the right, not its lack of fundamental character. At least that is what they show (Justice STEVENS would agree) for other rights. Once again, principles are applied selectively.

Justice STEVENS' final reason for rejecting incorporation of the Second Amendment reveals, more clearly than any of the others, the game that is afoot. Assuming that there is a "plausible constitutional basis" for holding that the right to keep and bear arms is incorporated, he asserts that we ought not to do so for prudential reasons. Even if we had the authority to withhold rights that are within the Constitution's command (and we assuredly do not), two of the reasons Justice STEVENS gives for abstention show just how much power he would hand to judges. The States' "right to experiment" with solutions to the problem of gun violence, he says, is at its apex here because "the best solution is far from clear." That is true of most serious social problems— whether, for example, "the best solution" for rampant crime is to admit confessions unless they are affirmatively shown to have been coerced, or to permit jurors to impose the death penalty without a requirement that they be free to consider "any relevant mitigating factor," which in turn leads to the conclusion that defense counsel has provided inadequate defense if he has not conducted a "reasonable investigation" into potentially mitigating factors, inquiry into which question tends to destroy any prospect of prompt justice. The obviousness of the optimal answer is in the eye of the beholder. The implication of Justice STEVENS' call for abstention is that if We The Court conclude that They The People's answers to a problem are silly, we are free to "interven[e]," but if we too are uncertain of the right answer, or merely think the States may be on to something, we can loosen the leash.

A second reason Justice STEVENS says we should abstain is that the States have shown they are "capable" of protecting the right at issue, and if anything have protected it too much. That reflects an assumption that judges can distinguish between a proper democratic decision to leave things alone (which we should honor), and a case of democratic market failure (which we should step in to correct). I would not—and no judge should—presume to have that sort of omniscience, which seems to me far more "arrogant" than confining courts' focus to our own national heritage. . . .

☐ *Justice THOMAS, concurring in part and concurring in the judgment.*

I agree with the Court that the Fourteenth Amendment makes the right to keep and bear arms set forth in the Second Amendment "fully applicable to the States." I write separately because I believe there is a more straightforward path to this conclusion, one that is more faithful to the Fourteenth Amendment's text and history.

Applying what is now a well-settled test, the plurality opinion concludes that the right to keep and bear arms applies to the States through the Fourteenth Amendment's Due Process Clause because it is "fundamental" to the American "scheme of ordered liberty," and "'deeply rooted in this Nation's history and Tradition.'" I agree with that description of the right. But I cannot agree that it is enforceable against the States through a clause that speaks only to "process." Instead, the right to keep and bear arms is a privilege of American citizenship that applies to the States through the Fourteenth Amendment's Privileges or Immunities Clause. . . .

[E]vidence plainly shows that the ratifying public understood the Privileges or Immunities Clause to protect constitutionally enumerated rights, including the right to keep and bear arms. As the Court demonstrates, there can be no doubt that Section 1 was understood to enforce the Second Amendment against the States. In my view, this is because the right to keep and bear arms was understood to be a privilege of American citizenship guaranteed by the Privileges or Immunities Clause. . . .

I agree with the Court that the Second Amendment is fully applicable to the States. I do so because the right to keep and bear arms is guaranteed by the Fourteenth Amendment as a privilege of American citizenship.

☐ *Justice STEVENS, dissenting.*

In *District of Columbia v. Heller* (2008) the Court answered the question whether a federal enclave's "prohibition on the possession of usable handguns in the home violates the Second Amendment to the Constitution." The question we should be answering in this case is whether the Constitution "guarantees individuals a fundamental right," enforceable against the States, "to possess a functional, personal firearm, including a handgun, within the home." That is a different—and more difficult—inquiry than asking if the Fourteenth Amendment "incorporates" the Second Amendment. The so-called incorporation question was squarely and, in my view, correctly resolved in the late 19th century. . . .

This is a substantive due process case. . . .

If text and history are inconclusive on this point, our precedent leaves no doubt: It has been "settled" for well over a century that the Due Process Clause "applies to matters of substantive law as well as to matters of procedure." Time and again, we have recognized that in the Fourteenth Amendment as well as the Fifth, the "Due Process Clause guarantees more than fair process, and the 'liberty' it protects includes more than the absence of physical restraint." "The Clause also includes a substantive component that 'provides heightened protection against government interference with certain fundamental rights and liberty interests.'" Some of our most enduring precedents, accepted today by virtually everyone, were substantive due process decisions. See, e.g., *Loving v. Virginia*, 388 U.S. 1 (1967) (recognizing due-process- as well as equal-protection-based right to marry person of another race); *Bolling v. Sharpe*, 347 U.S. 497 (1954) (outlawing racial segregation in District of Columbia public schools); *Pierce v. Society of Sisters*, 268 U.S. 510 (925) (vindicating right of parents to direct upbringing and education of their children); *Meyer v. Nebraska*, 62 U.S. 390 (1923) (striking down prohibition on teaching of foreign languages).

The second principle woven through our cases is that substantive due process is fundamentally a matter of personal liberty. For it is the liberty clause of the Fourteenth Amendment that grounds our most important holdings in this field. It is the liberty clause that enacts the Constitution's "promise" that a measure of dignity and self-rule will be afforded to all persons. . . .

[I]t is . . . an overstatement to say that the Court has "abandoned" a "two-track approach to incorporation." The Court moved away from that approach in the area of criminal procedure. But the Second Amendment differs in fundamental respects from its neighboring provisions in the Bill of Rights; and if some 1960's opinions purported to establish a general method of incorporation, that hardly binds us in this case. The Court has not hesitated to cut back on perceived WARREN Court excesses in more areas than I can count. . . .

Furthermore, there is a real risk that, by demanding the provisions of the Bill of Rights apply identically to the States, federal courts will cause those provisions to "be watered down in the needless pursuit of uniformity." *Duncan v. Louisiana*, 391 U.S. 145 (1968) (HARLAN, J., dissenting). When one legal standard must prevail across dozens of jurisdictions with disparate needs and customs, courts will often settle on a relaxed standard. This watering-down risk is particularly acute when we move beyond the narrow realm of criminal procedure and into the relatively vast domain of substantive rights. So long as the requirements of fundamental fairness are always and everywhere respected, it is not clear that greater liberty results from the jot-for-jot application of a provision of the Bill of Rights to the States. Indeed, it is far from clear that proponents of an individual right to keep and bear arms ought to celebrate today's decision.

Our precedents have established, not an exact methodology, but rather a framework for decisionmaking. In this respect, too, the Court's narrative fails to capture the continuity and flexibility in our doctrine. The basic inquiry was described by Justice CARDOZO more than 70 years ago. When confronted with a substantive due process claim, we must ask whether the allegedly unlawful practice violates values "implicit in the concept of ordered liberty." *Palko v. Connecticut*, 302 U.S. 319 (1937). If the practice in question lacks any "oppressive and arbitrary" character, if judicial enforcement of the asserted right would not materially contribute to "a fair and enlightened system of justice," then the claim is unsuitable for substantive due process protection. Implicit in Justice CARDOZO's test is a recognition that the postulates of liberty have a universal character. Liberty claims that are inseparable from the customs that prevail in a certain region, the idiosyncratic expectations of a certain group, or the personal preferences of their champions, may be valid claims in some sense; but they are not of constitutional stature. Whether conceptualized as a "rational continuum" of legal precepts, or a seamless web of moral commitments, the rights embraced by the liberty clause transcend the local and the particular.

Justice CARDOZO's test undeniably requires judges to apply their own reasoned judgment, but that does not mean it involves an exercise in abstract philosophy. In addition to other constraints . . . historical and empirical data of various kinds ground the analysis. Textual commitments laid down elsewhere in the Constitution, judicial precedents, English common law, legislative and social facts, scientific and professional developments, practices of other civilized societies, and, above all else, the "'traditions and conscience of our people,'" are critical variables. They can provide evidence about which rights really are vital to ordered liberty, as well as a spur to judicial action.

The Court errs both in its interpretation of *Palko* and in its suggestion that later cases rendered *Palko*'s methodology defunct. . . .

A rigid historical test is inappropriate in this case, most basically, because our substantive due process doctrine has never evaluated substantive rights in purely, or even predominantly, historical terms. When the Court applied many of the procedural guarantees in the Bill of Rights to the States in the 1960's, it often asked whether the guarantee in question was "fundamental in the context of the criminal processes maintained by the American States." That inquiry could extend back through time, but it was focused not so much on historical conceptions of the guarantee as on its functional significance within the States' regimes. This contextualized approach made sense, as the choice to employ any given trial-type procedure means little in the abstract. It is only by inquiring into how that procedure intermeshes with other procedures and practices in a criminal justice system that its relationship to "liberty" and "due process" can be determined.

Yet when the Court has used the Due Process Clause to recognize rights distinct from the trial context—rights relating to the primary conduct of free individuals—Justice CARDOZO's test has been our guide. The right to free speech, for instance, has been safeguarded from state infringement not because the States have always honored it, but because it is "essential to free government" and "to the maintenance of democratic institutions"—that is, because the right to free speech is implicit in the concept of ordered liberty. While the verbal formula has varied, the Court has largely been consistent in its liberty-based approach to substantive interests outside of the adjudicatory system. As the question before us indisputably concerns such an interest, the answer cannot be found in a granular inspection of state constitutions or congressional debates. . . .

[T]he liberty safeguarded by the Fourteenth Amendment is not merely preservative in nature but rather is a "dynamic concept." Its dynamism provides a central means through which the Framers enabled the Constitution to "endure for ages to come," a central example of how they "wisely spoke in general language and left to succeeding generations the task of applying that language to the unceasingly changing environment in which they would live." "The task of giving concrete meaning to the term 'liberty,'" I have elsewhere explained at some length, "was a part of the work assigned to future generations." The judge who would outsource the interpretation of "liberty" to historical sentiment has turned his back on a task the Constitution assigned to him and drained the document of its intended vitality.

At this point a difficult question arises. In considering such a majestic term as "liberty" and applying it to present circumstances, how are we to do justice to its urgent call and its open texture—and to the grant of interpretive discretion the latter embodies—without injecting excessive subjectivity or unduly restricting the States' "broad latitude in experimenting with possible solutions to problems of vital local concern"? One part of the answer, already discussed, is that we must ground the analysis in historical experience and reasoned judgment, and never on "merely personal and private notions." Our precedents place a number of additional constraints on the decisional process. Although "guideposts for responsible decisionmaking in this unchartered area are scarce and open-ended."

The most basic is that we have eschewed attempts to provide any all-purpose, top-down, totalizing theory of "liberty." . . .

Yet while "the 'liberty' specially protected by the Fourteenth Amendment " is "perhaps not capable of being fully clarified," it is capable of being refined and delimited. . . .

Rather than seek a categorical understanding of the liberty clause, our precedents have thus elucidated a conceptual core. The clause safeguards, most basically, "the ability independently to define one's identity," "the individual's right to make certain unusually important decisions that will affect his own, or his family's, destiny," and the right to be respected as a human being. Self-determination, bodily integrity, freedom of conscience, intimate relationships, political equality, dignity and respect—these are the central values we have found implicit in the concept of ordered liberty.

Another key constraint on substantive due process analysis is respect for the democratic process. . . .

This sensitivity is an aspect of a deeper principle: the need to approach our work with humility and caution. Because the relevant constitutional language is so "spacious," I have emphasized that "[t]he doctrine of judicial self-restraint requires us to exercise the utmost care whenever we are asked to break new ground in this field." . . .

Several rules of the judicial process help enforce such restraint. In the substantive due process field as in others, the Court has applied both the doctrine of *stare decisis*—adhering to precedents, respecting reliance interests, prizing stability and order in the law—and the common-law method—taking cases and controversies as they present themselves, proceeding slowly and incrementally, building on what came before. This restrained methodology was evident even in the heyday of "incorporation" during the 1960's. Although it would have been much easier for the Court simply to declare certain Amendments in the Bill of Rights applicable to the States in toto, the Court took care to parse each Amendment into its component guarantees, evaluating them one by one. This piecemeal approach allowed the Court to scrutinize more closely the right at issue in any given dispute, reducing both the risk and the cost of error. . . .

The question in this case, then, is not whether the Second Amendment right to keep and bear arms (whatever that right's precise contours) applies to the States because the Amendment has been incorporated into the Fourteenth Amendment. It has not been. The question, rather, is whether the particular right asserted by petitioners applies to the States because of the Fourteenth Amendment itself, standing on its own bottom. And to answer that question, we need to determine, first, the nature of the right that has been asserted and, second, whether that right is an aspect of Fourteenth Amendment "liberty." Even accepting the Court's holding in *Heller*, it remains entirely possible that the right to keep and bear arms identified in that opinion is not judicially enforceable against the States, or that only part of the right is so enforceable. It is likewise possible for the Court to find in this case that some part of the *Heller* right applies to the States, and then to find in later cases that other parts of the right also apply, or apply on different terms. . . .

[W]hile the utility of firearms, and handguns in particular, to the defense of hearth and home is certainly relevant to an assessment of petitioners' asserted right, there is no freestanding self-defense claim in this case. The question we must decide is whether the interest in keeping in the home a firearm of one's choosing—a handgun, for petitioners—is one that is "comprised within the term liberty" in the Fourteenth Amendment.

While I agree with the Court that our substantive due process cases offer a principled basis for holding that petitioners have a constitutional right to possess a usable firearm in the home, I am ultimately persuaded that a better reading of our case law supports the city of Chicago. I would not foreclose the possibility that a particular plaintiff—say, an elderly widow who lives in a dangerous neighborhood and does not have the strength to operate a long gun—may have a cognizable liberty interest in possessing a handgun. But I cannot accept petitioners' broader submission. A number of factors, taken together, lead me to this conclusion.

First, firearms have a fundamentally ambivalent relationship to liberty. Just as they can help homeowners defend their families and property from intruders, they can help thugs and insurrectionists murder innocent victims. The threat that firearms will be misused is far from hypothetical, for gun crime has devastated many of our communities. . . .

Hence, in evaluating an asserted right to be free from particular gun-control regulations, liberty is on both sides of the equation. Guns may be useful for self-defense, as well as for hunting and sport, but they also have a unique potential to facilitate death and destruction and thereby to destabilize ordered liberty. Your interest in keeping and bearing a certain firearm may diminish my interest in being and feeling safe from armed violence. And while granting you the right to own a handgun might make you safer on any given day—assuming the handgun's marginal contribution to self-defense outweighs its marginal contribution to the risk of accident, suicide, and criminal mischief—it may make you and the community you live in less safe overall, owing to the increased number of handguns in circulation. It is at least reasonable for a democratically elected legislature to take such concerns into account in considering what sorts of regulations would best serve the public welfare. . . .

Second, the right to possess a firearm of one's choosing is different in kind from the liberty interests we have recognized under the Due Process Clause. Despite the plethora of substantive due process cases that have been decided in the post-*Lochner* century, I have found none that holds, states, or even suggests that the term "liberty" encompasses either the common-law right of self-defense or a right to keep and bear arms. I do not doubt for a moment that many Americans feel deeply passionate about firearms, and see them as critical to their way of life as well as to their security. Nevertheless, it does not appear to be the case that the ability to own a handgun, or any particular type of firearm, is critical to leading a life of autonomy, dignity, or political equality: The marketplace offers many tools for self-defense, even if they are imperfect substitutes, and neither petitioners nor their *amici* make such a contention. Petitioners' claim is not the kind of substantive interest, accordingly, on which a uniform, judicially enforced national standard is presumptively appropriate. . . .

Third, the experience of other advanced democracies, including those that share our British heritage, undercuts the notion that an expansive right to keep and bear arms is intrinsic to ordered liberty. Many of these countries place restrictions on the possession, use, and carriage of firearms far more onerous than the restrictions found in this Nation (England, Canada, Australia, Japan, Denmark, Finland, Luxembourg, and New Zealand). That the United States is an international outlier in the permissiveness of its approach to guns does not suggest that our laws are bad laws. It does suggest that this Court may not need to assume responsibility for making our laws still more permissive. . . .

Fourth, the Second Amendment differs in kind from the Amendments that surround it, with the consequence that its inclusion in the Bill of Rights is not merely unhelpful but positively harmful to petitioners' claim. Generally, the inclusion of a liberty interest in the Bill of Rights points toward the conclusion that it is of fundamental significance and ought to be enforceable against the States. But the Second Amendment plays a peculiar role within the Bill, as announced by its peculiar opening clause. Even accepting the *Heller* Court's view that the Amendment protects an individual right to keep and bear arms disconnected from militia service, it remains undeniable that "the purpose for which the right was codified" was "to prevent elimination of the militia." It was the States, not private persons, on whose immediate behalf the Second Amendment was adopted. Notwithstanding the *Heller* Court's efforts to write the Second Amendment's preamble out of the Constitution, the Amendment still serves the structural function of protecting the States from encroachment by an overreaching Federal Government.

The Second Amendment, in other words, "is a federalism provision." It is directed at preserving the autonomy of the sovereign States, and its logic therefore "resists" incorporation by a federal court against the States. No one suggests that the Tenth Amendment, which provides that powers not given to the Federal Government remain with "the States," applies to the States;

such a reading would border on incoherent, given that the Tenth Amendment exists (in significant part) to safeguard the vitality of state governance. The Second Amendment is no different. . . .

Fifth, although it may be true that Americans' interest in firearm possession and state-law recognition of that interest are "deeply rooted" in some important senses, it is equally true that the States have a long and unbroken history of regulating firearms. The idea that States may place substantial restrictions on the right to keep and bear arms short of complete disarmament is, in fact, far more entrenched than the notion that the Federal Constitution protects any such right. Federalism is a far "older and more deeply rooted tradition than is a right to carry," or to own, "any particular kind of weapon." . . .

Finally, even apart from the States' long history of firearms regulation and its location at the core of their police powers, this is a quintessential area in which federalism ought to be allowed to flourish without this Court's meddling. Whether or not we can assert a plausible constitutional basis for intervening, there are powerful reasons why we should not do so.

Across the Nation, States and localities vary significantly in the patterns and problems of gun violence they face, as well as in the traditions and cultures of lawful gun use they claim. The city of Chicago, for example, faces a pressing challenge in combating criminal street gangs. Most rural areas do not. The city of Chicago has a high population density, which increases the potential for a gunman to inflict mass terror and casualties. Most rural areas do not. The city of Chicago offers little in the way of hunting opportunities. Residents of rural communities are, one presumes, much more likely to stock the dinner table with game they have personally felled.

Given that relevant background conditions diverge so much across jurisdictions, the Court ought to pay particular heed to state and local legislatures' "right to experiment." . . .

The fact that the right to keep and bear arms appears in the Constitution should not obscure the novelty of the Court's decision to enforce that right against the States. By its terms, the Second Amendment does not apply to the States; read properly, it does not even apply to individuals outside of the militia context. The Second Amendment was adopted to protect the States from federal encroachment. And the Fourteenth Amendment has never been understood by the Court to have "incorporated" the entire Bill of Rights. There was nothing foreordained about today's outcome.

Although the Court's decision in this case might be seen as a mere adjunct to its decision in *Heller*, the consequences could prove far more destructive—quite literally—to our Nation's communities and to our constitutional structure. Thankfully, the Second Amendment right identified in *Heller* and its newly minted Fourteenth Amendment analogue are limited, at least for now, to the home. But neither the "assurances" provided by the plurality, nor the many historical sources cited in its opinion should obscure the reality that today's ruling marks a dramatic change in our law—or that the Justices who have joined it have brought to bear an awesome amount of discretion in resolving the legal question presented by this case. . . .

Accordingly, I respectfully dissent.

□ *Justice BREYER, with whom Justice GINSBURG and Justice SOTOMAYOR join, dissenting.*

In my view, Justice STEVENS has demonstrated that the Fourteenth Amendment's guarantee of "substantive due process" does not include a general right to keep and bear firearms for purposes of private self-defense. As he argues, the Framers did not write the Second Amendment with this objective in view. Unlike other forms of substantive liberty, the carrying of arms for that purpose often puts others' lives at risk. And the use of arms for private self-defense does not warrant federal constitutional protection from state regulation.

The Court, however, does not expressly rest its opinion upon "substantive due process" concerns. Rather, it directs its attention to this Court's "incorporation" precedents and asks whether the Second Amendment right to private self-defense is "fundamental" so that it applies to the States through the Fourteenth Amendment. . . .

[H]istorians now tell us . . . that the right to which Blackstone referred had, not nothing, but everything, to do with the militia. As properly understood at the time of the English Civil Wars, the historians claim, the right to bear arms "ensured that Parliament had the power" to arm the citizenry: "to defend the realm" in the case of a foreign enemy, and to "secure the right of 'self-preservation,'" or "self-defense," should "the sovereign usurp the English Constitution." *English Historians' Brief*. Thus, the Declaration of Right says that private persons can possess guns only "as allowed by law." Moreover, when Blackstone referred to "'the right of having and using arms for self-preservation and defence,'" he was referring to the right of the people "to take part in the militia to defend their political liberties," and to the right of Parliament (which represented the people) to raise a militia even when the King sought to deny it that power. Nor can the historians find any convincing reason to believe that the Framers had something different in mind than what Blackstone himself meant. The historians concede that at least one historian takes a different position, but the Court, they imply, would lose a poll taken among professional historians of this period, say, by a vote of 8 to 1.

If history, and history alone, is what matters, why would the Court not now reconsider *Heller* in light of these more recently published historical views?

My aim in referring to this history is to illustrate the reefs and shoals that lie in wait for those nonexpert judges who place virtually determinative weight upon historical considerations. In my own view, the Court should not look to history alone but to other factors as well—above all, in cases where the history is so unclear that the experts themselves strongly disagree. It should, for example, consider the basic values that underlie a constitutional provision and their contemporary significance. And it should examine as well the relevant consequences and practical justifications that might, or might not, warrant removing an important question from the democratic decisionmaking process.

In my view, taking *Heller* as a given, the Fourteenth Amendment does not incorporate the Second Amendment right to keep and bear arms for purposes of private self-defense. Under this Court's precedents, to incorporate the private self-defense right the majority must show that the right is, e.g., "fundamental to the American scheme of justice," *Duncan v. Louisiana*, 391 U.S. 145 (1968).

The majority here, like that in *Heller*, relies almost exclusively upon history to make the necessary showing. But to do so for incorporation purposes is both wrong and dangerous. As Justice STEVENS points out, our society has historically made mistakes—for example, when considering certain 18th- and 19th-century property rights to be fundamental. And in the incorporation context, as elsewhere, history often is unclear about the answers.

Accordingly, this Court, in considering an incorporation question, has never stated that the historical status of a right is the only relevant consideration. Rather, the Court has either explicitly or implicitly made clear in its opinions that the right in question has remained fundamental over time.

I thus think it proper, above all where history provides no clear answer, to look to other factors in considering whether a right is sufficiently "fundamental" to remove it from the political process in every State. I would include among those factors the nature of the right; any contemporary disagreement about whether the right is fundamental; the extent to which incorporation will further other, perhaps more basic, constitutional aims; and the extent to which incorporation will advance or hinder the Constitution's structural aims, including its division of powers among different governmental institutions (and the people as well). Is incorporation needed, for example, to further the Constitution's effort to ensure that the government treats each individual with equal respect? Will it help maintain the democratic form of government that the Constitution foresees? In a word, will incorporation prove consistent, or inconsistent, with the Constitution's efforts to create governmental institutions well suited to the carrying out of its constitutional promises?

Finally, I would take account of the Framers' basic reason for believing the Court ought to have the power of judicial review. Alexander Hamilton feared granting that power to Congress alone, for he feared that Congress, acting as judges, would not overturn as unconstitutional a popular statute that it had recently enacted, as legislators. *The Federalist* No. 78 ("This independence of the judges is equally requisite to guard the constitution and the rights of individuals from the effects of those ill humours, which" can, at times, lead to "serious oppressions of the minor part in the community"). Judges, he thought, may find it easier to resist popular pressure to suppress the basic rights of an unpopular minority. That being so, it makes sense to ask whether that particular comparative judicial advantage is relevant to the case at hand.

How do these considerations apply here? For one thing, I would apply them only to the private self-defense right directly at issue. After all, the Amendment's militia-related purpose is primarily to protect States from federal regulation, not to protect individuals from militia-related regulation. Moreover, the Civil War Amendments, the electoral process, the courts, and numerous other institutions today help to safeguard the States and the people from any serious threat of federal tyranny. How are state militias additionally necessary? It is difficult to see how a right that, as the majority concedes, has "largely faded as a popular concern" could possibly be so fundamental that it would warrant incorporation through the Fourteenth Amendment. Hence, the incorporation of the Second Amendment cannot be based on the militia-related aspect of what *Heller* found to be more extensive Second Amendment rights.

For another thing, as *Heller* concedes, the private self-defense right that the Court would incorporate has nothing to do with "the reason" the Framers "codified" the right to keep and bear arms "in a written Constitution." *Heller* immediately adds that the self-defense right was nonetheless "the central component of the right." In my view, this is the historical equivalent of a claim that water runs uphill. . . .

Further, there is no popular consensus that the private self-defense right described in *Heller* is fundamental. . . .

Moreover, there is no reason here to believe that incorporation of the private self-defense right will further any other or broader constitutional objective. . . .

Finally, incorporation of the right will work a significant disruption in the constitutional allocation of decisionmaking authority, thereby interfering with the Constitution's ability to further its objectives.

First, on any reasonable accounting, the incorporation of the right recognized in *Heller* would amount to a significant incursion on a traditional and important area of state concern, altering the constitutional relationship between the States and the Federal Government. Private gun regulation is the quintessential exercise of a State's "police power"—i.e., the power to "protec[t] . . . the lives, limbs, health, comfort, and quiet of all persons, and the protection of all property within the State," by enacting "all kinds of restraints and burdens" on both "persons and property." . . .

Second, determining the constitutionality of a particular state gun law requires finding answers to complex empirically based questions of a kind that legislatures are better able than courts to make. . . .

Third, the ability of States to reflect local preferences and conditions—both key virtues of federalism—here has particular importance. The incidence of gun ownership varies substantially as between crowded cities and uncongested rural communities, as well as among the different geographic regions of the country. Thus, approximately 60 percent of adults who live in the relatively sparsely populated Western States of Alaska, Montana, and Wyoming report that their household keeps a gun, while fewer than 15 percent of adults in the densely populated Eastern States of Rhode Island, New Jersey, and Massachusetts say the same. . . .

Fourth, although incorporation of any right removes decisions from the democratic process, the incorporation of this particular right does so without strong offsetting justification—as the example of Oak Park's handgun ban helps to show. Oak Park decided to ban handguns in 1983, after a local attorney was shot to death with a handgun that his assailant had smuggled into a courtroom in a blanket. A citizens committee spent months gathering information about handguns. It secured 6,000 signatures from community residents in support of a ban. And the village board enacted a ban into law. . . .

Given the empirical and local value-laden nature of the questions that lie at the heart of the issue, why, in a Nation whose Constitution foresees democratic decisionmaking, is it so fundamental a matter as to require taking that power from the people? What is it here that the people did not know? What is it that a judge knows better?

In sum, the police power, the superiority of legislative decisionmaking, the need for local decisionmaking, the comparative desirability of democratic decisionmaking, the lack of a manageable judicial standard, and the life-threatening harm that may flow from striking down regulations all argue against incorporation. Where the incorporation of other rights has been at issue, some of these problems have arisen. But in this instance all these problems are present, all at the same time, and all are likely to be present in most, perhaps nearly all, of the cases in which the constitutionality of a gun regulation is at issue. At the same time, the important factors that favor incorporation in other instances—e.g., the protection of broader constitutional objectives—are not present here. The upshot is that all factors militate against incorporation—with the possible exception of historical factors. . . .

With respect, I dissent.

B | *The Rise and Retreat of the "Due Process Revolution"*

■ THE DEVELOPMENT OF LAW

Other Recent Rulings on Substantive and Procedural Due Process

CASE	VOTE	RULING
Rivera v. Illinois, 129 S.Ct. 1446 (2009)	9:0	During jury selection for Michael Rivera's first-degree murder trial, his counsel sought to use a pe-

remptory challenge to excuse a venire member Deloris Gomez. Rivera had already used peremptory against women, and it was conceded that there was no basis to challenge Gomez for cause. The trial court rejected the peremptory challenge out of concern that it was discriminatory under *Batson v. Kentucky,* 476 U.S. 79 (1986) (see Vol. 2, Ch. 12), holding that parties may not use peremptory challenges to exclude jurors based on race, ethnicity, or gender. Writing for a unanimous Court, Justice Ginsburg held that even though the trial court erred and the composed jury might have otherwise decided the case differently, because there was no juror removed for cause, Rivera's Sixth Amendment right to an impartial jury and Fourteenth Amendment right to due process was not violated. In short, due process does not meticulously observe state procedures, but only "the fundamental elements of fairness in a criminal trial."

Caperton v. A. T. Massey Coal Co., 129 S.Ct. 2252 (2009)	5:4	By a five-to-four vote, the Court held that it is unconstitutional for a state supreme court justice to sit on a case involving the finan-

cial interests of a major donor to the justices election campaign. Writing for the majority, Justice Kennedy held that West Virginia Supreme Court Chief Justice Brent Benjamin should have recused himself from a case that overturned a $50-million verdict against a company headed by a man who contributed $3 million to the justice's election. The failure to do so ran afoul of the Due Process Clause, which incorporates the common-law rule requiring recusal when a judge has "a direct, personal, substantial, pecuniary interest" in a case. According to the Court's precedents, recusal is required where "the probability of actual bias on the part of the judge or decisionmaker is too high to be constitutionally tolerable." In Justice Kennedy's words: "Not every campaign contribution by a litigant or attorney creates a probability of bias that requires a judge's recusal, but this is an exceptional case." By contrast, dissenting Chief Justice Roberts, joined by Justices Scalia, Thomas, and Alito, countered that the ruling "requires state and federal judges simultaneously to act as political scientists (why did candidate X win the election?), economists (was the financial support disproportionate?), and psychologists (is there likely to be a debt of gratitude?)."

District Attorney's Office for   5:4   Alaska is one of three states that
Third District v. Osborne,   do not allow postconviction ac-
129 S.Ct. 2308 (2009)   cess to DNA and other biological
                                          evidence in order to challenge a
defendant's conviction. Writing for a bare majority, Chief Justice Roberts re-jected a due process challenge and observed that it was up to the states and Congress to decide who has a right to testing that might prove innocence after a conviction. In his words, "[The] challenges DNA technology poses to our criminal justice system and our traditional notions of finality" are better left to elected officials than federal judges. "To suddenly constitutionalize this area would short-circuit what looks to be a prompt and considered legislative response." Justices Stevens, Souter, Ginsburg, and Breyer dissented.

5

FREEDOM OF EXPRESSION AND ASSOCIATION

A | *Judicial Approaches to the First Amendment*

In *Pleasant Grove City v. Summum* (2009) (excerpted below) the Roberts Court further extended the doctrine that the First Amendment does not apply to *government-sponsored speech*. In reversing the appellate court, Justice Alito held that under the First Amendment Free Speech Clause a small religious sect, the Summum, could not compel a city to erect a statue in a public park that contained a monument inscribed with the Ten Commandments and several other public displays. In so holding the Court extended prior rulings on government speech; see, e.g., *Rust v. Sullivan*, 500 U.S. 173 (1991) (excerpted in Vol. 2, Ch. 5), and *Rosenberger v. Rector and Visitors of the University of Virginia*, 515 U.S. 819 (1995) (excerpted in Vol. 2, Ch. 6).

In its 2009-2010 term, the Roberts Court considered the constitutionality of a 1999 federal statute, 18 U.S.C. Sec. 48, making it a crime to depict animal cruelty in interstate or foreign commerce for commercial gain, carrying a fine and five-year sentence. In a broad ruling, Chief Justice Roberts struck down the statute and declined to recognize depictions of animal cruelty as outside the scope of First Amendment protection.

Pleasant Grove City v. Summum
129 S.Ct. 1125 (2009)

Pioneer Park is a two-and-a-half acre public park located in Pleasant Grove City, Utah. The park contains fifteen permanent displays, of which eleven were donated by private groups or individuals. They include an historic granary, a wishing well, the city's first fire station, a September 11, 2001 monument, and a Ten Commandments monument donated by the Fraternal Order of Eagles in 1971. Summum, a religious organization founded in 1975 and headquartered in Salt Lake City, requested permission to erect a "stone monument," which would contain "the Seven Aphorisms of SUMMUM," such as "Summum is mind, thought; the universe is a mental creation." The city denied the requests and explained that its practice was to limit monuments in the Park to those that "either (1) directly relate to the history of Pleasant Grove, or (2) were donated by groups with longstanding ties to the Pleasant Grove community." Subsequently, the city passed a resolution putting this policy into writing. The resolution also mentioned other criteria, such as safety and esthetics.

In 2005, Summum sued the city, asserting that it violated the Free Speech Clause of the First Amendment by accepting the Ten Commandments monument but rejecting the proposed Seven Aphorisms monument. After a federal district court denied Summum's preliminary injunction request, Summum appealed and a panel of the Tenth Circuit reversed. The panel noted that it had previously found the Ten Commandments monument to be private rather than government speech and held that public parks have traditionally been regarded as public forums; thus, the city could not reject the Seven Aphorisms monument unless it had a compelling justification.

The appellate court's decision was reversed. Justice Alito delivered the opinion for the Court. Justices Stevens, Breyer, Souter, and Scalia each filed concurring opinions.

□ *Justice ALITO delivered the opinion of the Court.*

No prior decision of this Court has addressed the application of the Free Speech Clause to a government entity's acceptance of privately donated, permanent monuments for installation in a public park, and the parties disagree sharply about the line of precedents that governs this situation. . . .

If petitioners were engaging in their own expressive conduct, then the Free Speech Clause has no application. The Free Speech Clause restricts government regulation of private speech; it does not regulate government speech. See *Johanns v. Livestock Marketing Assn.*, 544 U.S. 550 (2005). A government entity has the right to "speak for itself." *Board of Regents of Univ. of Wis. System v. Southworth*, 529 U.S. 217 (2000). "[I]t is entitled to say what it wishes,"

Rosenberger v. Rector and Visitors of Univ. of Va., 515 U.S. 819 (1995), and to select the views that it wants to express. See *Rust v. Sullivan*, 500 U.S. 173 (1991). Indeed, it is not easy to imagine how government could function if it lacked this freedom. "If every citizen were to have a right to insist that no one paid by public funds express a view with which he disagreed, debate over issues of great concern to the public would be limited to those in the private sector, and the process of government as we know it radically transformed." *Keller v. State Bar of Cal.*, 496 U.S. 1 (1990).

A government entity may exercise this same freedom to express its views when it receives assistance from private sources for the purpose of delivering a government-controlled message.

This does not mean that there are no restraints on government speech. For example, government speech must comport with the Establishment Clause. The involvement of public officials in advocacy may be limited by law, regulation, or practice. And of course, a government entity is ultimately "accountable to the electorate and the political process for its advocacy." "If the citizenry objects, newly elected officials later could espouse some different or contrary position."

While government speech is not restricted by the Free Speech Clause, the government does not have a free hand to regulate private speech on government property. This Court long ago recognized that members of the public retain strong free speech rights when they venture into public streets and parks, "which 'have immemorially been held in trust for the use of the public and, time out of mind, have been used for purposes of assembly, communicating thoughts between citizens, and discussing public questions.'" *Perry Ed. Assn. v. Perry Local Educators' Assn.*, 460 U.S. 37 (1983)(quoting *Hague v. Committee for Industrial Organization*, 307 U.S. 496 (1939). In order to preserve this freedom, government entities are strictly limited in their ability to regulate private speech in such "traditional public fora." Reasonable time, place, and manner restrictions are allowed, but any restriction based on the content of the speech must satisfy strict scrutiny, that is, the restriction must be narrowly tailored to serve a compelling government interest, and restrictions based on viewpoint are prohibited.

With the concept of the traditional public forum as a starting point, this Court has recognized that members of the public have free speech rights on other types of government property and in certain other government programs that share essential attributes of a traditional public forum. We have held that a government entity may create "a designated public forum" if government property that has not traditionally been regarded as a public forum is intentionally opened up for that purpose. Government restrictions on speech in a designated public forum are subject to the same strict scrutiny as restrictions in a traditional public forum. The Court has also held that a government entity may create a forum that is limited to use by certain groups or dedicated solely to the discussion of certain subjects. In such a forum, a government entity may impose restrictions on speech that are reasonable and viewpoint-neutral.

There may be situations in which it is difficult to tell whether a government entity is speaking on its own behalf or is providing a forum for private speech, but this case does not present such a situation. Permanent monuments displayed on public property typically represent government speech.

Governments have long used monuments to speak to the public. Since ancient times, kings, emperors, and other rulers have erected statues of themselves to remind their subjects of their authority and power. Triumphal arches, columns, and other monuments have been built to commemorate military victories and sacrifices and other events of civic importance. A monument, by definition, is a structure that is designed as a means of expression. When a government entity arranges for the construction of a monument, it does so because it wishes to convey some thought or instill some feeling in those who see the structure. . . .

Just as government-commissioned and government-financed monuments speak for the government, so do privately financed and donated monuments that the government accepts and displays to the public on government land. It certainly is not common for property owners to open up their property for the installation of permanent monuments that convey a message with which they do not wish to be associated. And because property owners typically do not permit the construction of such monuments on their land, persons who observe donated monuments routinely—and reasonably—interpret them as conveying some message on the property owner's behalf. In this context, there is little chance that observers will fail to appreciate the identity of the speaker. This is true whether the monument is located on private property or on public property, such as national, state, or city park land. . . .

But while government entities regularly accept privately funded or donated monuments, they have exercised selectivity. An example discussed by the city of New York as *amicus curiae* is illustrative. In the wake of the controversy generated in 1876 when the city turned down a donated monument to honor Daniel Webster, the city adopted rules governing the acceptance of artwork for permanent placement in city parks, requiring, among other things, that "any proposed gift of art had to be viewed either in its finished condition or as a model before acceptance." Across the country, "municipalities generally exercise editorial control over donated monuments through prior submission requirements, design input, requested modifications, written criteria, and legislative approvals of specific content proposals." . . .

In this case, it is clear that the monuments in Pleasant Grove's Pioneer Park represent government speech. Although many of the monuments were not designed or built by the City and were donated in completed form by private entities, the City decided to accept those donations and to display them in the Park. Respondent does not claim that the City ever opened up the Park for the placement of whatever permanent monuments might be offered by private donors. Rather, the City has "effectively controlled" the messages sent by the monuments in the Park by exercising "final approval authority" over their selection. The City has selected those monuments that it wants to display for the purpose of presenting the image of the City that it wishes to project to all who frequent the Park; it has taken ownership of most of the monuments in the Park, including the Ten Commandments monument that is the focus of respondent's concern; and the City has now expressly set forth the criteria it will use in making future selections. . . .

Respondent seems to think that a monument can convey only one "message"—which is, presumably, the message intended by the donor—and that, if a government entity that accepts a monument for placement on its property does not formally embrace that message, then the government has not engaged in expressive conduct.

This argument fundamentally misunderstands the way monuments convey meaning. The meaning conveyed by a monument is generally not a simple one like " 'Beef. It's What's for Dinner.' " Even when a monument features the written word, the monument may be intended to be interpreted, and may in fact be interpreted by different observers, in a variety of ways. Monuments called to our attention by the briefing in this case illustrate this phenomenon.

What, for example, is "the message" of the Greco-Roman mosaic of the word "Imagine" that was donated to New York City's Central Park in memory of John Lennon? Some observers may "imagine" the musical contributions that John Lennon would have made if he had not been killed. Others may think of the lyrics of the Lennon song that obviously inspired the mosaic and may "imagine" a world without religion, countries, possessions, greed, or hunger. . . .

Contrary to respondent's apparent belief, it frequently is not possible to identify a single "message" that is conveyed by an object or structure, and consequently, the thoughts or sentiments expressed by a government entity that accepts and displays such an object may be quite different from those of either its creator or its donor. By accepting a privately donated monument and placing it on city property, a city engages in expressive conduct, but the intended and perceived significance of that conduct may not coincide with the thinking of the monument's donor or creator. Indeed, when a privately donated memorial is funded by many small donations, the donors themselves may differ in their interpretation of the monument's significance. By accepting such a monument, a government entity does not necessarily endorse the specific meaning that any particular donor sees in the monument.

The message that a government entity conveys by allowing a monument to remain on its property may also be altered by the subsequent addition of other monuments in the same vicinity. For example, following controversy over the original design of the Vietnam Veterans Memorial, a compromise was reached that called for the nearby addition of a flagstaff and bronze Three Soldiers statue, which many believed changed the overall effect of the memorial. . . .

A striking example of how the interpretation of a monument can evolve is provided by one of the most famous and beloved public monuments in the United States, the Statue of Liberty. The statue was given to this country by the Third French Republic to express republican solidarity and friendship between the two countries. . . . Only later did the statue come to be viewed as a beacon welcoming immigrants to a land of freedom.

[P]ublic parks can accommodate only a limited number of permanent monuments. Public parks have been used, "'time out of mind, . . . for purposes of assembly, communicating thoughts between citizens, and discussing public questions,'" but "one would be hard pressed to find a 'long tradition' of allowing people to permanently occupy public space with any manner of monuments."

Speakers, no matter how long-winded, eventually come to the end of their remarks; persons distributing leaflets and carrying signs at some point tire and go home; monuments, however, endure. They monopolize the use of the land on which they stand and interfere permanently with other uses of public space. A public park, over the years, can provide a soapbox for a very large number of orators—often, for all who want to speak—but it is hard to imagine how a public park could be opened up for the installation of permanent monuments by every person or group wishing to engage in that form of expression. . . .

In sum, we hold that the City's decision to accept certain privately donated monuments while rejecting respondent's is best viewed as a form of government speech. As a result, the City's decision is not subject to the Free

Speech Clause, and the Court of Appeals erred in holding otherwise. We therefore reverse.

☐ *Justice STEVENS with whom Justice GINSBURG joins, concurring.*

This case involves a property owner's rejection of an offer to place a permanent display on its land. While I join the Court's persuasive opinion, I think the reasons justifying the city's refusal would have been equally valid if its acceptance of the monument, instead of being characterized as "government speech," had merely been deemed an implicit endorsement of the donor's message. . . .

☐ *Justice BREYER, concurring.*

I agree with the Court and join its opinion. I do so, however, on the understanding that the "government speech" doctrine is a rule of thumb, not a rigid category. Were the City to discriminate in the selection of permanent monuments on grounds unrelated to the display's theme, say solely on political grounds, its action might well violate the First Amendment. In my view, courts must apply categories such as "government speech," "public forums," "limited public forums," and "nonpublic forums" with an eye towards their purposes—lest we turn "free speech" doctrine into a jurisprudence of labels. Consequently, we must sometimes look beyond an initial categorization. And, in doing so, it helps to ask whether a government action burdens speech disproportionately in light of the action's tendency to further a legitimate government objective[.] Were we to do so here, we would find—for reasons that the Court sets forth—that the City's action, while preventing Summum from erecting its monument, does not disproportionately restrict Summum's freedom of expression. After all, parks do not serve speech-related interests alone. To the contrary, cities use park space to further a variety of recreational, historical, educational, aesthetic, and other civic interests. To reserve to the City the power to pick and choose among proposed monuments according to criteria reasonably related to one or more of these legitimate ends restricts Summum's expression, but, given the impracticality of alternatives and viewed in light of the City's legitimate needs, the restriction is not disproportionate. Analyzed either way, as "government speech" or as a proportionate restriction on Summum's expression, the City's action here is lawful.

☐ *Justice SOUTER, concurring in the judgment.*

I agree with the Court that the Ten Commandments monument is government speech, that is, an expression of a government's position on the moral and religious issues raised by the subject of the monument. I have qualms, however, about accepting the position that public monuments are government speech categorically.

Because the government speech doctrine, as Justice Stevens notes, is "recently minted," it would do well for us to go slow in setting its bounds, which will affect existing doctrine in ways not yet explored. Even though, for example, Establishment Clause issues have been neither raised nor briefed before us, there is no doubt that this case and its government speech claim has been litigated by the parties with one eye on the Establishment Clause. The interaction between the "government speech doctrine" and Establishment Clause principles has not, however, begun to be worked out.

The case shows that it may not be easy to work out. After today's decision, whenever a government maintains a monument it will presumably be understood to be engaging in government speech. If the monument has some religious character, the specter of violating the Establishment Clause will behoove it to take care to avoid the appearance of a flat-out establishment of religion, in the sense of the government's adoption of the tenets expressed or symbolized. In such an instance, there will be safety in numbers, and it will be in the interest of a careful government to accept other monuments to stand nearby, to dilute the appearance of adopting whatever particular religious position the single example alone might stand for. As mementoes and testimonials pile up, however, the chatter may well make it less intuitively obvious that the government is speaking in its own right simply by maintaining the monuments. . . .

☐ *Justice SCALIA with whom Justice THOMAS joins, concurring.*

As framed and argued by the parties, this case presents a question under the Free Speech Clause of the First Amendment. I agree with the Court's analysis of that question and join its opinion in full. But it is also obvious that from the start, the case has been litigated in the shadow of the First Amendment's Establishment Clause . . . .

The city ought not fear that today's victory has propelled it from the Free Speech Clause frying pan into the Establishment Clause fire. Contrary to respondent's intimations, there are very good reasons to be confident that the park displays do not violate any part of the First Amendment.

In *Van Orden v. Perry*, 545 U.S. 677 (2005), this Court upheld against Establishment Clause challenge a virtually identical Ten Commandments monument, donated by the very same organization (the Fraternal Order of Eagles), which was displayed on the grounds surrounding the Texas State Capitol. Nothing in that decision suggested that the outcome turned on a finding that the monument was only "private" speech. To the contrary, all the Justices agreed that government speech was at issue, but the Establishment Clause argument was nonetheless rejected. For the plurality, that was because the Ten Commandments "have an undeniable historical meaning" in addition to their "religious significance." Justice BREYER, concurring in the judgment, agreed that the monument conveyed a permissible secular message, as evidenced by its location in a park that contained multiple monuments and historical markers; by the fact that it had been donated by the Eagles "as part of that organization's efforts to combat juvenile delinquency"; and by the length of time (40 years) for which the monument had gone unchallenged.

Even accepting the narrowest reading of the narrowest opinion necessary to the judgment in *Van Orden*, there is little basis to distinguish the monument in this case: Pioneer Park includes "15 permanent displays;" it was donated by the Eagles as part of its national effort to combat juvenile delinquency; and it was erected in 1971, which means it is approaching its (momentous!) 40th anniversary.

The city can safely exhale. Its residents and visitors can now return to enjoying Pioneer Park's wishing well, its historic granary—and, yes, even its Ten Commandments monument—without fear that they are complicit in an establishment of religion.

United States v. Stevens
130 S.Ct. 1577 (2010)

In 1999, Congress enacted and President Bill Clinton signed into law an Act to Establish Federal Criminal Penalties for Commerce in Depiction of Animal Cruelty, 18 U.S. Code Section 48. That law made the interstate commercial use of depictions of animal cruelty a crime. Subsequently, Robert Stevens was prosecuted under the law for operating a business called "Dogs of Velvet and Steel" and a Web site, Pitbull.com, on which he sold videos of dog fights. The Court of Appeals for the Third Circuit, however, declared the law overly broad and in violation of the First Amendment.

The appellate court's decision was affirmed by an eight-to-one vote. Chief Justice John Roberts delivered the opinion for the Court, and Justice Alito filed a dissenting opinion.

☐ *CHIEF JUSTICE ROBERTS delivered the opinion of the Court.*

Congress enacted 18 U.S.C. Sec. 48 to criminalize the commercial creation, sale, or possession of certain depictions of animal cruelty. The statute does not address underlying acts harmful to animals, but only portrayals of such conduct. The question presented is whether the prohibition in the statute is consistent with the freedom of speech guaranteed by the First Amendment.

Section 48 establishes a criminal penalty of up to five years in prison for anyone who knowingly "creates, sells, or possesses a depiction of animal cruelty," if done "for commercial gain" in interstate or foreign commerce. A depiction of "animal cruelty" is defined as one "in which a living animal is intentionally maimed, mutilated, tortured, wounded, or killed," if that conduct violates federal or state law where "the creation, sale, or possession takes place." In what is referred to as the "exceptions clause," the law exempts from prohibition any depiction "that has serious religious, political, scientific, educational, journalistic, historical, or artistic value." The legislative background of Sec. 48 focused primarily on the interstate market for "crush videos." According to the House Committee Report on the bill, such videos feature the intentional torture and killing of helpless animals, including cats, dogs, monkeys, mice, and hamsters. Crush videos often depict women slowly crushing animals to death "with their bare feet or while wearing high heeled shoes," sometimes while "talking to the animals in a kind of dominatrix patter" over "[t]he cries and squeals of the animals, obviously in great pain." . . .

The Government's primary submission is that Sec. 48 necessarily complies with the Constitution because the banned depictions of animal cruelty, as a class, are categorically unprotected by the First Amendment. We disagree.

The First Amendment provides that "Congress shall make no law . . . abridging the freedom of speech." "[A]s a general matter, the First Amendment means that government has no power to restrict expression because of its message, its ideas, its subject matter, or its content." *Ashcroft v. American Civil Liberties Union*, 535 U.S. 564 (2002). Section 48 explicitly regulates expression based on content: The statute restricts "visual [and] auditory depiction[s]," such as photographs, videos, or sound recordings, depending on whether they depict conduct in which a living animal is intentionally harmed. As such, Sec. 48 is "'presumptively invalid,' and the Government bears the burden to rebut that presumption." *United States v. Playboy Entertainment Group, Inc.*, 529 U.S. 803 (2000).

"From 1791 to the present," however, the First Amendment has "permitted restrictions upon the content of speech in a few limited areas," and has never "include[d] a freedom to disregard these traditional limitations." These "historic and traditional categories long familiar to the bar," *Simon & Schuster, Inc. v. Members of N.Y. State Crime Victims Bd.*, 502 U.S. 105 (1991)—including obscenity, defamation, fraud, incitement, and speech integral to criminal conduct—are "well-defined and narrowly limited classes of speech, the prevention and punishment of which have never been thought to raise any Constitutional problem."

The Government argues that "depictions of animal cruelty" should be added to the list. It contends that depictions of "illegal acts of animal cruelty" that are "made, sold, or possessed for commercial gain" necessarily "lack expressive value," and may accordingly "be regulated as unprotected speech." The claim is not just that Congress may regulate depictions of animal cruelty subject to the First Amendment, but that these depictions are outside the reach of that Amendment altogether—that they fall into a "'First Amendment Free Zone.'" . . .

[T]he Government points to Congress's "'legislative judgment that . . . depictions of animals being intentionally tortured and killed [are] of such minimal redeeming value as to render [them] unworthy of First Amendment protection,'" and asks the Court to uphold the ban on the same basis. The Government thus proposes that a claim of categorical exclusion should be considered under a simple balancing test: "Whether a given category of speech enjoys First Amendment protection depends upon a categorical balancing of the value of the speech against its societal costs."

As a free-floating test for First Amendment coverage, that sentence is startling and dangerous. The First Amendment's guarantee of free speech does not extend only to categories of speech that survive an ad hoc balancing of relative social costs and benefits. The First Amendment itself reflects a judgment by the American people that the benefits of its restrictions on the Government outweigh the costs. Our Constitution forecloses any attempt to revise that judgment simply on the basis that some speech is not worth it. . . .

To be fair to the Government, its view did not emerge from a vacuum. As the Government correctly notes, this Court has often described historically unprotected categories of speech as being "'of such slight social value as a step to truth that any benefit that may be derived from them is clearly outweighed by the social interest in order and morality.'" In *New York v. Ferber*, 458 U.S. 747 (1982), we noted that within these categories of unprotected speech, "the evil to be restricted so overwhelmingly outweighs the expressive interests, if any, at stake, that no process of case-by-case adjudication is required," because "the balance of competing interests is clearly struck." The Government derives its proposed test from these descriptions in our precedents.

But such descriptions are just that—descriptive. They do not set forth a test that may be applied as a general matter to permit the Government to imprison any speaker so long as his speech is deemed valueless or unnecessary, or so long as an ad hoc calculus of costs and benefits tilts in a statute's favor.

When we have identified categories of speech as fully outside the protection of the First Amendment, it has not been on the basis of a simple cost-benefit analysis. In *Ferber*, for example, we classified child pornography as such a category. We noted that the State of New York had a compelling interest in protecting children from abuse, and that the value of using children in these works (as opposed to simulated conduct or adult actors) was *de minimis*. But our decision did not rest on this "balance of competing interests" alone. We made clear that *Ferber* presented a special case: The market for child pornography was "intrinsically related" to the underlying abuse, and was therefore "an integral part of the production of such materials, an activity illegal throughout the Nation." As we noted, "'[i]t rarely has been suggested that the constitutional freedom for speech and press extends its immunity to speech or writing used as an integral part of conduct in violation of a valid criminal statute.'" *Ferber* thus grounded its analysis in a previously recognized, long-established category of unprotected speech, and our subsequent decisions have shared this understanding.

Our decisions in *Ferber* and other cases cannot be taken as establishing a freewheeling authority to declare new categories of speech outside the scope of the First Amendment. Maybe there are some categories of speech that have been historically unprotected, but have not yet been specifically identified or discussed as such in our case law. But if so, there is no evidence that "depictions of animal cruelty" is among them. We need not foreclose the future recognition of such additional categories to reject the Government's highly manipulable balancing test as a means of identifying them.

Because we decline to carve out from the First Amendment any novel exception for Sec. 48, we review Stevens' First Amendment challenge under our existing doctrine.

Stevens challenged Sec. 48 on its face, arguing that any conviction secured under the statute would be unconstitutional. The court below decided the case on that basis, and we granted the Solicitor General's petition for *certiorari* to determine "whether 18 U.S.C. 48 is facially invalid under the Free Speech Clause of the First Amendment."

To succeed in a typical facial attack, Stevens would have to establish "that no set of circumstances exists under which [Sec. 48] would be valid," or that the statute lacks any "plainly legitimate sweep." Here the Government asserts that Stevens cannot prevail because Sec. 48 is plainly legitimate as applied to crush videos and animal fighting depictions. Deciding this case through a traditional facial analysis would require us to resolve whether these applications of Sec. 48 are in fact consistent with the Constitution.

In the First Amendment context, however, this Court recognizes "a second type of facial challenge," whereby a law may be invalidated as overbroad if "a substantial number of its applications are unconstitutional, judged in relation to the statute's plainly legitimate sweep." Stevens argues that Sec. 48 applies to common depictions of ordinary and lawful activities, and that these depictions constitute the vast majority of materials subject to the statute. The Government makes no effort to defend such a broad ban as constitutional. Instead, the Government's entire defense of Sec. 48 rests on interpreting the statute as narrowly limited to specific types of "extreme" material. As the parties have presented the issue, therefore, the constitutionality of Sec. 48 hinges on how broadly it is construed. It is to that question that we now turn.

We read Sec. 48 to create a criminal prohibition of alarming breadth. To begin with, the text of the statute's ban on a "depiction of animal cruelty"

nowhere requires that the depicted conduct be cruel. That text applies to "any
. . . depiction" in which "a living animal is intentionally maimed, mutilated,
tortured, wounded, or killed." "[M]aimed, mutilated, [and] tortured" convey
cruelty, but "wounded" or "killed" do not suggest any such limitation. . . .
    While not requiring cruelty, Sec. 48 does require that the depicted con-
duct be "illegal." But this requirement does not limit Sec. 48 along the lines
the Government suggests. There are myriad federal and state laws concerning
the proper treatment of animals, but many of them are not designed to guard
against animal cruelty. Protections of endangered species, for example, restrict
even the humane "wound[ing] or kill[ing]" of "living animal[s]." Livestock
regulations are often designed to protect the health of human beings, and
hunting and fishing rules (seasons, licensure, bag limits, weight requirements)
can be designed to raise revenue, preserve animal populations, or prevent
accidents. The text of Sec. 48(c) draws no distinction based on the reason the
intentional killing of an animal is made illegal, and includes, for example, the
humane slaughter of a stolen cow. . . .
    The only thing standing between defendants who sell such depictions
and five years in federal prison—other than the mercy of a prosecutor—is
the statute's exceptions clause. Subsection (b) exempts from prohibition "any
depiction that has serious religious, political, scientific, educational, journalistic, historical, or artistic value." The Government argues that this clause substantially narrows the statute's reach: News reports about animal cruelty have
"journalistic" value; pictures of bullfights in Spain have "historical" value; and
instructional hunting video have "educational" value. Thus, the Government
argues, Sec. 48 reaches only crush videos, depictions of animal fighting (other
than Spanish bullfighting), and perhaps other depictions of "extreme acts of
animal cruelty." The Government's attempt to narrow the statutory ban, however, requires an unrealistically broad reading of the exceptions clause. As the
Government reads the clause, any material with "redeeming societal value,"
"'at least some minimal value,'" or anything more than "scant social value." . . .
But the text says "serious" value, and "serious" should be taken seriously.
We decline the Government's invitation—advanced for the first time in this
Court—to regard as "serious" anything that is not "scant." . . .
    Quite apart from the requirement of "serious" value in Sec. 48(b), the
excepted speech must also fall within one of the enumerated categories.
Much speech does not. Most hunting videos, for example, are not obviously
instructional in nature, except in the sense that all life is a lesson. According
to Safari Club International and the Congressional Sportsmen's Foundation,
many popular videos "have primarily entertainment value" and are designed
to "entertai[n] the viewer, marke[t] hunting equipment, or increas[e] the
hunting community."
    The Government explains that the language of Sec. 48(b) was largely
drawn from our opinion in *Miller v. California*, 413 U.S. 15 (1973), which
excepted from its definition of obscenity any material with "serious literary,
artistic, political, or scientific value." According to the Government, this incorporation of the *Miller* standard into Sec. 48 is therefore surely enough to
answer any First Amendment objection.
    In *Miller* we held that "serious" value shields depictions of sex from
regulation as obscenity. Limiting *Miller's* exception to "serious" value ensured
that "'[a] quotation from Voltaire in the flyleaf of a book [would] not constitutionally redeem an otherwise obscene publication.'" We did not, however,
determine that serious value could be used as a general precondition to

protecting other types of speech in the first place. Most of what we say to one another lacks "religious, political, scientific, educational, journalistic, historical, or artistic value" (let alone serious value), but it is still sheltered from government regulation. Even "'[w]holly neutral futilities . . . come under the protection of free speech as fully as do Keats' poems or Donne's sermons.'" *Cohen v. California*, 403 U.S. 15 (1971).

Thus, the protection of the First Amendment presumptively extends to many forms of speech that do not qualify for the serious-value exception of Sec. 48(b), but nonetheless fall within the broad reach of Sec. 48(c). . . .

However "growing" and "lucrative" the markets for crush videos and dog fighting depictions might be, they are dwarfed by the market for other depictions, such as hunting magazines and videos, that we have determined to be within the scope of Sec. 48. We therefore need not and do not decide whether a statute limited to crush videos or other depictions of extreme animal cruelty would be constitutional. We hold only that Sec. 48 is not so limited but is instead substantially overbroad, and therefore invalid under the First Amendment.

☐ *Justice ALITO, dissenting.*

The Court strikes down in its entirety a valuable statute that was enacted not to suppress speech, but to prevent horrific acts of animal cruelty—in particular, the creation and commercial exploitation of "crush videos," a form of depraved entertainment that has no social value. The Court's approach, which has the practical effect of legalizing the sale of such videos and is thus likely to spur a resumption of their production, is unwarranted. . . .

B | *Obscenity, Pornography, and Offensive Speech*

In its 2007–2008 term, the Court upheld the so-called PROTECT Act of 2003 aimed at curbing the pandering and proliferation of child pornography on the Internet. The law makes it a federal crime for any person who "knowingly . . . advertises, promotes, distributes, or solicits . . . any material or purported material in a manner that reflects the belief, or that is intended to cause another to believe, that the material or purported material is, or contains – (i) an obscene visual depiction of a minor engaging in sexually explicit conduct; or (ii) a visual depiction of an actual minor engaging in sexually explicit conduct." In doing so, the majority extended its earlier rulings on permitting the prosecution of pandering allegedly obscene materials (as discussed in Vol. 2, Ch. 5), but departed from its more recent decisions extending First Amendment protection to the Internet. Writing for the Court, Justice Scalia held that the law was neither overly broad in violation of the First Amendment nor unconstitutionally vague under the due process clause. Justice Souter, joined by Justice Ginsburg, dissented, arguing that the law swept too broadly in covering artistic works, such as *Romeo and Juliet*, and "virtual child pornography," which the Court ruled the First Amendment protects in *Ashcroft v. Free Speech Coalition*, 534 U.S. 234 (2002) (excerpted in Vol. 2, Ch. 5). The Court's ruling in *United States v. Williams* (2008) is excerpted below in Section F.

In its 2009–2010 term, the Roberts Court struck down a federal statute criminalizing the selling of so-called "crush videos," depicting animal cruelty, in *United States v. Stevens* (2010) (excerpted in Section A of this chapter).

In its 2010–2011 term, the Court will consider the constitutionality of a California law banning the sale or rental of violent video games to minors—those under eighteen—in *Schwarzenegger v. Entertainment Merchants Association* (Docket No. 08-1448). Under the law, blocked by a federal district court before it went into effect on January 1, 2006, video games containing violence must be labeled and civil penalties of $1,000 are incurred for violations. The law defines a violent video game as one that depicts "killing, maiming, dismembering, or sexually assaulting of an image of an humane being," in a manner that a reasonable person would find appeals to a "deviant or morbid interest" to minors, is "patently offensive" to prevailing standards of what is suitable for minors, and causes the game—as a whole—to lack "serious, artistic, political or scientific value" to minors. The Court of Appeals for the Ninth Circuit refused to apply that standard. Instead it applied the most rigorous constitutional standard—"strict scrutiny"—and concluded that there was no proof that such games would cause physical or psychological harm to minors. The appellate court also held that the law was not the least restrictive means to protecting children from exposure to such games.

F | *Regulating the Broadcast and Cable Media, and the Internet*

By a seven-to-two vote in *United States v. Williams* (2008) (excerpted below), the Court upheld the so-called PROTECT Act of 2003 aimed at curbing the pandering and proliferation of child pornography on the Internet. The law makes it a federal crime for any person who "knowingly . . . advertises, promotes, distributes, or solicits . . . any material or purported material in a manner that reflects the belief, or that is intended to cause another to believe, that the material or purported material is, or contains – (i) an obscene visual depiction of a minor engaging in sexually explicit conduct; or (ii) a visual depiction of an actual minor engaging in sexually explicit conduct." Writing for the Court, Justice Scalia held that the law was neither overly broad in violation of the First Amendment nor unconstitutionally vague under the due process clause. Justice Souter, joined by Justice Ginsburg, dissented, arguing that the law swept too broadly in covering artistic works, such as *Romeo and Juliet*, and "virtual child pornography," which the Court ruled the First Amendment protects in *Ashcroft v. Free Speech Coalition*, 534 U.S. 234 (2002) (excerpted in Vol. 2, Ch. 5).

In its 2008–2009 term, the Roberts Court reconsidered challenges to the Federal Communications Commission's enforcement of "indecency" standards in *Federal Communications Commission v. Fox Television Stations*. The Court last considered the matter thirty years ago, in *Federal Communications Commission v. Pacifica Foundation*, 438 U.S. 726 (1978) (excerpted in Vol. 2, Ch. 5), when it upheld the FCC's "indecency" standards in ruling on the satirist George Carlin's twelve-minute monologue on the "seven dirty words" that can't be said on the airwaves. The lawsuit in *Federal Communications Commission v. Fox Television Stations*, 129 S.Ct. 1800 (2009) was brought after the FCC reprimanded Fox Television for airing brief expletives of singer Cher in 2002 and Nicole Richie in 2003 at the Billboards Music Awards. In 2004, after Janet Jackson's "wardrobe malfunction" during a Super Bowl performance led to a $550,000 fine against CBS television stations, the FCC adopted the position that even brief, "fleeting" expletives expose networks to sanctions because new technology makes it easier to censor such "indecency." By contrast, Fox and other networks argued that the FCC exceeded its authority when an expletive does not convey a sexual message. The Court of Appeals for Second Circuit agreed that the FCC's policy was "arbitrary and capricious" under the Administrative Procedure Act and the First Amendment. But the Roberts Court reversed the appellate court's decision. Writing for the majority, Justice Scalia upheld the FCC's change in policy on indecent broadcasts under the Administrative Procedure Act, holding that it was not "arbitrary" or "capricious" in sanctioning the broadcasting of fleeting expletives. Notably, though, the Court declined to rule on the constitutionality of the FCC's policy under the First Amendment. Justices Kennedy and Thomas filed concurring opinions. Justices Stevens, Ginsburg, and Breyer filed dissenting opinions; Justice Souter joined the latter's dissent. Dissenting Justice Stevens, who delivered the opinion in *Pacifica Foundation*, sharply criticized the majority for "assuming that *Pacifica* endorsed a construction of the term 'indecent' that would include any expletive that has a sexual or excretory origin.... Our holding was narrow in two critical respects. First, we concluded ... that the statutory term 'indecent' was not limited to material that had prurient appeal and instead included material that was in 'nonconformance with accepted standards of morality.' Second, we upheld the FCC's adjudication that a 12-minute, expletive-filled monologue by satiric humorist George Carlin was indecent 'as broadcast.' We did not decide whether an isolated expletive could qualify as indecent. And we certainly did not hold that any word with a sexual or scatological origin, however used, was indecent." Justice Stevens also emphasized that:

> There is a critical distinction between the use of an expletive to describe a sexual or excretory function and the use of such a word for an entirely different purpose, such as to express an emotion. One rests at the core of indecency; the other stands miles apart. As any golfer who has watched his partner shank a short approach knows, it would be absurd to accept the suggestion that the resultant four-letter word uttered on the golf course describes sex or excrement and is therefore indecent.

United States v. Williams
128 S.Ct. 1830 (2008)

In response to the Court's ruling in *Ashcroft v. Free Speech Coalition*, 534 U.S. 234 (2002) (excerpted in Vol. 2, Ch. 5), which struck down provisions of the Child Pornography Prevention Act of 1996 that made it a crime to distribute or possess "virtual child pornography," Congress enacted the Prosecutorial Remedies and Other Tools to end the Exploitation of Children Today Act of 2003 (the PROTECT Act). Part of that law, Section 2252(a)(3)(B), makes it a federal crime for any person who "knowingly . . . advertises, promotes, or solicits . . . any material or purported material in a manner that reflects the belief, or that is intended to cause another to believe, that the material or purported material is, or contains − (i) an obscene visual depiction of a minor engaging in sexually explicit conduct; or (ii) a visual depiction of an actual minor engaging in sexually explicit conduct." Subsequently, in 2004 Michael Williams, using a sexually explicit screen name, signed into an Internet chat room. A Secret Service agent had also signed into the chat room under the moniker "Lisa n Miami." The agent noticed that Williams had posted a message that read: "Dad of toddler has 'good' pics of her an [sic] me for swap of your toddler pics, or live cam." The agent struck up a conversation with Williams, leading to an electronic exchange of non-pornographic pictures of children. Later, Williams messaged that he had photographs of men molesting his four-year-old daughter. Suspicious that "Lisa n Miami" was a law-enforcement agent, before proceeding further Williams demanded that the agent produce additional pictures. When he did not, Williams posted the following public message in the chat room: "HERE ROOM; I CAN PUT UPLINK CUZ IM FOR REAL—SHE CANT." Appended to this declaration was a hyperlink that led to seven pictures of actual children, aged approximately five to fifteen, engaging in sexually explicit conduct and displaying their genitals. The Secret Service then obtained a search warrant for Williams' home, where agents seized two hard drives containing twenty-two images of real children engaged in sexually explicit conduct. Williams was charged with one count of pandering child pornography under Section 2252A (a)(3)(B) and one count of possessing child pornography under Section 2252A(a)(5)(B). He pleaded guilty to both counts but reserved the right to challenge the constitutionality of the pandering conviction. The District Court rejected his challenge and sentenced him to concurrent sixty-month sentences. The Court of Appeals for the Eleventh Circuit reversed the pandering conviction, holding that the statute was both overbroad and impermissibly vague. In its view, the statute was broad enough to include any "braggart, exaggerator, or outright liar" who claimed to have child pornography. The government appealed and the Supreme Court granted *certiorari*.

The appellate court's decision was reversed by a seven-to-two vote. Justice Scalia delivered the opinion of the Court. Justice Stevens filed a concurring opinion, while Justice Souter, joined by Justice Ginsburg, issued a dissenting opinion.

☐ *Justice SCALIA delivered the opinion of the Court.*

Section 2252A(a)(3)(B) of Title 18, United States Code, criminalizes, in certain specified circumstances, the pandering or solicitation of child pornography. This case presents the question whether that statute is overbroad under the First Amendment or impermissibly vague under the Due Process Clause of the Fifth Amendment.

We have long held that obscene speech—sexually explicit material that violates fundamental notions of decency—is not protected by the First Amendment. See *Roth v. United States*, 354 U.S. 476 (1957). But to protect explicit material that has social value, we have limited the scope of the obscenity exception, and have overturned convictions for the distribution of sexually graphic but nonobscene material. See *Miller v. California*, 413 U.S. 15 (1973); see also, e.g., *Jenkins v. Georgia*, 418 U.S. 153 (1974).

Over the last 25 years, we have confronted a related and overlapping category of proscribable speech: child pornography. See *Ashcroft v. Free Speech Coalition*, 535 U.S. 234 (2002); *New York v. Ferber*, 458 U.S. 747 (1982). This consists of sexually explicit visual portrayals that feature children. We have held that a statute which proscribes the distribution of all child pornography, even material that does not qualify as obscenity, does not on its face violate the First Amendment. Moreover, we have held that the government may criminalize the possession of child pornography, even though it may not criminalize the mere possession of obscene material involving adults.

The broad authority to proscribe child pornography is not, however, unlimited. Four Terms ago, we held facially overbroad two provisions of the federal Child Pornography Protection Act of 1996 (CPPA). *Free Speech Coalition.* The first of these banned the possession and distribution of "'any visual depiction'" that "'is, or appears to be, of a minor engaging in sexually explicit conduct,'" even if it contained only youthful-looking adult actors or virtual images of children generated by a computer. This was invalid, we explained, because the child-protection rationale for speech restriction does not apply to materials produced without children. The second provision at issue in *Free Speech Coalition* criminalized the possession and distribution of material that had been pandered as child pornography, regardless of whether it actually was that. A person could thus face prosecution for possessing unobjectionable material that someone else had pandered. We held that this prohibition, which did "more than prohibit pandering," was also facially overbroad.

After our decision in *Free Speech Coalition*, Congress went back to the drawing board and produced legislation with the unlikely title of the Prosecutorial Remedies and Other Tools to end the Exploitation of Children Today Act of 2003. We shall refer to it as the Act. Section 503 of the Act amended 18 U.S.C. Section 2252A to add a new pandering and solicitation provision, relevant portions of which now read as follows:

> (a) Any person who—
> (3) knowingly—
> (B) advertises, promotes, presents, distributes, or solicits through the mails, or in interstate or foreign commerce by any means, including by computer, any material or purported material in a manner that reflects the belief, or that is intended to cause another to believe, that the material or purported material is, or contains—
> (i) an obscene visual depiction of a minor engaging in sexually explicit conduct; or
> (ii) a visual depiction of an actual minor engaging in sexually explicit conduct, shall be punished as provided in subsection (b).

Section 2256(2)(A) defines "sexually explicit conduct" as "actual or simulated—

> (i) sexual intercourse, including genital-genital, oral-genital, anal-genital, or oral-anal, whether between persons of the same or opposite sex;
> (ii) bestiality;
> (iii) masturbation;
> (iv) sadistic or masochistic abuse; or
> (v) lascivious exhibition of the genitals or pubic area of any person.

Violation of Section 2252A(a)(3)(B) incurs a minimum sentence of five years' imprisonment and a maximum of twenty years.

The Act's express findings indicate that Congress was concerned that limiting the child-pornography prohibition to material that could be proved to feature actual children, as our decision in *Free Speech Coalition* required, would enable many child pornographers to evade conviction. The emergence of new technology and the repeated retransmission of picture files over the Internet could make it nearly impossible to prove that a particular image was produced using real children—even though "[t]here is no substantial evidence that any of the child pornography images being trafficked today were made other than by the abuse of real children," virtual imaging being prohibitively expensive. . . .

According to our First Amendment overbreadth doctrine, a statute is facially invalid if it prohibits a substantial amount of protected speech. The doctrine seeks to strike a balance between competing social costs. *Virginia v. Hicks*, 539 U.S. 113 (2003). On the one hand, the threat of enforcement of an overbroad law deters people from engaging in constitutionally protected speech, inhibiting the free exchange of ideas. On the other hand, invalidating a law that in some of its applications is perfectly constitutional—particularly a law directed at conduct so antisocial that it has been made criminal—has obvious harmful effects. In order to maintain an appropriate balance, we have vigorously enforced the requirement that a statute's overbreadth be substantial, not only in an absolute sense, but also relative to the statute's plainly legitimate sweep.

The first step in overbreadth analysis is to construe the challenged statute; it is impossible to determine whether a statute reaches too far without first knowing what the statute covers. Generally speaking, Section 2252A(a)(3)(B) prohibits offers to provide and requests to obtain child pornography. The statute does not require the actual existence of child pornography. In this respect, it differs from the statutes in *Ferber*, and *Free Speech Coalition*, which prohibited the possession or distribution of child pornography. Rather than targeting the underlying material, this statute bans the collateral speech that introduces such material into the child-pornography distribution network. Thus, an Internet user who solicits child pornography from an undercover agent violates the statute, even if the officer possesses no child pornography. Likewise, a person who advertises virtual child pornography as depicting actual children also falls within the reach of the statute.

The statute's definition of the material or purported material that may not be pandered or solicited precisely tracks the material held constitutionally proscribable in *Ferber* and *Miller*: obscene material depicting (actual or virtual) children engaged in sexually explicit conduct, and any other material depicting actual children engaged in sexually explicit conduct. . . .

We now turn to whether the statute, as we have construed it, criminalizes a substantial amount of protected expressive activity.

Offers to engage in illegal transactions are categorically excluded from First Amendment protection. *Pittsburgh Press Co. v. Pittsburgh Comm'n on Human Relations*, 413 U.S. 376 (1973). One would think that this principle resolves the present case, since the statute criminalizes only offers to provide or requests to obtain contraband—child obscenity and child pornography involving actual children, both of which are proscribed, and the proscription of which is constitutional. The Eleventh Circuit, however, believed that the exclusion of First Amendment protection extended only to commercial offers to provide or receive contraband.

This mistakes the rationale for the categorical exclusion. It is based not on the less privileged First Amendment status of commercial speech, see *Central Hudson Gas & Elec. Corp. v. Public Serv. Comm'n of N.Y.*, 447 U.S. 557 (1980), but on the principle that offers to give or receive what it is unlawful to possess have no social value and thus, like obscenity, enjoy no First Amendment protection. Many long established criminal proscriptions—such as laws against conspiracy, incitement, and solicitation—criminalize speech (commercial or not) that is intended to induce or commence illegal activities. Offers to provide or requests to obtain unlawful material, whether as part of a commercial exchange or not, are similarly undeserving of First Amendment protection. It would be an odd constitutional principle that permitted the government to prohibit offers to sell illegal drugs, but not offers to give them away for free....

In sum, we hold that offers to provide or requests to obtain child pornography are categorically excluded from the First Amendment....

Child pornography harms and debases the most defenseless of our citizens. Both the State and Federal Governments have sought to suppress it for many years, only to find it proliferating through the new medium of the Internet. This Court held unconstitutional Congress's previous attempt to meet this new threat, and Congress responded with a carefully crafted attempt to eliminate the First Amendment problems we identified. As far as the provision at issue in this case is concerned, that effort was successful.

The judgment of the Eleventh Circuit is reversed.

☐ *Justice STEVENS, with whom Justice BREYER joins, concurring.*

My conclusion that this statutory provision is not facially unconstitutional is buttressed by two interrelated considerations on which Justice SCALIA finds it unnecessary to rely. First, I believe the result to be compelled by the principle that "every reasonable construction must be resorted to, in order to save a statute from unconstitutionality," *Hooper v. California*, 155 U.S. 648 (1895).

Second, to the extent the statutory text alone is unclear, our duty to avoid constitutional objections makes it especially appropriate to look beyond the text in order to ascertain the intent of its drafters. It is abundantly clear from the provision's legislative history that Congress' aim was to target materials advertised, promoted, presented, distributed, or solicited with a lascivious purpose—that is, with the intention of inciting sexual arousal. The provision was described throughout the deliberations in both Houses of Congress as the "pandering," or "pandering and solicitation" provision, despite the fact that the term "pandering" appears nowhere in the statute....

The dissent argues that the statute impermissibly undermines our First Amendment precedents insofar as it covers proposals to transact in constitutionally protected material. It is true that proof that a pornographic but not obscene representation did not depict real children would place that representation on the protected side of the line. But any constitutional concerns that might arise on that score are surely answered by the construction the Court gives the statute's operative provisions; that is, proposing a transaction in such material would not give rise to criminal liability under the statute unless the defendant actually believed, or intended to induce another to believe, that the material in question depicted real children.

Accordingly, when material which is protected—particularly if it possesses serious literary, artistic, political, or scientific value—is advertised, promoted, presented, distributed, or solicited for some lawful and nonlascivious purpose, such conduct is not captured by the statutory prohibition.

☐ *Justice SOUTER, with whom Justice GINSBURG joins, dissenting.*

Dealing in obscenity is penalized without violating the First Amendment, but as a general matter pornography lacks the harm to justify prohibiting it. If, however, a photograph (to take the kind of image in this case) shows an actual minor child as a pornographic subject, its transfer and even its possession may be made criminal. *New York v. Ferber*, 458 U.S. 747 (1982). The exception to the general rule rests not on the content of the picture but on the need to foil the exploitation of child subjects, and the justification limits the exception: only pornographic photographs of actual children may be prohibited, see *Ashcroft v. Free Speech Coalition*, 535 U.S. 234(2002). Thus, just six years ago the Court struck down a statute outlawing particular material merely represented to be child pornography, but not necessarily depicting actual children.

The Prosecutorial Remedies and Other Tools to end the Exploitation of Children Today Act of 2003 (Act) was enacted in the wake of *Free Speech Coalition*. The Act responds by avoiding any direct prohibition of transactions in child pornography when no actual minors may be pictured; instead, it prohibits proposals for transactions in pornography when a defendant manifestly believes or would induce belief in a prospective party that the subject of an exchange or exhibition is or will be an actual child, not an impersonated, simulated or "virtual" one, or the subject of a composite created from lawful photos spliced together. The Act specifically prohibits three types of those proposals. It outlaws solicitation of child pornography, as well as two distinct kinds of offers: those "advertis[ing]" or "promot[ing]" prosecutable child pornography, which recommend the material with the implication that the speaker can make it available, and those "present[ing]" or "distribut[ing]" such child pornography, which make the material available to anyone who chooses to take it.

The Court holds it is constitutional to prohibit these proposals, and up to a point I do not disagree. In particular, I accept the Court's explanation that Congress may criminalize proposals unrelated to any extant image. I part ways from the Court, however, on the regulation of proposals made with regard to specific, existing representations. Under the new law, the elements of the pandering offense are the same, whether or not the images are of real children. As to those that do not show real children, of course, a transaction in the material could not be prosecuted consistently with the First Amendment, and I believe that maintaining the First Amendment protection of expression we have previously held to cover fake child pornography requires a limit to the law's criminalization of pandering proposals. In failing to confront the tension between ostensibly protecting the material pandered while approving prosecution of the pandering of that same material, and in allowing the new pandering prohibition to suppress otherwise protected speech, the Court undermines *Ferber* and *Free Speech Coalition* in both reasoning and result. This is the significant element of today's holding, and I respectfully dissent from it. . . .

G | *Fair Trial/Free Press Controversies*

In *Skilling v. United States*, 130 S.Ct. 2896 (2010), the Court reaffirmed that the media prominence of the defendant does not necessarily produce prejudice, that juror impartiality does not require ignorance of the case, and that a presumption of prejudice arises only in an extreme case. The case grew out of the collapse of the Enron Corporation in 2001 and the indictment of Jeffrey Skilling, Enron's chief executive officer, for manipulating publicly reported financial records and making false and misleading statements. Because of the publicity over Enron's collapse, Skilling had moved for a change of venue because of the hostility toward him in Houston and because the extensive pretrial publicity poisoned potential jurors. Writing for the Court, Justice Ginsburg rejected that argument.

H | Symbolic Speech and Speech-Plus-Conduct

In its 2010–2011 term, the Court will consider the issue of picketing protests at the funerals of soldiers killed in wartime, and whether to reinstate a 5-million-dollar damages award against a Kansas preacher and his antigay crusade in *Snyder v. Phelps* (Docket No. 09-751). In March 2006 Marine Lance Corporal Matthew Snyder was killed in Iraq. His family arranged for a private funeral at St. John's Catholic Church in Westminster, Maryland. Pastor Fred Phelps, Sr. of Westboro Baptist Church in Topeka, Kansas, staged a protest demonstration at the funeral. In response to similar protests, about forty states have passed laws regulating funeral demonstrations. Phelps' church preaches a strong antigay message and spreads its view on its Internet site. At Snyder's funeral, Phelps, two daughters, and four grandchildren staged a protest, carrying posters such as "God Hates the USA," "America is doomed," and "Thank God for dead soldiers." The protest broke no local laws and police kept them at a distance from the church. Albert Snyder, the soldier's father, sued Phelps and won a 5-million-dollar award based on three tort claims: intrusion into a private event, intentional infliction of emotional distress, and civil conspiracy. The verdict included $2.9 million for compensatory damages and $2.1 million for punitive damages. The Court of Appeals for the Fourth Circuit overturned the verdict upon concluding that the protestors' speech was protected by the First Amendment because it was only a form of hyperbole. While finding that Phelps' remarks were "utterly distasteful," the appellate court concluded that they involved matters of public concern. Snyder appealed that decision and the Supreme Court granted review.

■ THE DEVELOPMENT OF LAW

Places That Have Been Held Not to Be Public Forums

CASE	VOTE	RULING
Pleasant Grove City v. Summum, 129 S.Ct. 1446 (2009)	9:0	Unlike speech in a public park or other public forum, the Court held that a city's decision about

what kinds of permanent monuments to permit constituted *government speech*, and thus the public forum doctrine does not apply. (The case is excerpted in this chapter.)

6

FREEDOM FROM AND
OF RELIGION

A | *The (Dis)Establishment of Religion*

In its 2009–2010 term, the Roberts Court revisited the controversy over the public display of religious displays in *Salazar v. Buono*, 130 S.Ct. 1803 (2010). The case involved whether an eight-foot cross in the Mojave National Preserve is an unconstitutional governmental endorsement of religion. Erected in 1934 by the Veterans of Foreign Wars, the cross had been maintained as a war memorial by the National Park Service. The American Civil Liberties Union filed a suit in 2001 on behalf of a former park service officer, Frank Buono, a Catholic, who alleged that the cross violated the Establishment Clause of the First Amendment. The suit also noted that the Park Service had denied a request to have a Buddhist shrine erected near the cross. A federal district court agreed with Buono, ruling in 2002 that the "primary effect of the presence of the cross" was to "advance religion." Congress responded in 2004 by enacting legislation directing the Department of the Interior to transfer about an acre of land to the Veterans of Foreign Wars in exchange for a privately owned plot nearby. In 2007, a three-judge panel of the U.S. Court of Appeals for the Ninth Circuit upheld the lower court's decision and invalidated the land transfer, observing that "carving out a tiny parcel of property in the midst of this vast preserve—like a donut hole with the cross atop it—will do nothing to minimize the impermissible government endorsement" of a religious symbol. The ruling was appealed to the Supreme Court, contending that it would require the government to "tear down a cross that has stood without incident for 70 years

126 | FREEDOM FROM AND OF RELIGION

as a memorial to fallen service members." The government also questioned whether Buono had standing to sue, since he lived in Oregon and suffered no specific harm because of the cross.

In a fragmented five-to-four decision, the Court reversed the appellate court and reopened the possibility of maintaining the cross as a war memorial. Writing for a plurality, Justice Kennedy, joined only by Chief Justice Roberts and Justice Alito, overturned the district court's order rejecting Congress's solution to the earlier ruling that the cross conveyed a constitutionally impermissible endorsement of religion, and remanded the case for further consideration. Concurring Justice Alito would have upheld the land transfer and found no violation of the First Amendment, while concurring Justice Scalia, joined by Justice Thomas, agreed with the result but would have denied Buono standing to bring the suit in the first place. Justice Stevens dissented, joined by Justices Ginsburg and Sotomayor, and emphasized that a "solitary cross . . . conveys an inescapably sectarian message" in violation of the First Amendment. In a separate dissent, Justice Breyer contended that the district court should have been allowed to decide whether the landtransfer law violated its earlier injunctions and would have not reached the First Amendment claim.

A bare majority held that public universities may require officially recognized student groups to accept all students who want to join, and such a requirement does not violate the constitutional rights of religious groups that want to exclude homosexuals. Writing the majority in *Christian Legal Society v. Martinez*, 130 S.Ct. 2971 (2010), Justice Ginsburg ruled that the University of California's Hastings College of Law's nondiscrimination policy did not unfairly target faith-based groups. In her words: "CLS, it bears emphasis, seeks not parity with other organizations, but a preferential exemption from Hastings' policy" in being officially recognized but with an exemption from the university's nondiscrimination policy with regard to homosexuals. Justice Ginsburg distinguished prior rulings on discrimination against a group's viewpoints and emphasized that Hastings solved that problem by protecting its "all comers" policy: "It is, after all, hard to imagine a more viewpoint-neutral policy than one requiring *all* student groups to accept *all* comers." By contrast, dissenting Justice Alito, joined by Chief Justice Roberts and Justices Scalia and Thomas, countered that, "The loudest boast of our free speech jurisprudence is that we protect the freedom to express 'the thought that we hate.'"

In its 2010–2011 term, the Court will consider whether a state statute granting tax credits to individual taxpayers who contribute to nonprofit organizations that provide scholarship funds for private schooling violates the Establishment Clause in *Arizona Christian School Tuition Organization v. Winn* (No. 09-087). Arizona grants dollar-for-dollar tax credits to individual taxpayers who contribute to nonprofit organizations that provide private school scholarships. A group of Arizona taxpayers alleged that because some of the nonprofit organizations restrict the availability of these scholarships to religious private schools, Arizona effectively deprived parents of a genuine choice when selecting between private secular and private sectarian schools. A federal district court dismissed the suit, finding that taxpayers lacked standing. The Ninth Circuit Court of Appeals reversed, finding that the taxpayers had standing because there was an exception to the general rule against taxpayer standing when the claim alleges that the government uses the funds to violate the (Dis)establishment Clause. In addition, the appellate court held that the allegations constituted a sufficient claim that Arizona's tax-credit funded scholarship program, as applied, violated the (Dis)establishment Clause, because it lacked religious neutrality and did not provide a true private choice for parents deciding where to send their children.

7

THE FOURTH AMENDMENT
GUARANTEE AGAINST
UNREASONABLE SEARCHES
AND SEIZURES

B | *Exceptions to the Fourth Amendment Warrant Requirement*

In *Arizona v. Johnson* 129 S.Ct. 781(2009), the Court further extended the "stop and frisk" exception to the Fourth Amendment laid down in *Terry v. Ohio*, 392 U.S. 1 (1968) (excerpted in Vol. 2, Ch. 7). In *Terry* the Court ruled that a "stop and frisk" may be conducted without violating the Fourth Amendment guarantee against unreasonable searches and seizures if (a) in an investigatory stop police have a reasonable suspicion that a person is committing or has committed a crime, and (b) police proceed from a stop to a pat-down search for weapons based on a reasonable suspicion the individual is armed and dangerous. Subsequent decisions expanded that exception with respect to traffic stops. In *Brendlin v. California*, 591 U.S. 249 (2007), for instance, the Court held that during a traffic stop police may seize "everyone in the vehicle"—the driver and all passengers. In *Arizona v. Johnson*, Justice Ginsburg held for a unanimous Court that police may order a passenger out of a stopped vehicle and conduct a pat-down search if they have reason to believe that the rider is armed and dangerous, and therefore poses a threat to police and the public.

Arizona v. Johnson stemmed from a police patrol of gang activity in a neighborhood associated with gangs in Tucson, Arizona. When one car passed, an officer ran a check on the license plate and found that insurance on the vehicle was suspended. Hence, although there was no suspicion of crime, the officers stopped the car to question the driver and one of the officers engaged a back-seat passenger, Lemon Montrea Johnson, who was wearing a blue bandanna—a gang emblem of the Crips. The officer learned from her conversation with Johnson that he was from town, he was associated with gang activity, and he had done time on a burglary conviction. Whereupon the officer ordered him out of the car, frisked him, and felt a gun near his waist. Johnson was arrested, tried, and convicted for illegal weapons possession. A state appellate court, however, reversed his conviction on the ground that police based the search only on their conversation with him, and on no reasonable suspicion that he had committed a crime. The Supreme Court reversed that decision.

In its 2008–2009 term, a bare majority of the Roberts Court limited warrantless car searches and reaffirmed the holding in *Chimel v. California*, 395 U.S. 752 (1969)(excerpted in Vol. 2, Ch. 7), as extended to automobiles in *New York v. Belton*, 453 U.S. 454 (1981), and in *Arizona v. Gant* (2009) (excerpted in Section C of this chapter).

C | *The Special Problems of Automobiles in a Mobile Society*

The Roberts Court ruled unanimously that police do not act unconstitutionally in conducting a search of a driver following an arrest based on probable cause, even if the arrest violates a state law. Delivering the decision in *Virginia v. Moore* (excerpted below), Justice Scalia upheld the conviction of David Moore for possession of crack cocaine after he was stopped for driving on a suspended license, which under state law authorized a traffic citation, not an arrest. As long as police have probable cause to make an arrest, Justice Scalia held, it makes no difference that a state law bars police from making an arrest when the crime involved is only a misdemeanor traffic offense. "An arrest based on probable cause serves interests that have long been seen as sufficient to justify the seizure" of evidence after an arrest. Justice Scalia noted that with its policy of ticketing after a traffic offense, "Virginia chooses to protect individual privacy and dignity more than the Fourth Amendment requires." But he ruled that choice does not make a resulting search invalid under the Fourth Amendment. "Moore would allow Virginia to accord enhanced protection only on pain of accompanying that protection with federal remedies for Fourth Amendment violations, which often include the exclusionary rule. States unwilling to lose control over the remedy would have to abandon restrictions on arrest altogether. This is an odd consequence of a provision designed to protect against searches and seizures."

In its 2008–2009 term, the Court also considered whether police violated the Fourth Amendment, during a routine traffic stop, by conducting a pat-down search of a passenger, based on an articulable basis to believe the passenger might be armed and dangerous, but not probable cause to believe the passenger is committing or has committed a criminal offense. The case, *Arizona v. Johnson*, 129 S.Ct. 781 (2009) is further discussed in Section B of this chapter.

In its 2008–2009 term, the Roberts Court split five to four in limiting warrantless car searches. Writing for the Court, Justice Stevens reaffirmed the holding in *Chimel v. California*, 895 U.S. 752 (1969) (excerpted in Vol. 2, Ch. 7), as extended in *New York v. Belton*, 453 U.S. 454 (1981), that police may search only the immediate area in order to protect the safety of officers in a search-incident-to-arrest; the police must have a warrant to search a car after the driver or passenger is taken into custody and may conduct a warrantless search only for evidence related to the arrest. Justice Scalia cast the deciding vote and issued a concurring opinion. Chief Justice Roberts and Justices Thomas, Breyer, and Alito dissented in *Arizona v. Gant* (2009) (excerpted below).

Arizona v. Gant
129 S.Ct. 1710 (2009)

Arizona police went to the home of Rodney Gant in search of drugs and to arrest him for failing to appear in court for having a suspended driver's license. When they arrived Gant was not there, but while the police were still there Gant pulled into the driveway. While Gant was in the car, an officer shined a flashlight into the vehicle, but made no other contact with him until he stepped out of the car. He was then arrested for driving with a suspended license, handcuffed, and locked in the back of a patrol car. Afterward, police officers searched his car and discovered cocaine in the pocket of a jacket on the backseat. Because Gant could not have accessed his car to retrieve weapons or evidence at the time of the search, on appeal, the Arizona Supreme Court held that the search-incident-to-arrest exception to the Fourth Amendment's warrant requirement, as defined in *Chimel v. California*, 395 U.S. 752 (1969), and applied to vehicle searches in *New York v. Belton*, 453 U.S. 454 (1981), did not justify the search in this case. The state appealed and the Supreme Court granted review.

The state supreme court's decision was affirmed by a five-to-four vote. Justice Stevens delivered the opinion of the Court. Justice Scalia issued a concurring opinion. Justices Breyer and Alito filed dissenting opinions; the latter's was joined by Chief Justice Roberts and Justice Thomas.

☐ *Justice STEVENS delivered the opinion of the Court.*

Under *Chimel*, police may search-incident-to-arrest only the space within an arrestee's "'immediate control,'" meaning "the area from within which he might gain possession of a weapon or destructible evidence." The safety and evidentiary justifications underlying *Chimel*'s reaching-distance rule determine *Belton*'s scope. Accordingly, we hold that *Belton* does not authorize a vehicle search incident to a recent occupant's arrest after the arrestee has been secured and cannot access the interior of the vehicle. Consistent with the holding in *Thornton v. United States*, 541 U.S. 615 (2004), and following the suggestion in Justice SCALIA's opinion concurring in the judgment in that case, we also conclude that circumstances unique to the automobile context justify a search-incident-to-arrest when it is reasonable to believe that evidence of the offense of arrest might be found in the vehicle. . . .

Consistent with our precedent, our analysis begins, as it should in every case addressing the reasonableness of a warrantless search, with the basic rule that "searches conducted outside the judicial process, without prior approval by judge or magistrate, are per se unreasonable under the Fourth Amendment— subject only to a few specifically established and well-delineated exceptions." *Katz v. United States*, 389 U.S. 347 (1967). Among the exceptions to the warrant requirement is a search incident to a lawful arrest. The exception derives from interests in officer safety and evidence preservation that are typically implicated in arrest situations.

In *Chimel*, we held that a search-incident-to-arrest may only include "the arrestee's person and the area 'within his immediate control'—construing that phrase to mean the area from within which he might gain possession of a weapon or destructible evidence." That limitation, which continues to define the boundaries of the exception, ensures that the scope of a search-incident-to-arrest is commensurate with its purposes of protecting arresting officers and safeguarding any evidence of the offense of arrest that an arrestee might conceal or destroy. If there is no possibility that an arrestee could reach into the area that law enforcement officers seek to search, both justifications for the search-incident-to-arrest exception are absent and the rule does not apply.

In *Belton*, we considered *Chimel*'s application to the automobile context. A lone police officer in that case stopped a speeding car in which Belton was one of four occupants. While asking for the driver's license and registration, the officer smelled burnt marijuana and observed an envelope on the car floor marked "Supergold"—a name he associated with marijuana. Thus having probable cause to believe the occupants had committed a drug offense, the officer ordered them out of the vehicle, placed them under arrest, and patted them down. Without handcuffing the arrestees, the officer "'split them up into four separate areas of the Thruway . . . so they would not be in physical touching area of each other'" and searched the vehicle, including the pocket of a jacket on the backseat, in which he found cocaine. . . .

[W]e held that when an officer lawfully arrests "the occupant of an automobile, he may, as a contemporaneous incident of that arrest, search the passenger compartment of the automobile" and any containers therein. That holding was based in large part on our assumption "that articles inside the relatively narrow compass of the passenger compartment of an automobile are in fact generally, even if not inevitably, within 'the area into which an arrestee might reach.' "

The Arizona Supreme Court read our decision in *Belton* as merely delineating "the proper scope of a search of the interior of an automobile" incident to an arrest. That is, when the passenger compartment is within an arrestee's reaching distance, *Belton* supplies the generalization that the entire compartment and any containers therein may be reached. On that view of *Belton*, the state court concluded that the search of Gant's car was unreasonable because Gant clearly could not have accessed his car at the time of the search. It also found that no other exception to the warrant requirement applied in this case.

Despite the textual and evidentiary support for the Arizona Supreme Court's reading of *Belton*, our opinion has been widely understood to allow a vehicle search incident to the arrest of a recent occupant even if there is no possibility the arrestee could gain access to the vehicle at the time of the search. This reading may be attributable to Justice BRENNAN's dissent in *Belton*, in which he characterized the Court's holding as resting on the "fiction . . . that the interior of a car is always within the immediate control of an arrestee who has recently been in the car." Under the majority's approach, he argued, "the result would presumably be the same even if [the officer] had handcuffed Belton and his companions in the patrol car" before conducting the search.

Since we decided *Belton*, Courts of Appeals have given different answers to the question whether a vehicle must be within an arrestee's reach to justify a vehicle search incident to arrest, but Justice BRENNAN's reading of the Court's opinion has predominated. . . .

Under this broad reading of *Belton*, a vehicle search would be authorized incident to every arrest of a recent occupant notwithstanding that in most cases the vehicle's passenger compartment will not be within the arrestee's reach at the time of the search. To read *Belton* as authorizing a vehicle search incident to every recent occupant's arrest would thus untether the rule from the justifications underlying the *Chimel* exception—a result clearly incompatible with our statement in *Belton* that it "in no way alters the fundamental principles established in the *Chimel* case regarding the basic scope of searches incident to lawful custodial arrests." Accordingly, we reject this reading of *Belton* and hold that the *Chimel* rationale authorizes police to search a vehicle incident to a recent occupant's arrest only when the arrestee is unsecured and within reaching distance of the passenger compartment at the time of the search.

Although it does not follow from *Chimel*, we also conclude that circumstances unique to the vehicle context justify a search incident to a lawful arrest when it is "reasonable to believe evidence relevant to the crime of arrest might be found in the vehicle." *Thornton*. In many cases, as when a recent occupant is arrested for a traffic violation, there will be no reasonable basis to believe the vehicle contains relevant evidence. See, e.g., *Atwater v. Lago Vista*, 532 U.S. 318 (2001); *Knowles v. Iowa*, 525 U.S. 113 (1998). But in others, including *Belton* and *Thornton*, the offense of arrest will supply a basis for searching the passenger compartment of an arrestee's vehicle and any containers therein. . . .

The State argues that *Belton* searches are reasonable regardless of the possibility of access in a given case because that expansive rule correctly balances law enforcement interests, including the interest in a bright-line rule, with an arrestee's limited privacy interest in his vehicle.

For several reasons, we reject the State's argument. First, the State seriously undervalues the privacy interests at stake. Although we have recognized that a motorist's privacy interest in his vehicle is less substantial than in his home, the former interest is nevertheless important and deserving of constitutional protection. It is particularly significant that *Belton* searches authorize police officers to search not just the passenger compartment but every purse, briefcase, or other container within that space. A rule that gives police the power to conduct such a search whenever an individual is caught committing a traffic offense, when there is no basis for believing evidence of the offense might be found in the vehicle, creates a serious and recurring threat to the privacy of countless individuals. Indeed, the character of that threat implicates the central concern underlying the Fourth Amendment—the concern about giving police officers unbridled discretion to rummage at will among a person's private effects.

At the same time as it undervalues these privacy concerns, the State exaggerates the clarity that its reading of *Belton* provides. Courts that have read *Belton* expansively are at odds regarding how close in time to the arrest and how proximate to the arrestee's vehicle an officer's first contact with the arrestee must be to bring the encounter within *Belton's* purview and whether a search is reasonable when it commences or continues after the arrestee has been removed from the scene. The rule has thus generated a great deal of uncertainty, particularly for a rule touted as providing a "bright line."

Contrary to the State's suggestion, a broad reading of *Belton* is also unnecessary to protect law enforcement safety and evidentiary interests. Under our view, *Belton* and *Thornton* permit an officer to conduct a vehicle search when an arrestee is within reaching distance of the vehicle or it is reasonable to believe the vehicle contains evidence of the offense of arrest. Other established exceptions to the warrant requirement authorize a vehicle search under additional circumstances when safety or evidentiary concerns demand. For instance, *Michigan v. Long*, 463 U.S. 1032 (1983), permits an officer to search a vehicle's passenger compartment when he has reasonable suspicion that an individual, whether or not the arrestee, is "dangerous" and might access the vehicle to "gain immediate control of weapons." If there is probable cause to believe a vehicle contains evidence of criminal activity, *United States v. Ross*, 456 U.S. 798 (1982), authorizes a search of any area of the vehicle in which the evidence might be found. Unlike the searches permitted by Justice SCALIA's opinion concurring in the judgment in *Thornton*, which we conclude today are reasonable for purposes of the Fourth Amendment, *Ross* allows searches for evidence relevant to offenses other than the offense of arrest, and the scope of the search authorized is broader. Finally, there may be still other circumstances in which safety or evidentiary interests would justify a search. *Maryland v. Buie*, 494 U.S. 325 (1990) (holding that, incident to arrest, an officer may conduct a limited protective sweep of those areas of a house in which he reasonably suspects a dangerous person may be hiding).

These exceptions together ensure that officers may search a vehicle when genuine safety or evidentiary concerns encountered during the arrest of a vehicle's recent occupant justify a search. Construing *Belton* broadly to allow vehicle searches incident to any arrest would serve no purpose except to provide a police entitlement, and it is anathema to the Fourth Amendment to permit a warrantless search on that basis. For these reasons, we are unpersuaded by the State's arguments that a broad reading of *Belton* would meaningfully further law enforcement interests and justify a substantial intrusion on individuals' privacy....

Police may search a vehicle incident to a recent occupant's arrest only if the arrestee is within reaching distance of the passenger compartment at the time of the search or it is reasonable to believe the vehicle contains evidence of the offense of arrest. When these justifications are absent, a search of an arrestee's vehicle will be unreasonable unless police obtain a warrant or show that another exception to the warrant requirement applies. The Arizona Supreme Court correctly held that this case involved an unreasonable search. Accordingly, the judgment of the State Supreme Court is affirmed.

☐ *Justice SCALIA concurring.*

To determine what is an "unreasonable" search within the meaning of the Fourth Amendment, we look first to the historical practices the Framers sought to preserve; if those provide inadequate guidance, we apply traditional standards of reasonableness. Since the historical scope of officers' authority to search vehicles incident to arrest is uncertain, see *Thornton v. United States*, 541 U.S. 615 (2004) (SCALIA, J., concurring in judgment), traditional standards of reasonableness govern. It is abundantly clear that those standards do not justify what I take to be the rule set forth in *New York v. Belton*, 453 U.S. 454 (1981), and *Thornton*: that arresting officers may always search an arrestee's vehicle in order to protect themselves from hidden weapons. When an arrest is made in connection with a roadside stop, police virtually always have a less intrusive and more effective means of ensuring their safety—and a means that is virtually always employed: ordering the arrestee away from the vehicle, patting him down in the open, handcuffing him, and placing him in the squad car. . . .

It must be borne in mind that we are speaking here only of a rule automatically permitting a search when the driver or an occupant is arrested. Where no arrest is made, we have held that officers may search the car if they reasonably believe "the suspect is dangerous and . . . may gain immediate control of weapons." *Michigan v. Long*, 463 U.S. 1032 (1983). In the no-arrest case, the possibility of access to weapons in the vehicle always exists, since the driver or passenger will be allowed to return to the vehicle when the interrogation is completed. The rule of *Michigan v. Long* is not at issue here.

Justice STEVENS acknowledges that an officer-safety rationale cannot justify all vehicle searches-incident-to-arrest, but asserts that that is not the rule *Belton* and *Thornton* adopted. (As described above, I read those cases differently). Justice STEVENS would therefore retain the application of *Chimel v. California*, 395 U.S. 752 (1969), in the car-search context but would apply in the future what he believes our cases held in the past: that officers making a roadside stop may search the vehicle so long as the "arrestee is within reaching distance of the passenger compartment at the time of the search." I believe that this standard fails to provide the needed guidance to arresting officers and also leaves much room for manipulation, inviting officers to leave the scene unsecured (at least where dangerous suspects are not involved) in order to conduct a vehicle search. In my view we should simply abandon the *Belton-Thornton* charade of officer safety and overrule those cases. I would hold that a vehicle search-incident-to-arrest is *ipso facto* "reasonable" only when the object of the search is evidence of the crime for which the arrest was made, or of another crime that the officer has probable cause to believe occurred. Because respondent was arrested for driving without a license (a crime for which no evidence could be expected to be found in the vehicle), I would hold in the present case that the search was unlawful. . . .

No other Justice, however, shares my view that application of *Chimel* in this context should be entirely abandoned. It seems to me unacceptable for the Court to come forth with a 4-to-1-to-4 opinion that leaves the governing rule uncertain. I am therefore confronted with the choice of either leaving the current understanding of *Belton* and *Thornton* in effect, or acceding to what seems to me the artificial narrowing of those cases adopted by Justice STEVENS. The latter, as I have said, does not provide the degree of certainty I think desirable in this field; but the former opens the field to what I think are plainly unconstitutional searches—which is the greater evil. I therefore join the opinion of the Court.

□ *Justice ALITO, with whom THE CHIEF JUSTICE and Justice KENNEDY join, and with whom Justice BREYER joins except as to Part II-E, dissenting.*

Twenty-eight years ago, in *New York v. Belton*, 453 U.S. 454 (1981), this Court held that "when a policeman has made a lawful custodial arrest of the occu-pant of an automobile, he may, as a contemporaneous incident of that arrest, search the passenger compartment of that automobile." Five years ago, in *Thorn-ton v. United States*, 541 U.S. 615 (2004)—a case involving a situation not materially distinguishable from the situation here—the Court not only reaf-firmed but extended the holding of *Belton*, making it applicable to recent occupants. Today's decision effectively overrules those important decisions, even though respondent Gant has not asked us to do so.

To take the place of the overruled precedents, the Court adopts a new two-part rule under which a police officer who arrests a vehicle occupant or recent occupant may search the passenger compartment if (1) the arrestee is within reaching distance of the vehicle at the time of the search or (2) the officer has reason to believe that the vehicle contains evidence of the offense of arrest. The first part of this new rule may endanger arresting officers and is truly endorsed by only four Justices; Justice SCALIA joins solely for the purpose of avoiding a "4-to-1-to 4 opinion." The second part of the new rule is taken from Justice SCALIA's separate opinion in *Thornton* without any inde-pendent explanation of its origin or justification and is virtually certain to con-fuse law enforcement officers and judges for some time to come. The Court's decision will cause the suppression of evidence gathered in many searches carried out in good-faith reliance on well-settled case law, and although the Court purports to base its analysis on the landmark decision in *Chimel v. California*, 395 U.S. 752 (1969), the Court's reasoning undermines *Chimel*. I would follow *Belton*, and I therefore respectfully dissent. . . .

The precise holding in *Belton* could not be clearer. The Court stated un-equivocally: "[W]e hold that when a policeman has made a lawful custodial arrest of the occupant of an automobile, he may, as a contemporaneous incident of that arrest, search the passenger compartment of that automobile."

Despite this explicit statement, the opinion of the Court in the present case curiously suggests that *Belton* may reasonably be read as adopting a hold-ing that is narrower than the one explicitly set out in the *Belton* opinion, namely, that an officer arresting a vehicle occupant may search the passenger compartment "when the passenger compartment is within an arrestee's reach-ing distance." According to the Court, the broader reading of *Belton* that has gained wide acceptance "may be attributable to Justice BRENNAN's dissent."

Contrary to the Court's suggestion, however, Justice BRENNAN's *Belton* dissent did not mischaracterize the Court's holding in that case or cause that holding to be misinterpreted. As noted, the *Belton* Court explicitly stated precisely what it held. . . .

Respondent in this case has not asked us to overrule *Belton*, much less *Chimel*. Respondent's argument rests entirely on an interpretation of *Belton* that is plainly incorrect, an interpretation that disregards *Belton*'s explicit delin-eation of its holding. I would therefore leave any reexamination of our prior precedents for another day, if such a reexamination is to be undertaken at all. In this case, I would simply apply *Belton* and reverse the judgment below.

Virginia v. Moore
128 S.Ct. 1598 (2008)

Rather than issuing a summons required by Virginia law, police arrested David Moore for the misdemeanor of driving with a suspended license. A search incident to the arrest found crack cocaine and Moore was charged and tried on drug charges. The trial court rejected a motion to suppress the evidence on Fourth Amendment grounds and Moore was convicted. The Virginia state supreme court reversed, reasoning that the search violated the Fourth Amendment because the arresting officers should have issued a citation under state law, and the Fourth Amendment does not permit a search incident to an arrest for a traffic citation. Moore appealed and the Supreme Court granted review.

The state supreme court's decision was reversed by a unanimous Court. Justice Scalia delivered the opinion of the Court. Justice Ginsburg filed a concurring opinion.

☐ *Justice SCALIA delivered the opinion of the Court.*

We consider whether a police officer violates the Fourth Amendment by making an arrest based on probable cause but prohibited by state law.

On February 20, 2003, two City of Portsmouth police officers stopped a car driven by David Lee Moore. They had heard over the police radio that a person known as "Chubs" was driving with a suspended license, and one of the officers knew Moore by that nickname. The officers determined that Moore's license was in fact suspended, and arrested him for the misdemeanor of driving on a suspended license, which is punishable under Virginia law by a year in jail and a $2,500 fine. The officers subsequently searched Moore and found that he was carrying 16 grams of crack cocaine and $516 in cash. Under state law, the officers should have issued Moore a summons instead of arresting him. Driving on a suspended license, like some other misdemeanors, is not an arrestable offense except as to those who "fail or refuse to discontinue" the violation, and those whom the officer reasonably believes to be likely to disregard a summons, or likely to harm themselves or others. . . .

Moore was charged with possessing cocaine with the intent to distribute it in violation of Virginia law. He filed a pretrial motion to suppress the evidence from the arrest search. Virginia law does not, as a general matter, require suppression of evidence obtained in violation of state law. Moore argued, however, that suppression was required by the Fourth Amendment. The trial court denied the motion, and after a bench trial found Moore guilty of the drug charge and sentenced him to a 5-year prison term, with one year and six months of the sentence suspended. The conviction was reversed by a panel of Virginia's intermediate court on Fourth Amendment grounds, [but] reversed again by the Virginia Supreme Court. The Court reasoned that since the arresting officers should have issued Moore a citation under state law, and the Fourth Amendment does not permit search incident to citation, the arrest search violated the Fourth Amendment.

The Fourth Amendment protects "against unreasonable searches and seizures" of (among other things) the person. In determining whether a search or seizure is unreasonable, we begin with history. We look to the statutes and common law of the founding era to determine the norms that the Fourth Amendment was meant to preserve. See *Wyoming v. Houghton*, 526 U.S. 295 (1999). We are aware of no historical indication that those who ratified the Fourth Amendment understood it as a redundant guarantee of whatever limits on search and seizure legislatures might have enacted. The immediate object of the Fourth Amendment was to prohibit the general warrants and writs of assistance that English judges had employed against the colonists. That suggests, if anything, that founding-era citizens were skeptical of using the rules for search and seizure set by government actors as the index of reasonableness. . . .

Of course such a claim would not have been available against state officers, since the Fourth Amendment was a restriction only upon federal power. But early Congresses tied the arrest authority of federal officers to state laws of arrest. Moreover, even though several state constitutions also prohibited unreasonable searches and seizures, citizens who claimed officers had violated state restrictions on arrest did not claim that the violations also ran afoul of the state constitutions. The apparent absence of such litigation is particularly striking in light of the fact that searches incident to warrantless arrests (which is to say arrests in which the officer was not insulated from private suit) were, as one commentator has put it, "taken for granted" at the founding, as were warrantless arrests themselves. . . .

When history has not provided a conclusive answer, we have analyzed a search or seizure in light of traditional standards of reasonableness "by assessing, on the one hand, the degree to which it intrudes upon an individual's privacy and, on the other, the degree to which it is needed for the promotion of legitimate governmental interests." *Houghton*. That methodology provides no support for Moore's Fourth Amendment claim. In a long line of cases, we have said that when an officer has probable cause to believe a person committed even a minor crime in his presence, the balancing of private and public interests is not in doubt. The arrest is constitutionally reasonable.

Our decisions counsel against changing this calculus when a State chooses to protect privacy beyond the level that the Fourth Amendment requires. We have treated additional protections exclusively as matters of state law. . . .

We are convinced that the approach of our prior cases is correct, because an arrest based on probable cause serves interests that have long been seen as sufficient to justify the seizure. Arrest ensures that a suspect appears to answer charges and does not continue a crime, and it safeguards evidence and enables officers to conduct an in-custody investigation. Moore argues that a State has no interest in arrest when it has a policy against arresting for certain crimes. That is not so, because arrest will still ensure a suspect's appearance at trial, prevent him from continuing his offense, and enable officers to investigate the incident more thoroughly. State arrest restrictions are more accurately characterized as showing that the State values its interests in forgoing arrests more highly than its interests in making them, or as showing that the State places a higher premium on privacy than the Fourth Amendment requires. A State is free to prefer one search-and-seizure policy among the range of constitutionally permissible options, but its choice of a more restrictive option does not render the less restrictive ones unreasonable, and hence unconstitutional. If we concluded otherwise, we would often frustrate rather than further state policy. Virginia chooses to protect individual privacy and dignity more than the Fourth Amendment requires, but it also chooses not to attach to violations of its arrest rules the potent remedies that federal courts have applied to Fourth Amendment violations. Virginia does not, for example, ordinarily exclude from criminal trials evidence obtained in violation of its statutes. Moore would allow Virginia to accord enhanced protection against arrest only on pain of accompanying that protection with federal remedies for Fourth Amendment violations, which often include the exclusionary rule. States unwilling to lose control over the remedy would have to abandon restrictions on arrest altogether. This is an odd consequence of a provision designed to protect against searches and seizures.

Even if we thought that state law changed the nature of the Commonwealth's interests for purposes of the Fourth Amendment, we would adhere to the probable-cause standard. In determining what is reasonable under the Fourth Amendment, we have given great weight to the "essential interest in readily administrable rules." . . .

Finally, linking Fourth Amendment protections to state law would cause them to "vary from place to place and from time to time." Even at the same place and time, the Fourth Amendment's protections might vary if federal officers were not subject to the same statutory constraints as state officers. In *Elkins v. United States*, 364 U.S. 206 (1960), we noted the practical difficulties posed by the "silver-platter doctrine," which had imposed more stringent limitations on federal officers than on state police acting independent of them. It would be strange to construe a constitutional provision that did not apply to the States at all when it was adopted to now restrict state officers more than federal officers, solely because the States have passed search-and-seizure laws that are the prerogative of independent sovereigns.

We conclude that warrantless arrests for crimes committed in the presence of an arresting officer are reasonable under the Constitution, and that while States are free to regulate such arrests however they desire, state restrictions do not alter the Fourth Amendment's protections.

Moore argues that even if the Constitution allowed his arrest, it did not allow the arresting officers to search him. We have recognized, however, that officers may perform searches incident to constitutionally permissible arrests in order to ensure their safety and safeguard evidence. *United States v. Robinson*, 414 U.S. 218 (1973). We have described this rule as covering any "lawful arrest," with constitutional law as the reference point. . . .

The interests justifying search are present whenever an officer makes an arrest. A search enables officers to safeguard evidence, and, most critically, to ensure their safety during "the extended exposure which follows the taking of a suspect into custody and transporting him to the police station." *Robinson*. Officers issuing citations do not face the same danger, and we therefore held in *Knowles v. Iowa*, 525 U.S. 113 (1998), that they do not have the same authority to search. We cannot agree with the Virginia Supreme Court that *Knowles* controls here. The state officers arrested Moore, and therefore faced the risks that are "an adequate basis for treating all custodial arrests alike for purposes of search justification." *Robinson*.

The Virginia Supreme Court may have concluded that *Knowles* required the exclusion of evidence seized from Moore because, under state law, the officers who arrested Moore should have issued him a citation instead. This argument might have force if the Constitution forbade Moore's arrest, because we have sometimes excluded evidence obtained through unconstitutional methods in order to deter constitutional violations. But the arrest rules that the officers violated were those of state law alone, and as we have just concluded, it is not the province of the Fourth Amendment to enforce state law. That Amendment does not require the exclusion of evidence obtained from a constitutionally permissible arrest. We reaffirm against a novel challenge what we have signaled for more than half a century. When officers have probable cause to believe that a person has committed a crime in their presence, the Fourth Amendment permits them to make an arrest, and to search the suspect in order to safeguard evidence and ensure their own safety. The judgment of the Supreme Court of Virginia is reversed, and the case is remanded for further proceedings not inconsistent with this opinion.

☐ *Justice GINSBURG, concurring in the judgment.*

I find in the historical record more support for Moore's position than the Court does. Further, our decision in *United States v. Di Re*, 332 U.S. 581 (1948), requiring suppression of evidence gained in a search incident to an unlawful arrest, seems to me pinned to the Fourth Amendment and not to our "supervisory power." And I am aware of no "long line of cases" holding that, regardless of state law, probable cause renders every warrantless arrest for crimes committed in the presence of an arresting officer "constitutionally reasonable."

I agree with the Court's conclusion and its reasoning, however, to this extent. In line with the Court's decision in *Atwater v. Lago Vista*, 532 U.S. 318 (2001), Virginia could have made driving on a suspended license an arrestable offense. The Commonwealth chose not to do so. Moore asks us to credit Virginia law on a police officer's arrest authority, but only in part. He emphasizes Virginia's classification of driving on a suspended license as a nonarrestable misdemeanor. Moore would have us ignore, however, the limited consequences Virginia attaches to a police officer's failure to follow the Commonwealth's summons-only instruction. For such an infraction, the officer may be disciplined and the person arrested may bring a tort suit against the officer. But Virginia law does not demand the suppression of evidence seized. Virginia could have made driving on a suspended license an arrestable offense. The Commonwealth chose not to do so. Moore asks us to credit Virginia law on a police officer's arrest authority, but only in part. He emphasizes Virginia's classification of driving on a suspended license as a nonarrestable misdemeanor. Moore would have us ignore, however, the limited consequences Virginia attaches to a police officer's failure to follow the Commonwealth's summons-only instruction. For such an infraction, the officer may be disciplined and the person arrested by an officer who arrests when he should have issued a summons.

The Fourth Amendment, today's decision holds, does not put States to an all-or-nothing choice in this regard. A State may accord protection against arrest beyond what the Fourth Amendment requires, yet restrict the remedies available when police deny to persons they apprehend the extra protection state law orders. Because I agree that the arrest and search Moore challenges violated Virginia law, but did not violate the Fourth Amendment, I join the Court's judgment.

D | *Other Governmental Searches in the Administrative State*

In its 2008–2009 term, the Roberts Court held unconstitutional a strip search of a thirteen-year-old student in *Safford Unified School District No. 1 v. Redding* (2009) (excerpted below).

In its 2009–2010 term the Court decided whether the Fourth Amendment protects the privacy of text messages of government employees sent by electronic paging devices. The case arose in Ontario, California, from the police department's review of text messages sent and received by Sergeant Jeff Quon, a member of the department's SWAT team. The city had no official privacy policy for text messaging. However, it did have a general policy about computer and Internet use that indicated that Ontario reserved the right to monitor e-mail messages and Internet usage, which Quon agreed to. In 2002, Quon and another officer exceeded a 25,000-character limit for texting. The chief of police contacted the service provider who voluntarily disclosed the transcripts without notifying Quon. They showed that a large portion were personal and many sexually explicit. Subsequently, Quon and other officers sued, arguing that he wasn't aware that the city's policy applied to his department and that its informal policy permitted the use for personal messages so long as they paid for overage charges. A trial found that the officers had a reasonable expectation of privacy in their text messages but that the police chief's intent was to uncover misconduct. However, a three-judge panel of the Court of Appeals for the Ninth Circuit reversed, holding that the search was unreasonable as a matter of law and that the officers had "a reasonable expectation of privacy in the content of the text messages." The Supreme Court granted an appeal of that decision in *City of Ontario v. Quon*, 130 S.Ct. 2619 (2010), and held that the search was permissible because the government was reasonably investigating violations of workplace rules. The Court did not decide whether Quon had a reasonable expectation of privacy in his text messages because the search had a legitimate work-related purpose and the scope of the search was not excessive.

Safford Unified School District No. 1 v. Redding
129 S.Ct. 2633 (2009)

The facts are discussed in the excerpt below. The Court affirmed the Court of Appeals for the Ninth Circuit's holding that a strip search of a middle school student for Ibuprofen pills violated the Fourth Amendment, but reversed the appellate court's holding that school officials did not have qualified immunity from a suit for damages for violating constitutional rights. Justice Souter delivered the opinion for the Court. Justices Stevens, Ginsburg, and Thomas each issued separate opinions, in part concurring and dissenting.

☐ *Justice SOUTER delivered the opinion of the Court.*

The issue here is whether a 13-year-old student's Fourth Amendment right was violated when she was subjected to a search of her bra and underpants by school officials acting on reasonable suspicion that she had brought forbidden prescription and over-the-counter drugs to school. Because there were no reasons to suspect the drugs presented a danger or were concealed in her underwear, we hold that the search did violate the Constitution, but because there is reason to question the clarity with which the right was established, the official who ordered the unconstitutional search is entitled to qualified immunity from liability.

The events immediately prior to the search in question began in 13-year-old Savana Redding's math class at Safford Middle School one October day in 2003. The assistant principal of the school, Kerry Wilson, came into the room and asked Savana to go to his office. There, he showed her a day planner, unzipped and open flat on his desk, in which there were several knives, lighters, a permanent marker, and a cigarette. Wilson asked Savana whether the planner was hers; she said it was, but that a few days before she had lent it to her friend, Marissa Glines. Savana stated that none of the items in the planner belonged to her.

Wilson then showed Savana four white prescription-strength ibuprofen 400-mg pills, and one over-the-counter blue naproxen 200-mg pill, all used for pain and inflammation but banned under school rules without advance permission. He asked Savana if she knew anything about the pills. Savana answered that she did not. Wilson then told Savana that he had received a report that she was giving these pills to fellow students; Savana denied it and agreed to let Wilson search her belongings. Helen Romero, an administrative assistant, came into the office, and together with Wilson they searched Savana's backpack, finding nothing.

At that point, Wilson instructed Romero to take Savana to the school nurse's office to search her clothes for pills. Romero and the nurse, Peggy Schwallier, asked Savana to remove her jacket, socks, and shoes, leaving her in stretch pants and a T-shirt (both without pockets), which she was then asked to remove. Finally, Savana was told to pull her bra out and to the side and shake it, and to pull out the elastic on her underpants, thus exposing her breasts and pelvic area to some degree. No pills were found.

Savana's mother filed suit against Safford Unified School District No. 1, Wilson, Romero, and Schwallier for conducting a strip search in violation of Savana's Fourth Amendment rights. The individuals (hereinafter petitioners) moved for summary judgment, raising a defense of qualified immunity. The District Court for the District of Arizona granted the motion on the ground that there was no Fourth Amendment violation, and a panel of the Ninth Circuit affirmed.

A closely divided Circuit sitting *en banc*, however, reversed. Following the two-step protocol for evaluating claims of qualified immunity, the Ninth Circuit held that the strip search was unjustified under the Fourth Amendment test for searches of children by school officials set out in *New Jersey v. T. L. O.*, 469 U.S. 325 (1985). . . .

In *T. L. O.*, we recognized that the school setting "requires some modification of the level of suspicion of illicit activity needed to justify a search," and held that for searches by school officials "a careful balancing of governmental and private interests suggests that the public interest is best served by a Fourth Amendment standard of reasonableness that stops short of probable cause." We have thus applied a standard of reasonable suspicion to determine the legality of a school administrator's search of a student, and have held that a school search "will be permissible in its scope when the measures adopted are reasonably related to the objectives of the search and not excessively intrusive in light of the age and sex of the student and the nature of the infraction." . . .

In this case, the school's policies strictly prohibit the nonmedical use, possession, or sale of any drug on school grounds, including "'[a]ny prescription or over-the-counter drug, except those for which permission to use in school has been granted pursuant to Board policy.'" A week before Savana was searched, another student, Jordan Romero (no relation of the school's administrative assistant), told the principal and Assistant Principal Wilson that "certain students were bringing drugs and weapons on campus," and that he had been sick after taking some pills that "he got from a classmate." On the morning of October 8, the same boy handed Wilson a white pill that he said Marissa Glines had given him. He told Wilson that students were planning to take the pills at lunch.

Wilson learned from Peggy Schwallier, the school nurse, that the pill was Ibuprofen 400 mg, available only by prescription. Wilson then called Marissa out of class. Outside the classroom, Marissa's teacher handed Wilson the day planner, found within Marissa's reach, containing various contraband items. Wilson escorted Marissa back to his office.

In the presence of Helen Romero, Wilson requested Marissa to turn out her pockets and open her wallet. Marissa produced a blue pill, several white ones, and a razor blade. Wilson asked where the blue pill came from, and Marissa answered, "'I guess it slipped in when she gave me the IBU 400s.'" When Wilson asked whom she meant, Marissa replied, "'Savana Redding.'" Wilson then enquired about the day planner and its contents; Marissa denied knowing anything about them. Wilson did not ask Marissa any followup questions to determine whether there was any likelihood that Savana presently had pills: neither asking when Marissa received the pills from Savana nor where Savana might be hiding them.

Schwallier did not immediately recognize the blue pill, but information provided through a poison control hotline indicated that the pill was a 200-mg dose of an antiinflammatory drug, generically called naproxen, available over the counter. At Wilson's direction, Marissa was then subjected to a search of her bra and underpants by Romero and Schwallier, as Savana was later on. The search revealed no additional pills.

It was at this juncture that Wilson called Savana into his office and showed her the day planner. Their conversation established that Savana and Marissa were on friendly terms: while she denied knowledge of the contraband, Savana admitted that the day planner was hers and that she had lent it to Marissa. Wilson had other reports of their friendship from staff members, who had identified Savana and Marissa as part of an unusually rowdy group at the school's opening dance in August, during which alcohol and cigarettes were found in the girls' bathroom. Wilson had reason to connect the girls with this contraband, for Wilson knew that Jordan Romero had told the principal that before the dance, he had been at a party at Savana's house where alcohol was served. Marissa's statement that the pills came from Savana was thus sufficiently plausible to warrant suspicion that Savana was involved in pill distribution. This suspicion of Wilson's was enough to justify a search of Savana's backpack and outer clothing. If a student is reasonably suspected of giving out contraband pills, she is reasonably suspected of carrying them on her person and in the carryall that has become an item of student uniform in most places today. If Wilson's reasonable suspicion of pill distribution were not understood to support searches of outer clothes and backpack, it would not justify any search worth making. And the look into Savana's bag, in her presence and in the relative privacy of Wilson's office, was not excessively intrusive, any more than Romero's subsequent search of her outer clothing.

Here it is that the parties part company, with Savana's claim that extending the search at Wilson's behest to the point of making her pull out her underwear was constitutionally unreasonable. The exact label for this final step in the intrusion is not important, though strip search is a fair way to speak of it. Romero and Schwallier directed Savana to remove her clothes down to her underwear, and then "pull out" her bra and the elastic band on her underpants. Although Romero and Schwallier stated that they did not see anything when Savana followed their instructions, we would not define strip search and its Fourth Amendment consequences in a way that would guarantee litigation about who was looking and how much was seen. The very fact of Savana's pulling her underwear away from her body in the presence of the two officials who were able to see her necessarily exposed her breasts and pelvic area to some degree, and both subjective and reasonable societal expectations of personal privacy support the treatment of such a search as categorically distinct, requiring distinct elements of justification on the part of school authorities for going beyond a search of outer clothing and belongings.

Savana's subjective expectation of privacy against such a search is inherent in her account of it as embarrassing, frightening, and humiliating. The reasonableness of her expectation (required by the Fourth Amendment standard) is indicated by the consistent experiences of other young people similarly searched, whose adolescent vulnerability intensifies the patent intrusiveness of the exposure.

The indignity of the search does not, of course, outlaw it, but it does implicate the rule of reasonableness as stated in *T. L. O.*, that "the search as actually conducted [be] reasonably related in scope to the circumstances which justified the interference in the first place." The scope will be permissible, that is, when it is "not excessively intrusive in light of the age and sex of the student and the nature of the infraction."

Here, the content of the suspicion failed to match the degree of intrusion. Wilson knew beforehand that the pills were prescription-strength ibuprofen and over-the-counter naproxen, common pain relievers equivalent to two Advil, or one Aleve. He must have been aware of the nature and limited threat of the specific drugs he was searching for, and while just about anything can be taken in quantities that will do real harm, Wilson had no reason to suspect that large amounts of the drugs were being passed around, or that individual students were receiving great numbers of pills.

Nor could Wilson have suspected that Savana was hiding common painkillers in her underwear. . . .

In sum, what was missing from the suspected facts that pointed to Savana was any indication of danger to the students from the power of the drugs or their quantity, and any reason to suppose that Savana was carrying pills in her underwear. We think that the combination of these deficiencies was fatal to finding the search reasonable.

We do mean . . . to make it clear that the concern to limit a school search to reasonable scope requires the support of reasonable suspicion of danger or of resort to underwear for hiding evidence of wrongdoing before a search can reasonably make the quantum leap from outer clothes and backpacks to exposure of intimate parts. The meaning of such a search, and the degradation its subject may reasonably feel, place a search that intrusive in a category of its own demanding its own specific suspicions. . . .

☐ *Justice STEVENS, with whom Justice GINSBURG joins, concurring in part and dissenting in part.*

In *New Jersey v. T. L. O.*, 469 U.S. 325 (1985), the Court established a two-step inquiry for determining the reasonableness of a school official's decision to search a student. First, the Court explained, the search must be "'justified at its inception'" by the presence of "reasonable grounds for suspecting that the search will turn up evidence that the student has violated or is violating either the law or the rules of the school." Second, the search must be "permissible in its scope," which is achieved "when the measures adopted are reasonably related to the objectives of the search and not excessively intrusive in light of the age and sex of the student and the nature of the infraction."

Nothing the Court decides today alters this basic framework. It simply applies *T. L. O.* to declare unconstitutional a strip search of a 13-year-old honors student that was based on a groundless suspicion that she might be hiding medicine in her underwear. This is, in essence, a case in which clearly established law meets clearly outrageous conduct. I have long believed that "'[i]t does not require a constitutional scholar to conclude that a nude search of a 13-year-old child is an invasion of constitutional rights of some magnitude.'" The strip search of Savana Redding in this case was both more intrusive and less justified than the search of the student's purse in *T. L. O.* . . .

☐ *Justice THOMAS, concurring in the judgment in part and dissenting in part.*

I agree with the Court that the judgment against the school officials with respect to qualified immunity should be reversed. Unlike the majority, however, I would hold that the search of Savana Redding did not violate the Fourth Amendment. The majority imposes a vague and amorphous standard on school administrators. It also grants judges sweeping authority to second-guess the measures that these officials take to maintain discipline in their schools and ensure the health and safety of the students in their charge. This deep intrusion into the administration of public schools exemplifies why the Court should return to the common-law doctrine of *in loco parentis* under which "the judiciary was reluctant to interfere in the routine business of school administration, allowing schools and teachers to set and enforce rules and to maintain order." *Morse v. Frederick*, 551 U.S. 393 (2007) (THOMAS, J., concurring). But even under the prevailing Fourth Amendment test established by *New Jersey v. T. L. O.* (1985), all petitioners, including the school district, are entitled to judgment as a matter of law in their favor.

"Although the underlying command of the Fourth Amendment is always that searches and seizures be reasonable, what is reasonable depends on the context within which a search takes place." Thus, although public school students retain Fourth Amendment rights under this Court's precedent, those rights "are different . . . than elsewhere; the 'reasonableness' inquiry cannot disregard the schools' custodial and tutelary responsibility for children," *Vernonia School Dist. 47J v. Acton*, 515 U.S. 646 (1995). For nearly 25 years this Court has understood that "[m]aintaining order in the classroom has never been easy, but in more recent years, school disorder has often taken particularly ugly forms: drug use and violent crime in the schools have become major social problems." In schools, "[e]vents calling for discipline are frequent occurrences and sometimes require immediate, effective action." *Goss v. Lopez*, 419 U.S. 565 (1975).

For this reason, school officials retain broad authority to protect students and preserve "order and a proper educational environment" under the Fourth Amendment. This authority requires that school officials be able to engage in the "close supervision of schoolchildren, as well as . . . enforc[e] rules against conduct that would be perfectly permissible if undertaken by an adult." Seeking to reconcile the Fourth Amendment with this unique public school setting, the Court in *T. L. O.* held that a school search is "reasonable" if it is "'justified at its inception'" and "'reasonably related in scope to the circumstances which justified the interference in the first place.'" . . .

F | *The Exclusionary Rule*

In an important ruling, a bare majority of the Court in *Herring v. United States* (2009) (excerpted below) held that negligent errors and illegal seizures do not automatically trigger the exclusionary rule. Writing for the Court, Chief Justice Roberts emphasized that "Our cases establish that suppression [of illegally obtained evidence] is not an automatic consequence of a Fourth Amendment violation. Instead, the question turns on the culpability of the police and the potential of exclusion to deter wrongful police conduct." In other words if police make an objectively reasonable mistake—i.e., are merely negligent—the exclusionary rule does not apply to whatever evidence is found. In so holding, the majority extended the "good faith" exception to ordinary police conduct; see *United States v. Leon* and *Massachusetts v. Sheppard* (1984) (excerpted in Vol. 2, Ch. 7) and *Arizona v. Evans* (1995) (excerpted in Vol. 2, Ch. 7). As Chief Justice Roberts put it: "To trigger the exclusionary rule, police conduct must be sufficiently deliberate that exclusion can meaningfully deter it, and sufficiently culpable that such deterrence is worth the price paid by the justice system. As laid out in our cases, the exclusionary rule serves to deter deliberate, reckless, or grossly negligent conduct, or in some circumstances recurring or systemic negligence."

Notably, Justice Kennedy cast the deciding vote in *Herring*, joining Justices Scalia, Thomas, Alito, and Chief Justice Roberts, in holding that the exclusionary rule does not apply to evidence obtained after an arrest even if the police had no basis for it in the first place. However, in *Corley v. United States* (2009) (excerpted in Vol. 2, Ch. 8), Justice Kennedy joined Justices Stevens, Souter, Ginsburg, and Breyer, in holding that, when federal agents do not bring a suspect before a judge for "presentment" within six hours of an arrest, a defendant's confession made six hours after an arrest should be excluded as evidence at trial.

In addition, in *Pearson v. Callahan*, 129 S.Ct. 808 (2009), the Roberts Court unanimously held that police may not be sued for entering a house without a warrant after receiving a signal from an informant on the inside that a drug transaction is taking place. Writing for the Court, Justice Alito observed that the law in this area was not "clearly established" and therefore police are immune from liability for entering the house without a warrant. Together, *Herring* and *Pearson* further cut back on the scope and application of the exclusionary rule.

Herring v. United States
129 S.Ct. 695 (2009)

In July 2004, police investigator Mark Anderson learned that Bennie Dean Herring had gone to the Coffee County Sheriff's Department to retrieve something from his impounded truck. Herring was no stranger to law enforcement, and Anderson asked the county's warrant clerk to check for any outstanding warrants for Herring's arrest. When she found none, Anderson asked the clerk to check with her counterpart in neighboring Dale County. After checking Dale County's computer database, the clerk replied that there was an active arrest warrant for Herring's failure to appear on a felony charge, and information was relayed to Anderson, while a request was made for a fax copy of the warrant as confirmation. Subsequently, Anderson and a deputy followed Herring as he left the impound lot, pulled him over, and arrested him. A search incident to the arrest revealed methamphetamine in his pocket and a pistol (which as a felon he could not possess) in his vehicle. There was, however, a mistake about the warrant. The Dale County sheriff's computer records are supposed to correspond to actual arrest warrants, which the office also maintains. But the clerk discovered that the warrant had been recalled five months earlier. Normally when a warrant is recalled the court clerk's office or a judge's chambers calls the clerk, who enters the information in the sheriff's computer database and disposes of the physical copy. For whatever reason, the information about the recall of the warrant for Herring did not appear in the database.

After Herring was indicted in federal district court for illegally possessing the gun and drugs, he moved to suppress the evidence on the ground that his initial arrest had been illegal because the warrant had been rescinded. A magistrate judge recommended denying the motion because the arresting officers had acted in a good-faith belief that the warrant was still outstanding. Thus, even if there were a Fourth Amendment violation, there was "no reason to believe that application of the exclusionary rule here would deter the occurrence of any future mistakes." The district court adopted that recommendation and the Court of Appeals for the Eleventh Circuit affirmed. Herring appealed that decision and the Supreme Court granted review.

The appellate court's decision was affirmed by a five-to-four vote. Chief Justice Roberts delivered the opinion for the Court. Justices Ginsburg and Breyer issued dissenting opinions, which Justices Stevens and Souter joined.

☐ *CHIEF JUSTICE ROBERTS delivered the opinion of the Court.*

The Fourth Amendment forbids "unreasonable searches and seizures," and this usually requires the police to have probable cause or a warrant before making an arrest. What if an officer reasonably believes there is an outstanding arrest warrant, but that belief turns out to be wrong because of a negligent bookkeeping error by another police employee? The parties here agree that the ensuing arrest is still a violation of the Fourth Amendment, but dispute whether contraband found during a search incident to that arrest must be excluded in a later prosecution.

Our cases establish that of isolated negligence attenuated from the arrest. We hold that in these circumstances the jury should not be barred from considering all the evidence. . . .

When a probable-cause determination was based on reasonable but mistaken assumptions, the person subjected to a search or seizure has not necessarily been the victim of a constitutional violation. The very phrase "probable cause" confirms that the Fourth Amendment does not demand all possible precision. And whether the error can be traced to a mistake by a state actor or some other source may bear on the analysis. For purposes of deciding this case, however, we accept the parties' assumption that there was a Fourth Amendment violation. The issue is whether the exclusionary rule should be applied.

The Fourth Amendment protects "[t]he right of the people to be secure in their persons, houses, papers, and effects, against unreasonable searches and seizures," but "contains no provision expressly precluding the use of evidence obtained in violation of its commands," *Arizona v. Evans*, 514 U.S. 1 (1995). Nonetheless, our decisions establish an exclusionary rule that, when applicable, forbids the use of improperly obtained evidence at trial. See, e.g., *Weeks v. United States*, 232 U.S. 383 (1914). We have stated that this judicially created rule is "designed to safeguard Fourth Amendment rights generally through its deterrent effect." *United States v. Calandra*, 414 U.S. 338 (1974).

In analyzing the applicability of the rule, [*United States v.*] *Leon* [468 U.S. 897 (1984)], admonished that we must consider the actions of all the police officers involved. The Coffee County officers did nothing improper. Indeed, the error was noticed so quickly because Coffee County requested a faxed confirmation of the warrant.

The Eleventh Circuit concluded, however, that somebody in Dale County should have updated the computer database to reflect the recall of the arrest warrant. The court also concluded that this error was negligent, but did not find it to be reckless or deliberate. That fact is crucial to our holding that this error is not enough by itself to require "the extreme sanction of exclusion."

The fact that a Fourth Amendment violation occurred—i.e., that a search or arrest was unreasonable—does not necessarily mean that the exclusionary rule applies. *Illinois v. Gates*, 462 U.S. 213 (1983). Indeed, exclusion "has always been our last resort, not our first impulse," *Hudson v. Michigan*, 547 U.S. 586 (2006), and our precedents establish important principles that constrain application of the exclusionary rule.

First, the exclusionary rule is not an individual right and applies only where it "'result[s] in appreciable deterrence.'" *Leon*. We have repeatedly rejected the argument that exclusion is a necessary consequence of a Fourth Amendment violation. *Leon, Evans*. Instead we have focused on the efficacy of the rule in deterring Fourth Amendment violations in the future. See *Calandra; Stone v. Powell*, 428 U.S. 465 (1976).

In addition, the benefits of deterrence must outweigh the costs. "[T]o the extent that application of the exclusionary rule could provide some incremental deterrent, that possible benefit must be weighed against [its] substantial social costs." *Illinois v. Krull*, 480 U.S. 340 (1987). The principal cost of applying the rule is, of course, letting guilty and possibly dangerous defendants go free—something that "offends basic concepts of the criminal justice system." *Leon*.

These principles are reflected in the holding of *Leon*: When police act under a warrant that is invalid for lack of probable cause, the exclusionary rule does not apply if the police acted "in objectively reasonable reliance" on the subsequently invalidated search warrant. We (perhaps confusingly) called this objectively reasonable reliance "good faith." In a companion case, *Massachusetts v. Sheppard*, 468 U.S. 981 (1984), we held that the exclusionary rule did not apply when a warrant was invalid because a judge forgot to make "clerical corrections" to it.

Shortly thereafter we extended these holdings to warrantless administrative searches performed in good-faith reliance on a statute later declared unconstitutional. Finally, in *Evans*, we applied this good-faith rule to police who reasonably relied on mistaken information in a court's database that an arrest warrant was outstanding. We held that a mistake made by a judicial employee could not give rise to exclusion for three reasons: The exclusionary rule was crafted to curb police rather than judicial misconduct; court employees were unlikely to try to subvert the Fourth Amendment; and "most important, there [was] no basis for believing that application of the exclusionary rule in [those] circumstances" would have any significant effect in deterring the errors. *Evans* left unresolved "whether the evidence should be suppressed if police personnel were responsible for the error," an issue not argued by the State in that case, but one that we now confront.

The extent to which the exclusionary rule is justified by these deterrence principles varies with the culpability of the law enforcement conduct. As we said in *Leon*, "an assessment of the flagrancy of the police misconduct constitutes an important step in the calculus" of applying the exclusionary rule. . . .

Indeed, the abuses that gave rise to the exclusionary rule featured intentional conduct that was patently unconstitutional. In *Weeks*, a foundational exclusionary rule case, the officers had broken into the defendant's home (using a key shown to them by a neighbor), confiscated incriminating papers, then returned again with a U.S. Marshal to confiscate even more. Not only did they have no search warrant, which the Court held was required, but they could not have gotten one had they tried. They were so lacking in sworn and particularized information that "not even an order of court would have justified such procedure."

Equally flagrant conduct was at issue in *Mapp v. Ohio*, 367 U.S. 643 (1961), which overruled *Wolf v. Colorado*, 338 U.S. 25 (1949), and extended the exclusionary rule to the States. Officers forced open a door to Ms. Mapp's house, kept her lawyer from entering, brandished what the court concluded was a false warrant, then forced her into handcuffs and canvassed the house for obscenity. An error that arises from nonrecurring and attenuated negligence is thus far removed from the core concerns that led us to adopt the rule in the first place. And in fact since *Leon*, we have never applied the rule to exclude evidence obtained in violation of the Fourth Amendment, where the police conduct was no more intentional or culpable than this.

To trigger the exclusionary rule, police conduct must be sufficiently deliberate that exclusion can meaningfully deter it, and sufficiently culpable that such deterrence is worth the price paid by the justice system. As laid out in our cases, the exclusionary rule serves to deter deliberate, reckless, or grossly negligent conduct, or in some circumstances recurring or systemic negligence. The error in this case does not rise to that level.

Our decision in *Franks v. Delaware*, 438 U.S. 154 (1978), provides an analogy. In *Franks*, we held that police negligence in obtaining a warrant did not even rise to the level of a Fourth Amendment violation, let alone meet the more stringent test for triggering the exclusionary rule. We held that the Constitution allowed defendants, in some circumstances, "to challenge the truthfulness of factual statements made in an affidavit supporting the warrant," even after the warrant had issued. If those false statements were necessary to the Magistrate Judge's probable-cause determination, the warrant would be "voided." But we did not find all false statements relevant: "There must be allegations of deliberate falsehood or of reckless disregard for the truth," and "[a]llegations of negligence or innocent mistake are insufficient."

Both this case and *Franks* concern false information provided by police. Under *Franks*, negligent police miscommunications in the course of acquiring a warrant do not provide a basis to rescind a warrant and render a search or arrest invalid. Here, the miscommunications occurred in a different context— after the warrant had been issued and recalled—but that fact should not require excluding the evidence obtained.

The pertinent analysis of deterrence and culpability is objective, not an "inquiry into the subjective awareness of arresting officers." We have already held that "our good-faith inquiry is confined to the objectively ascertainable question whether a reasonably well trained officer would have known that the search was illegal" in light of "all of the circumstances." *Leon*. These circumstances frequently include a particular officer's knowledge and experience, but that does not make the test any more subjective than the one for probable cause, which looks to an officer's knowledge and experience, but not his subjective intent.

We do not suggest that all recordkeeping errors by the police are immune from the exclusionary rule. In this case, however, the conduct at issue was not so objectively culpable as to require exclusion. In *Leon* we held that "the marginal or nonexistent benefits produced by suppressing evidence obtained in objectively reasonable reliance on a subsequently invalidated search warrant cannot justify the substantial costs of exclusion."The same is true when evidence is obtained in objectively reasonable reliance on a subsequently recalled warrant.

If the police have been shown to be reckless in maintaining a warrant system, or to have knowingly made false entries to lay the groundwork for future false arrests, exclusion would certainly be justified under our cases should such misconduct cause a Fourth Amendment violation. We said as much in *Leon*, explaining that an officer could not "obtain a warrant on the basis of a 'bare bones' affidavit and then rely on colleagues who are ignorant of the circumstances under which the warrant was obtained to conduct the search."

The dissent also adverts to the possible unreliability of a number of databases not relevant to this case. In a case where systemic errors were demonstrated, it might be reckless for officers to rely on an unreliable warrant system. But there is no evidence that errors in Dale County's system are routine or widespread. . . .

Petitioner's claim that police negligence automatically triggers suppression cannot be squared with the principles underlying the exclusionary rule, as they have been explained in our cases. In light of our repeated holdings that the deterrent effect of suppression must be substantial and outweigh any harm to the justice system, we conclude that when police mistakes are the result of negligence such as that described here, rather than systemic error or reckless disregard of constitutional requirements, any marginal deterrence does not "pay its way." In such a case, the criminal should not "go free because the constable has blundered." *People v. Defore*, 242 N.Y. 13 (1926) (opinion of the Court by CARDOZO, J.).

□ *Justice GINSBURG, with whom Justice STEVENS, Justice SOUTER, and Justice BREYER join, dissenting.*

The exclusionary rule provides redress for Fourth Amendment violations by placing the government in the position it would have been in had there been no unconstitutional arrest and search. The rule thus strongly encourages police compliance with the Fourth Amendment in the future. The Court, however, holds the rule inapplicable because careless recordkeeping by the police—not flagrant or deliberate misconduct—accounts for Herring's arrest.

I would not so constrict the domain of the exclusionary rule and would hold the rule dispositive of this case: "[I]f courts are to have any power to discourage [police] error of [the kind here at issue], it must be through the application of the exclusionary rule." *Arizona v. Evans*, 514 U.S. 1 (1995) (STEVENS, J., dissenting). The unlawful search in this case was contested in court because the police found methamphetamine in Herring's pocket and a pistol in his truck. But the "most serious impact" of the Court's holding will be on innocent persons "wrongfully arrested based on erroneous information [carelessly maintained] in a computer data base." . . .

Beyond doubt, a main objective of the rule "is to deter—to compel respect for the constitutional guaranty in the only effectively available way—by removing the incentive to disregard it." *Elkins v. United States*, 364 U.S. 206 (1960). But the rule also serves other important purposes: It "enabl[es] the judiciary to avoid the taint of partnership in official lawlessness," and it "assur[es] the people—all potential victims of unlawful government conduct—that the government would not profit from its lawless behavior, thus minimizing the risk of seriously undermining popular trust in government." *United States v. Calandra*, 414 U.S. 338 (1974) (BRENNAN, J., dissenting).

The Court maintains that Herring's case is one in which the exclusionary rule could have scant deterrent effect and therefore would not "pay its way." I disagree.

The exclusionary rule, the Court suggests, is capable of only marginal deterrence when the misconduct at issue is merely careless, not intentional or reckless. The suggestion runs counter to a foundational premise of tort law—that liability for negligence, i.e., lack of due care, creates an incentive to act with greater care. The Government so acknowledges.

That the mistake here involved the failure to make a computer entry hardly means that application of the exclusionary rule would have minimal value.

Consider the potential impact of a decision applying the exclusionary rule in this case. As earlier observed, the record indicates that there is no electronic connection between the warrant database of the Dale County Sheriff's Department and that of the County Circuit Clerk's office, which is located in the basement of the same building. When a warrant is recalled, one of the "many different people that have access to th[e] warrants," must find the hard copy of the warrant in the "two or three different places" where the department houses warrants, return it to the Clerk's office, and manually update the Department's database. The record reflects no routine practice of checking the database for accuracy, and the failure to remove the entry for Herring's warrant was not discovered until Investigator Anderson sought to pursue Herring five months later. Is it not altogether obvious that the Department could take further precautions to ensure the integrity of its database? The Sheriff's Department "is in a position to remedy the situation and might well do so if the exclusionary rule is there to remove the incentive to do otherwise."

Is the potential deterrence here worth the costs it imposes? In light of the paramount importance of accurate recordkeeping in law enforcement, I would answer yes, and next explain why, as I see it, Herring's motion presents a particularly strong case for suppression.

Electronic databases form the nervous system of contemporary criminal justice operations. In recent years, their breadth and influence have dramatically expanded. Police today can access databases that include not only the updated National Crime Information Center (NCIC), but also terrorist watchlists, the Federal Government's employee eligibility system, and various commercial databases. . . . As a result, law enforcement has an increasing supply of information within its easy electronic reach.

The risk of error stemming from these databases is not slim. Herring's *amici* warn that law enforcement databases are insufficiently monitored and often out of date. Government reports describe, for example, flaws in NCIC databases, terrorist watchlist databases, and databases associated with the Federal Government's employment eligibility verification system.

Inaccuracies in expansive, interconnected collections of electronic information raise grave concerns for individual liberty. . . .

First, by restricting suppression to bookkeeping errors that are deliberate or reckless, the majority leaves Herring, and others like him, with no remedy for violations of their constitutional rights. There can be no serious assertion that relief is available under 42 U.S.C. Section 1983. The arresting officer would be sheltered by qualified immunity, and the police department itself is not liable for the negligent acts of its employees. Moreover, identifying the department employee who committed the error may be impossible.

Second, I doubt that police forces already possess sufficient incentives to maintain up-to-date records. The Government argues that police have no desire to send officers out on arrests unnecessarily, because arrests consume resources and place officers in danger. The facts of this case do not fit that description of police motivation. Here the officer wanted to arrest Herring and consulted the Department's records to legitimate his predisposition.

Third, even when deliberate or reckless conduct is afoot, the Court's assurance will often be an empty promise: How is an impecunious defendant to make the required showing? If the answer is that a defendant is entitled to discovery (and if necessary, an audit of police databases), then the Court has imposed a considerable administrative burden on courts and law enforcement.

Negligent recordkeeping errors by law enforcement threaten individual liberty, are susceptible to deterrence by the exclusionary rule, and cannot be remedied effectively through other means. Such errors present no occasion to further erode the exclusionary rule. The rule "is needed to make the Fourth Amendment something real; a guarantee that does not carry with it the exclusion of evidence obtained by its violation is a chimera." *Calandra.* (BRENNAN, J., dissenting). In keeping with the rule's "core concerns" suppression should have attended the unconstitutional search in this case.

For the reasons stated, I would reverse the judgment of the Eleventh Circuit.

☐ *Justice BREYER, with whom Justice Souter joins, dissenting.*

I agree with Justice GINSBURG and join her dissent. I write separately to note one additional supporting factor that I believe important. In *Arizona v. Evans*, 514 U.S. 1 (1995), we held that recordkeeping errors made by a court clerk do not trigger the exclusionary rule, so long as the police reasonably relied upon the court clerk's recordkeeping. The rationale for our decision was premised on a distinction between judicial errors and police errors, and we gave several reasons for recognizing that distinction.

First, we noted that "the exclusionary rule was historically designed as a means of deterring police misconduct, not mistakes by court employees." Second, we found "no evidence that court employees are inclined to ignore or subvert the Fourth Amendment or that lawlessness among these actors requires application of the extreme sanction of exclusion." Third, we recognized that there was "no basis for believing that application of the exclusionary rule . . . [would] have a significant effect on court employees responsible for informing the police that a warrant has been quashed. Because court clerks are not adjuncts to the law enforcement team engaged in the often competitive enterprise of ferreting out crime, they have no stake in the outcome of particular criminal prosecutions." Taken together, these reasons explain why police recordkeeping errors should be treated differently than judicial ones. . . .

Distinguishing between police recordkeeping errors and judicial ones not only is consistent with our precedent, but also is far easier for courts to administer than THE CHIEF JUSTICE's case-by-case, multifactored inquiry into the degree of police culpability. I therefore would apply the exclusionary rule when police personnel are responsible for a recordkeeping error that results in a Fourth Amendment violation.

The need for a clear line, and the recognition of such a line in our precedent, are further reasons in support of the outcome that Justice GINSBURG's dissent would reach.

8

THE FIFTH AMENDMENT GUARANTEE AGAINST SELF-ACCUSATION

A | Coerced Confessions and Police Interrogations

A bare majority in *Corley v. United States*, 129 S.Ct. 1558 (2009), reaffirmed a Warren Court ruling that if federal agents wait too long to take a suspect to be informed of the charges against him, a confession is barred even if voluntary. In a controversial ruling in *Mallory v. United States*, 354 U.S. 449 (1957), Justice Frankfurter held for a unanimous Court that a confession given seven hours after an arrest could not be used if there was an "unnecessary delay" in presenting the suspect to a magistrate to learn of the charge. The decision reaffirmed *McNabb v. United States*, 318 U.S. 332 (1943), but along the ruling in *Miranda v. Arizona*, 384 U.S. 436 (1966) (excerpted in Vol. 2, Ch. 8), inspired a reaction and Congress enacted the Crime Control and Safe Streets Act of 1968, which sought to limit the *Mallory-McNabb* rule and *Miranda*. In *Dickerson v. United States*, 530 U.S. 428 (2000) (excerpted in Vol. 2, Ch. 8) the Rehnquist Court reaffirmed *Miranda* as a constitutional ruling. And in *Corley*, although not a constitutional ruling, reaffirmed *Mallory-McNabb* in holding that confessions made six hours after an arrest were impermissible and that Congress had not discarded *Mallory* but "merely [sought] to narrow" it. Thus, voluntary confessions to federal crimes may not be admitted into evidence if the suspect was not fairly soon after confessing taken to court.

In Justice Souter's words for the majority: "In a world without *McNabb-Mallory*, federal agents would be free to question suspects for extended periods before bringing them out in the open, and we have always known what custodial secrecy leads to . . . No one with any smattering of the history of the twentieth century dictatorships needs a lecture on the subject . . . and there is mounting empirical evidence that these pressures can induce a frightening high percentage of people to confess to crimes they never committed." Chief Justice Roberts and Justices Scalia, Thomas, and Alito dissented.

In its 2009–2010 term, the Roberts Court handed down other rulings on the Fifth Amendment and the Sixth Amendment right to counsel. *Florida v. Powell*, 130 S.Ct. 1195 (2010), held that police need not give the precise language of informing a suspect of the right to counsel during an interrogation as laid down in *Miranda v. Arizona*, 384 U.S. 436 (1966) (excerpted in Vol. 2, Ch. 8), as interpreted in *Duckworth v. Eagan*, 492 U.S. 195 (1989) (excerpted in Vol. 2, Ch. 8). Writing for the Court in *Florida v. Powell*, Justice Ginsburg reaffirmed *Duckworth*'s holding that the precise language of *Miranda* need not be followed. In this case police officers informed a suspect of "the right to talk to a lawyer before answering any of [the law enforcement officers'] questions," and that he could invoke that right "at anytime . . . during th[e] interview." That was held to satisfy *Miranda*. By contrast, dissenting Justices Stevens and Breyer countered that *Miranda* mandated that suspects be informed of "the right to consult with a lawyer *and to have the lawyer with him during interrogation*" (emphasis added).

In *Maryland v. Shatzer*, 130 S.Ct. 1213 (2010), Justice Scalia ruled that a suspect's incriminating statements could be used at trial, even though made in a second interrogation in which he waived his right to counsel that took place more than two weeks after he was first interrogated and informed of his right to counsel. Justice Scalia held that the break in his custody, even though he was in jail, satisfied the rulings in *Edwards v. Arizona*, 451 U.S. 477 (1981), and *Minnick v. Mississippi*, 498 U.S. 146 (1990) (both discussed in Vol. 2, Ch. 8).

Even more broadly chipping back on the right to remain silent during police interrogations in *Miranda v. Arizona*, a bare majority ruled that (1) a suspect must say unequivocally and unambiguously the he or she is invoking the right to remain silent; and (2) if the suspect answers any questions—even with a one-word response—that amount to a confession, it may be considered a waiver of the right to remain silent and may be used as evidence at trial. In short, police need not obtain an explicit waiver of a suspect's *Miranda* rights. In *Berghuis v. Thompkins* (2010) (excerpted below), Justices Stevens, Ginsburg, Breyer, and Sotomayor dissented.

Berghuis v. Thompkins

130 S.Ct. 2250 (2010)

Justice Kennedy's opinion for the Court, and Justice Sotomayor's dissenting opinion, discuss the facts in the case. The appellate court's decision was reversed by a five to four vote. Justice Sotomayor's dissent was joined by Justices Stevens, Ginsburg, and Breyer.

☐ *Justice KENNEDY delivered the opinion of the Court.*

On January 10, 2000, a shooting occurred outside a mall in Southfield, Michigan. Among the victims was Samuel Morris, who died from multiple gunshot wounds. The other victim, Frederick France, recovered from his injuries and later testified. [Van Chester] Thompkins, who was a suspect, fled. About one year later he was found in Ohio and arrested there.

Two Southfield police officers traveled to Ohio to interrogate Thompkins, then awaiting transfer to Michigan. The interrogation began around 1:30 P.M. and lasted about three hours. The interrogation was conducted in a room that was 8 by 10 feet, and Thompkins sat in a chair that resembled a school desk (it had an arm on it that swings around to provide a surface to write on). At the beginning of the interrogation, one of the officers, Detective Helgert, presented Thompkins with a form derived from the *Miranda* rule. It stated:

"NOTIFICATION OF CONSTITUTIONAL
RIGHTS AND STATEMENT

1. You have the right to remain silent.
2. Anything you say can and will be used against you in a court of law.
3. You have a right to talk to a lawyer before answering any questions and you have the right to have a lawyer present with you while you are answering any questions.
4. If you cannot afford to hire a lawyer, one will be appointed to represent you before any questioning, if you wish one.
5. You have the right to decide at any time before or during questioning to use your right to remain silent and your right to talk with a lawyer while you are being questioned."

Helgert asked Thompkins to read the fifth warning out loud. Thompkins complied. Helgert later said this was to ensure that Thompkins could read, and Helgert concluded that Thompkins understood English. Helgert then read the other four *Miranda* warnings out loud and asked Thompkins to sign the form to demonstrate that he understood his rights. Thompkins declined to sign the form. . . .

Officers began an interrogation. At no point during the interrogation did Thompkins say that he wanted to remain silent, that he did not want to talk with the police, or that he wanted an attorney. Thompkins was "[l]argely" silent during the interrogation, which lasted about three hours. He did give a few limited verbal responses, however, such as "yeah," "no," or "I don't know."

And on occasion he communicated by nodding his head. Thompkins also said that he "didn't want a peppermint" that was offered to him by the police and that the chair he was "sitting in was hard."

About 2 hours and 45 minutes into the interrogation, Helgert asked Thompkins, "Do you believe in God?" Thompkins made eye contact with Helgert and said "Yes," as his eyes "well[ed] up with tears." Helgert asked, "Do you pray to God?" Thompkins said "Yes." Helgert asked, "Do you pray to God to forgive you for shooting that boy down?" Thompkins answered "Yes" and looked away. Thompkins refused to make a written confession, and the interrogation ended about 15 minutes later.

Thompkins was charged with first-degree murder, assault with intent to commit murder, and certain firearms-related offenses. He moved to suppress the statements made during the interrogation. He argued that he had invoked his Fifth Amendment right to remain silent, requiring police to end the interrogation at once, see *Michigan v. Mosley*, 423 U.S. 96 (1975), that he had not waived his right to remain silent, and that his inculpatory statements were involuntary. The trial court denied the motion. . . .

The jury found Thompkins guilty on all counts. He was sentenced to life in prison without parole.

The trial court denied a motion for new trial filed by Thompkins' appellate counsel. . . .

Thompkins appealed this ruling, along with the trial court's refusal to suppress his pretrial statements under *Miranda*. The Michigan Court of Appeals rejected the *Miranda* claim, ruling that Thompkins had not invoked his right to remain silent and had waived it. . . .

Thompkins filed a petition for a writ of *habeas corpus* in the United States District Court for the Eastern District of Michigan. The District Court rejected Thompkins' *Miranda* and ineffective-assistance claims.

The United States Court of Appeals for the Sixth Circuit reversed, ruling for Thompkins on both his *Miranda* and ineffective-assistance-of-counsel claims. The Court of Appeals ruled that the state court, in rejecting Thompkins' *Miranda* claim, unreasonably applied clearly established federal law and based its decision on an unreasonable determination of the facts. The Court of Appeals acknowledged that a waiver of the right to remain silent need not be express, as it can be "'inferred from the actions and words of the person interrogated.'" The panel held, nevertheless, that the state court was unreasonable in finding an implied waiver in the circumstances here. The Court of Appeals found that the state court unreasonably determined the facts because "the evidence demonstrates that Thompkins was silent for two hours and forty-five minutes." . . .

The *Miranda* Court formulated a warning that must be given to suspects before they can be subjected to custodial interrogation. The substance of the warning still must be given to suspects today. A suspect in custody must be advised as follows:

> "He must be warned prior to any questioning that he has the right to remain silent, that anything he says can be used against him in a court of law, that he has the right to the presence of an attorney, and that if he cannot afford an attorney one will be appointed for him prior to any questioning if he so desires."

All concede that the warning given in this case was in full compliance with these requirements. The dispute centers on the response—or nonresponse—from the suspect.

Thompkins makes various arguments that his answers to questions from the detectives were inadmissible. He first contends that he "invoke[d] his privilege" to remain silent by not saying anything for a sufficient period of time, so the interrogation should have "cease[d]" before he made his inculpatory statements.

This argument is unpersuasive. In the context of invoking the *Miranda* right to counsel, the Court in *Davis v. United States*, 512 U.S. 452 (1994), held that a suspect must do so "unambiguously." If an accused makes a statement concerning the right to counsel "that is ambiguous or equivocal" or makes no statement, the police are not required to end the interrogation, or ask questions to clarify whether the accused wants to invoke his or her *Miranda* rights.

The Court has not yet stated whether an invocation of the right to remain silent can be ambiguous or equivocal, but there is no principled reason to adopt different standards for determining when an accused has invoked the *Miranda* right to remain silent and the *Miranda* right to counsel at issue in *Davis*.

There is good reason to require an accused who wants to invoke his or her right to remain silent to do so unambiguously. A requirement of an unambiguous invocation of *Miranda* rights results in an objective inquiry that "avoid[s] difficulties of proof and . . . provide[s] guidance to officers" on how to proceed in the face of ambiguity. *Davis*.

Thompkins did not say that he wanted to remain silent or that he did not want to talk with the police. Had he made either of these simple, unambiguous statements, he would have invoked his "'right to cut off questioning.'" *Mosley*. Here he did neither, so he did not invoke his right to remain silent.

We next consider whether Thompkins waived his right to remain silent. Even absent the accused's invocation of the right to remain silent, the accused's statement during a custodial interrogation is inadmissible at trial unless the prosecution can establish that the accused "in fact knowingly and voluntarily waived [*Miranda*] rights" when making the statement. The waiver inquiry "has two distinct dimensions": waiver must be "voluntary in the sense that it was the product of a free and deliberate choice rather than intimidation, coercion, or deception," and "made with a full awareness of both the nature of the right being abandoned and the consequences of the decision to abandon it."

Some language in *Miranda* could be read to indicate that waivers are difficult to establish absent an explicit written waiver or a formal, express oral statement. *Miranda* said "a valid waiver will not be presumed simply from the silence of the accused after warnings are given or simply from the fact that a confession was in fact eventually obtained." In addition, the *Miranda* Court stated that "a heavy burden rests on the government to demonstrate that the defendant knowingly and intelligently waived his privilege against self-incrimination and his right to retained or appointed counsel."

The course of decisions since *Miranda*, informed by the application of *Miranda* warnings in the whole course of law enforcement, demonstrates that waivers can be established even absent formal or express statements of waiver that would be expected in, say, a judicial hearing to determine if a guilty plea has been properly entered. The main purpose of *Miranda* is to ensure that an accused is advised of and understands the right to remain silent and the right to counsel. Thus, "[i]f anything, our subsequent cases have reduced the impact of the *Miranda* rule on legitimate law enforcement while reaffirming the decision's core ruling that unwarned statements may not be used as evidence in the prosecution's case in chief." *Dickerson v. United States*, 530 U.S. 428 (2000). . . .

The prosecution therefore does not need to show that a waiver of *Miranda* rights was express. An "implicit waiver" of the "right to remain silent" is sufficient to admit a suspect's statement into evidence. [A] waiver of *Miranda* rights may be implied through "the defendant's silence, coupled with an understanding of his rights and a course of conduct indicating waiver."

If the State establishes that a *Miranda* warning was given and the accused made an uncoerced statement, this showing, standing alone, is insufficient to demonstrate "a valid waiver" of *Miranda* rights. The prosecution must make the additional showing that the accused understood these rights. Where the prosecution shows that a *Miranda* warning was given and that it was understood by the accused, an accused's uncoerced statement establishes an implied waiver of the right to remain silent.

Although *Miranda* imposes on the police a rule that is both formalistic and practical when it prevents them from interrogating suspects without first providing them with a *Miranda* warning, it does not impose a formalistic waiver procedure that a suspect must follow to relinquish those rights. As a general proposition, the law can presume that an individual who, with a full understanding of his or her rights, acts in a manner inconsistent with their exercise has made a deliberate choice to relinquish the protection those rights afford.

The record in this case shows that Thompkins waived his right to remain silent. There is no basis in this case to conclude that he did not understand his rights; and on these facts it follows that he chose not to invoke or rely on those rights when he did speak. First, there is no contention that Thompkins did not understand his rights; and from this it follows that he knew what he gave up when he spoke. There was more than enough evidence in the record to conclude that Thompkins understood his *Miranda* rights. Thompkins received a written copy of the *Miranda* warnings; Detective Helgert determined that Thompkins could read and understand English; and Thompkins was given time to read the warnings. Thompkins, furthermore, read aloud the fifth warning, which stated that "you have the right to decide at any time before or during questioning to use your right to remain silent and your right to talk with a lawyer while you are being questioned." He was thus aware that his right to remain silent would not dissipate after a certain amount of time and that police would have to honor his right to be silent and his right to counsel during the whole course of interrogation. Those rights, the warning made clear, could be asserted at any time. Helgert, moreover, read the warnings aloud.

Second, Thompkins' answer to Detective Helgert's question about whether Thompkins prayed to God for forgiveness for shooting the victim is a "course of conduct indicating waiver" of the right to remain silent. If Thompkins wanted to remain silent, he could have said nothing in response to Helgert's questions, or he could have unambiguously invoked his *Miranda* rights and ended the interrogation. . . .

Third, there is no evidence that Thompkins' statement was coerced. Thompkins does not claim that police threatened or injured him during the interrogation or that he was in any way fearful. The interrogation was conducted in a standard-sized room in the middle of the afternoon. It is true that apparently he was in a straight-backed chair for three hours, but there is no authority for the proposition that an interrogation of this length is inherently coercive. . . .

In order for an accused's statement to be admissible at trial, police must have given the accused a *Miranda* warning. If that condition is established, the court can proceed to consider whether there has been an express or implied waiver of *Miranda* rights. In making its ruling on the admissibility of a statement made during custodial questioning, the trial court, of course, considers whether there is evidence to support the conclusion that, from the whole course of questioning, an express or implied waiver has been established. Thus, after giving a *Miranda* warning, police may interrogate a suspect who has neither invoked nor waived his or her *Miranda* rights. On these premises, it follows the police were not required to obtain a waiver of Thompkins' *Miranda* rights before commencing the interrogation.

In sum, a suspect who has received and understood the *Miranda* warnings, and has not invoked his *Miranda* rights, waives the right to remain silent by making an uncoerced statement to the police. Thompkins did not invoke his right to remain silent and stop the questioning. Understanding his rights in full, he waived his right to remain silent by making a voluntary statement to the police. The police, moreover, were not required to obtain a waiver of Thompkins' right to remain silent before interrogating him. . . .

The judgment of the Court of Appeals is reversed, and the case is remanded with instructions to deny the petition.

☐ *Justice SOTOMAYOR, with whom Justice STEVENS, Justice GINSBURG, and Justice BREYER join, dissenting.*

The Court concludes today that a criminal suspect waives his right to remain silent if, after sitting tacit and uncommunicative through nearly three hours of police interrogation, he utters a few one-word responses. The Court also concludes that a suspect who wishes to guard his right to remain silent against such a finding of "waiver" must, counterintuitively, speak—and must do so with sufficient precision to satisfy a clear-statement rule that construes ambiguity in favor of the police. Both propositions mark a substantial retreat from the protection against compelled self-incrimination that *Miranda v. Arizona* has long provided during custodial interrogation. The broad rules the Court announces today are also troubling because they are unnecessary to decide this case, which is governed by the deferential standard of review set forth in the Antiterrorism and Effective Death Penalty Act of 1996 (AEDPA). Because I believe Thompkins is entitled to relief under AEDPA on the ground that his statements were admitted at trial without the prosecution having carried its burden to show that he waived his right to remain silent; because longstanding principles of judicial restraint counsel leaving for another day the questions of law the Court reaches out to decide; and because the Court's answers to those questions do not result from a faithful application of our prior decisions, I respectfully dissent. . . .

The strength of Thompkins' *Miranda* claims depends in large part on the circumstances of the 3-hour interrogation, at the end of which he made inculpatory statements later introduced at trial. The Court's opinion downplays record evidence that Thompkins remained almost completely silent and unresponsive throughout that session. One of the interrogating officers, Detective Helgert, testified that although Thompkins was administered *Miranda* warnings, the last of which he read aloud, Thompkins expressly declined to sign a written acknowledgment that he had been advised of and understood his rights. There is conflicting evidence in the record about whether Thompkins ever verbally confirmed understanding his rights. The record contains no indication that the officers sought or obtained an express waiver.

As to the interrogation itself, Helgert candidly characterized it as "very, very one-sided" and "nearly a monologue." Thompkins was "[p]eculiar," "[s]ullen," and "[g]enerally quiet." Helgert and his partner "did most of the talking," as Thompkins was "not verbally communicative" and "[l]argely" remained silent. To the extent Thompkins gave any response, his answers consisted of "a word or two. A 'yeah,' or a 'no,' or 'I don't know.' . . . And sometimes . . . he simply sat down . . . with [his] head in [his] hands looking down. Sometimes . . . he would look up and make eye contact would be the only response." After proceeding in this fashion for approximately 2 hours and 45 minutes, Helgert asked Thompkins three questions relating to his faith in God. The prosecution relied at trial on Thompkins' one-word answers of "yes."

Thompkins' nonresponsiveness is particularly striking in the context of the officers' interview strategy, later explained as conveying to Thompkins that "this was his opportunity to explain his side [of the story]" because "[e]verybody else, including [his] co-[d]efendants, had given their version," and asking him "[w]ho is going to speak up for you if you don't speak up for yourself?" Yet, Helgert confirmed that the "only thing [Thompkins said] relative to his involvement [in the shooting]" occurred near the end of the interview—i.e., in response to the questions about God. . . .

Even when warnings have been administered and a suspect has not affirmatively invoked his rights, statements made in custodial interrogation may not be admitted as part of the prosecution's case in chief "unless and until" the prosecution demonstrates that an individual "knowingly and intelligently waive[d] [his] rights." The government must satisfy the "high standar[d] of proof for the waiver of constitutional rights [set forth in] *Johnson v. Zerbst*, 304 U.S. 458 (1938)." The question whether a suspect has validly waived his right is "entirely distinct" as a matter of law from whether he invoked that right. The questions are related, however, in terms of the practical effect on the exercise of a suspect's rights. A suspect may at any time revoke his prior waiver of rights—or, closer to the facts of this case, guard against the possibility of a future finding that he implicitly waived his rights—by invoking the rights and thereby requiring the police to cease questioning.

Like the Sixth Circuit, I begin with the question whether Thompkins waived his right to remain silent. Even if Thompkins did not invoke that right, he is entitled to relief because Michigan did not satisfy its burden of establishing waiver.

Miranda's discussion of the prosecution's burden in proving waiver speaks with particular clarity to the facts of this case and therefore merits reproducing at length:

> "If [an] interrogation continues without the presence of an attorney and a statement is taken, a heavy burden rests on the government to demonstrate that the defendant knowingly and intelligently waived his privilege against self-incrimination and his right to retained or appointed counsel. . . . Since the State is responsible for establishing the isolated circumstances under which [an] interrogation takes place and has the only means of making available corroborated evidence of warnings given during incommunicado interrogation, the burden is rightly on its shoulders.

> "An express statement that the individual is willing to make a statement and does not want an attorney followed closely by a statement could constitute a waiver. But a valid waiver will not be presumed simply from the silence of the accused after warnings are given or simply from the fact that a confession was in fact eventually obtained."

Miranda went further in describing the facts likely to satisfy the prosecution's burden of establishing the admissibility of statements obtained after a lengthy interrogation:

> "Whatever the testimony of the authorities as to waiver of rights by an accused, the fact of lengthy interrogation or incommunicado incarceration before a statement is made is strong evidence that the accused did not validly waive his rights. In these circumstances the fact that the individual eventually made a statement is consistent with the conclusion that the compelling influence of the interrogation finally forced him to do so. It is inconsistent with any notion of a voluntary relinquishment of the privilege."

This Court's decisions subsequent to *Miranda* have emphasized the prosecution's "heavy burden" in proving waiver. We have also reaffirmed that a court may not presume waiver from a suspect's silence or from the mere fact that a confession was eventually obtained. See *North Carolina v. Butler*, 441 U.S. 369 (1979).

Even in concluding that *Miranda* does not invariably require an express waiver of the right to silence or the right to counsel, this Court in *Butler* made clear that the prosecution bears a substantial burden in establishing an implied waiver. The Federal Bureau of Investigation had obtained statements after advising Butler of his rights and confirming that he understood them. When presented with a written waiver-of-rights form, Butler told the agents, "'I will talk to you but I am not signing any form.'" He then made inculpatory statements, which he later sought to suppress on the ground that he had not expressly waived his right to counsel.

Although this Court reversed the state-court judgment concluding that the statements were inadmissible, we quoted at length portions of the *Miranda* opinion reproduced above. We cautioned that even an "express written or oral statement of waiver of the right to remain silent or of the right to counsel" is not "inevitably . . . sufficient to establish waiver," emphasizing that "[t]he question is . . . whether the defendant in fact knowingly and voluntarily waived the rights delineated in the *Miranda* case." *Miranda*, we observed, "unequivocally said . . . mere silence is not enough." While we stopped short in *Butler* of announcing a per se rule that "the defendant's silence, coupled with an understanding of his rights and a course of conduct indicating waiver, may never support a conclusion that a defendant has waived his rights," we reiterated that "courts must presume that a defendant did not waive his rights; the prosecution's burden is great." Rarely do this Court's precedents provide clearly established law so closely on point with the facts of a particular case. Together, *Miranda* and *Butler* establish that a court "must presume that a defendant did not waive his right[s]"; the prosecution bears a "heavy burden" in attempting to demonstrate waiver; the fact of a "lengthy interrogation" prior to obtaining statements is "strong evidence" against a finding of valid waiver; "mere silence" in response to questioning is "not enough"; and waiver may not be presumed "simply from the fact that a confession was in fact eventually obtained."

It is undisputed here that Thompkins never expressly waived his right to remain silent. His refusal to sign even an acknowledgment that he understood his *Miranda* rights evinces, if anything, an intent not to waive those rights. That Thompkins did not make the inculpatory statements at issue until after approximately 2 hours and 45 minutes of interrogation serves as "strong evidence" against waiver. *Miranda* and *Butler* expressly preclude the possibility that the inculpatory statements themselves are sufficient to establish waiver. . . .

Today's dilution of the prosecution's burden of proof to the bare fact that a suspect made inculpatory statements after *Miranda* warnings were given and understood takes an unprecedented step away from the "high standards of proof for the waiver of constitutional rights" this Court has long demanded. Requiring proof of a course of conduct beyond the inculpatory statements themselves is critical to ensuring that those statements are voluntary admissions and not the dubious product of an overborne will.

Today's decision thus ignores the important interests *Miranda* safeguards. The underlying constitutional guarantee against self-incrimination reflects "many of our fundamental values and most noble aspirations," our society's "preference for an accusatorial rather than an inquisitorial system of criminal justice"; a "fear that self-incriminating statements will be elicited by inhumane treatment and abuses" and a resulting "distrust of self-deprecatory statements"; and a realization that while the privilege is "sometimes a shelter to the guilty, [it] is often a protection to the innocent." For these reasons, we have observed, a criminal law system "which comes to depend on the 'confession' will, in the long run, be less reliable and more subject to abuses than a system relying on independent investigation." "By bracing against 'the possibility of unreliable statements in every instance of in-custody interrogation,'" *Miranda*'s prophylactic rules serve to "'protect the fairness of the trial itself.'" Today's decision bodes poorly for the fundamental principles that *Miranda* protects. . . .

Today's decision turns *Miranda* upside down. Criminal suspects must now unambiguously invoke their right to remain silent—which, counterintuitively, requires them to speak. At the same time, suspects will be legally presumed to have waived their rights even if they have given no clear expression of their intent to do so. Those results, in my view, find no basis in *Miranda* or our subsequent cases and are inconsistent with the fair-trial principles on which those precedents are grounded. Today's broad new rules are all the more unfortunate because they are unnecessary to the disposition of the case before us. I respectfully dissent.

9

THE RIGHT TO COUNSEL AND OTHER PROCEDURAL GUARANTEES

A | *The Right to Counsel*

By a seven-to-two vote, the Court held in *Indiana v. Edwards*, 128 S.Ct. 2379 (2008), that states may require a criminal defendant who suffers from mental illness to have a court-appointed lawyer at trial, rather than acting in his own defense, even when the defendant is deemed competent to stand trial. Edwards, who suffered from schizophrenia, was deemed by the trial court competent to stand trial but not competent to defend himself. He appealed that ruling, arguing that it violated his Sixth Amendment right to counsel and the Court's holding in *Faretta v. California*, 422 U.S. 806 (1976), that a defendant deemed competent to stand trial has a right to self-representation. Justice Breyer delivered the opinion of the Court that declined to overrule *Faretta* on the ground that states have some flexibility and that there was "no empirical research" showing "that *Faretta*'s holding has proven counterproductive in practice" or that the right of representing one's self "furthers or inhibits" the fairness of a trial. Justices Scalia and Thomas dissented.

In another seven-to-two decision, the Roberts Court held that a defendant's incriminating statements made in violation of the Sixth Amendment right to counsel to a governmental informant in a prison cell may be used to impeach the defendant's trial testimony. Writing for the Court in *Kansas v. Ventris*, 129 S.Ct. 1841 (2009), Justice Scalia held that the core of the Sixth Amendment right to counsel is a trial right and covers pretrial interrogations only to ensure that the defendant has "effective representation by counsel at the only stage when legal aid and advice would help him." (quoting *Massiah v. United States*, 377 U.S. 201 [1964]). But, the right to be free of uncounseled interrogation applies only at the time of police interrogation and not when a confession is admitted as evidence against the defendant. Justices Stevens and Ginsburg dissented.

Writing for a bare majority in *Montejo v. Louisiana*, 129 S.Ct. 2079 (2009), Justice Scalia also overturned a long-standing decision in *Michigan v. Jackson*, 475 U.S. 625 (1986), that barred police from initiating questions unless a suspect's lawyer is present. *Michigan v. Jackson* held that police may not question a suspect who has a lawyer or who has asked for one unless an attorney is present, even if a suspect agreed to talk with officers in the absence of an attorney. Writing for the Court in *Montejo*, Justice Scalia dismissed the prior ruling as "poorly reasoned" because police could not even ask a suspect who had been appointed an attorney if he wanted to talk. In his words: "It would be completely unjustified to presume that a defendant's consent to police-initiated interrogation was involuntary or coerced simply because he had previously been appointed a lawyer." Moreover, he added that, "The considerable adverse effect of this rule upon society's ability to solve crimes and bring criminals to justice far outweighs its capacity to prevent a genuinely coerced agreement to speak without counsel present." Dissenting Justice Stevens, who had delivered the decision in *Michigan v. Jackson*, joined by Justices Souter, Ginsburg, and Breyer, countered that "The police interrogation in this case clearly violated petitioner's Sixth Amendment right to counsel," and would "only diminish the public's confidence in the reliability and fairness of our system of justice." Jesse Jay Montejo was found guilty of killing Lewis Ferrari. He had been appointed an attorney but never indicated that he wanted the assistance of counsel. After being given his *Miranda* rights to remain silent and to have counsel, in the absence of counsel, he showed police where to look for the murder weapon. While in the police car en route, he also wrote a letter to Ferrari's widow incriminating himself. That letter was later used against him at trial and he was convicted and sentenced to death.

In its 2009–2010 term, the Court also considered the scope of "*Miranda* rights" in *Florida v. Powell*, 130 S.Ct. 573 (2010) and whether those warnings to a suspect in police custody may exclude an explicit assurance that the individual may have a lawyer in the room while under interrogation. Powell was arrested for the possession of a firearm and was initially read his rights, and he also signed a waiver of those rights. The form, however, did not expressly state that he had the right to have an attorney present while police asked him questions. During the interrogation he admitted that the gun was his. A state trial court allowed the introduction of the confession, but on appeal Powell's conviction was reversed on the ground that the warning was insufficient because it only informed Powell that he had a right to counsel before questioning began. The Florida state supreme court affirmed that decision, holding that the warning given to Powell was inadequate because it did not expressly notify him of his right to counsel during questioning. The Court, however, reversed the state court's decision and held that the *Miranda* warnings were satisfied.

B | *Plea Bargaining and the Right to Effective Counsel*

In its 2009–2010 term, the justices considered whether the failure of counsel to present evidence of a defendant's mental impairment constitutes ineffective counsel under the Sixth Amendment, in *Wood v. Allen*, 130 S.Ct. 841 (2010). A jury convicted Wood of capital murder and a judge sentenced him to death for the killing of his girlfriend. He appealed, claiming that he is mentally retarded and cannot be executed under the Court's precedents, as well as that his counsel was ineffective in failing to present evidence of his low mental abilities. A state appellate and supreme court affirmed and the U.S. Supreme Court denied an appeal. But after a post-conviction court found that he was not mentally retarded and had effective counsel, Wood filed a petition for a writ of *habeas corpus* and a federal district court vacated his death sentence on the basis of ineffective counsel. On the state's appeal, the Court of Appeals for the Eleventh Circuit held that Wood was not mentally retarded and that he had had effective counsel. Wood appealed that decision; the Court granted review and affirmed the decision with only Justices Stevens and Bryer dissenting.

■ THE DEVELOPMENT OF LAW

Rulings on Plea Bargaining and Effective Counsel

CASE	VOTE	RULING
Wright v. VanPatten, 128 S.Ct. 743 (2008)	9:0	In a *per curiam* opinion, the Roberts Court held that during a plea bargaining hearing there was no violation of the Sixth Amendment right to counsel when the defendant's lawyer was present only on a speaker phone.
Padilla v. Kentucky, 130 S.Ct. 1473 (2010)	7:2	Writing for the Court, Justice Stevens held that counsel must inform alien defendants that a guilty plea carries the risk of deportation, because, under the *Strickland v. Washington*, 466 U.S. 668 (1984), test for ineffective counsel, deportation is "intimately related to the criminal process."

D | *The Right to an Impartial Jury Trial*

In *Kimbrough v. United States*, 128 S.Ct. 558 (2007), the Court reaffirmed an earlier ruling in *United States v. Booker*, 543 U.S. 2220 (2005), that the federal mandatory sentencing guidelines were only advisory for federal judges in sentencing. In *Booker* a bare majority ruled that the federal mandatory sentencing guidelines violate the Sixth Amendment because federal judges may impose enhanced sentences based on facts that a jury did not consider. The Court was badly fragmented in *Booker*, however, and two opinions for the Court were delivered for different bare majorities. On the one hand, Justice Stevens, joined by Justices Scalia, Souter, Thomas, and Ginsburg, ruled that federal judges are no longer bound by the guidelines and that they were only advisory. On the other hand, Justice Breyer, joined by Chief Justice Rehnquist and Justices O'Connor, Kennedy, and Ginsburg, held that the guidelines should still be consulted and that judges' sentences are subject to reversal if appellate courts find them unreasonable and defendants deserve longer or shorter sentences. The federal guidelines, in the words of Justice Breyer, who helped write them, serve to "avoid excessive sentencing disparities while maintaining flexibility sufficient to individualize sentences where necessary." Justice Ginsburg cast the crucial fifth vote for both opinions but issued no separate opinion. Justices Stevens, Scalia, Thomas, and Breyer, each filed dissenting opinions.

Over the last decade a controversy emerged over the differential sentencing under the guidelines for those convicted of crack cocaine (who are predominantly African American) and powder cocaine (who are predominantly white). Writing for the Court in *Kimbrough*, Justice Ginsburg reasserted that the federal guidelines were only advisory, over the dissents of Justices Thomas and Alito. Kimbrough had been convicted of selling fifty grams of crack cocaine and subject to a sentence under the guidelines of 228 to 270 months in prison. But the district court found that excessive and sentenced him to 180 months in prisons and five years of supervised release. An appellate court vacated that sentence because it was outside the guidelines, but the Supreme Court reversed, holding that the guidelines are only advisory and that appellate courts must review the imposition of sentences under an "abuse of discretion standard," not the prescriptions of the guidelines.

In a related case the Court reinforced that ruling. In *Gall v. United States*, 128 S.Ct. 586 (2007), Justice Stevens writing for the Court, with Justices Thomas and Alito again dissenting, held that appellate courts must review all sentences under the "deferential abuse of discretion standard" regardless of the range of variance between the sentence imposed and the guidelines' recommendations. Gall had been sentenced, based on the district court's evaluation of all facts, to thirty-six months of probation instead of the recommended thirty to thirty-seven months of prison.

In its 2008–2009 term, the Court limited the line of cases following *Apprendi v. New Jersey*, 536 U.S. 466 (2000) (see Vol. 2, Ch. 9), which limited judges' discretion in sentencing in holding that enhanced sentences may not be imposed unless based on facts found by a jury. In *Oregon v. Ice*, 129 S.Ct. 711 (2009), a bare majority held that the Sixth Amendment jury trial right limited judges' discretion to decide to require that sentences be served separately rather than simultaneously. Thomas Ice was tried for assaulting an eleven-year-old girl and charged with entering her home twice and sexually touching her four times; he was convicted on all six counts. Under Oregon law, sentences for multiple crimes are served concurrently, but the trial judge found that the two charges of burglary and four sex crimes were separate incidents. The judge sentenced Ice to a total of 340 months in prison, with three of the six sentences running consecutively. Writing for a bare majority Justice Ginsburg reasoned that both historic practice—that juries traditionally had no role in deciding for or against concurrent sentences—and "respect for state sovereignty" justified confining the ruling in *Apprendi* to "sentences for discrete crimes." By contrast, dissenting Justice Scalia, joined by Chief Justice Roberts and Justices Souter and Thomas, countered that the majority's decision was "a virtual copy of the dissents" in the *Apprendi* line of rulings and that the matter of enhanced sentencing—in this case, consecutive (instead of concurrent) sentencing on convictions—was a matter for juries, not judges, to decide.

E | *A Speedy and Public Trial*

In *Vermont v. Brillon*, 129 S.Ct. 1283 (2009) the Court held that trial delays caused by defense counsel, whether privately retained or appointed by a court, are attributable to the defendant unless the delays are the result of a "systematic breakdown in the public defender system." At issue was whether a three-year delay in bringing a defendant to trial violated the Sixth Amendment right to a speedy trial. Brillon was arrested and charged with felony domestic violence and as a habitual offender. During the three years prior to his trial, he was assigned six different public defenders. He was eventually found guilty and sentenced to twelve to twenty years in prison, and he appealed. Writing for the Court, Justice Ginsburg ruled that assigned counsel "act on behalf of their clients, and delays sought by counsel are ordinarily attributable to the defendants they represent." In this case, all but six months of the delays were attributable to the defense counsel, and thus to the defendant; the only time delay caused by defense counsel attributable to the state was the result of a "systematic breakdown in the public defender system." Justice Breyer, joined by Justice Stevens, dissented.

In addition, the Roberts Court in *per curiam* opinion, in *Presley v. Georgia*, 130 S.Ct. 721 (2010), with Justices Thomas and Scalia dissenting, reaffirmed prior holdings that the public has a right to attend *voir dire* examinations of potential juries, and did so on the basis of the Sixth Amendment guarantee of a public trial, rather than on the First Amendment.

F | *The Right to Be Informed of Charges and to Confront Accusers*

In a five-to-four ruling in *Melendez-Diaz v. Massachusetts*, 129 S.Ct. 2527 (2009), the majority held that chemists and other scientists who prepare crime lab reports may be summoned as witnesses in criminal trials to defend their analyses in order not to violate defendants' Sixth Amendment right to confront witnesses against them. Writing for the Court, Justice Scalia observed that "There is little reason to believe that confrontation will be useless in testing analysts' honesty, proficiency, and methodology—the features that are commonly the focus in a cross-examination of experts." In doing so, he recited reports about how defective crime labs and their results are and dismissed claims that crime lab reports are a product of "neutral scientific testing." "Forensic evidence," Justice Scalia wrote, "is not uniquely immune from the risk of manipulation." Chief Justice Roberts and Justices Kennedy, Breyer, and Alito dissented.

IO

CRUEL AND UNUSUAL PUNISHMENT

A | *Noncapital Punishment*

In its 2009–2010 term, the Roberts Court considered whether a sentence of lifetime imprisonment, without the possibility of parole, for a nonhomicide crime committed by a juvenile violates the Eighth Amendment in *Graham v. Florida*. Terrance Graham, at age 16, was on probation when he pled guilty to robbery. At the time of the crime, he was seventeen years old. A state appeals court found that, although the imposition of the death penalty on a minor violates the Eighth Amendment, under *Roper v. Simmons*, 543 U.S. 551 (2005) (excerpted in Vol. 2, Ch. 10), a lifetime sentence for a juvenile was distinguishable and did not per se violate the cruel and unusual punishment clause. The state court of appeals further reasoned that even if such a sentence runs afoul of international norms, the U.S. Supreme Court had held that the courts, not the international community, determine the scope of Eighth Amendment protections.

By a six-to-three vote in *Graham v. Florida*, 130 S.Ct. 2011 (2010), the Court held that the Eighth Amendment bars juvenile offenders from receiving life sentences without parole for nonhomicide crimes. Writing for the Court, Justice Kennedy ruled that societal views did not support lifetime sentences for juveniles and that juvenile nonhomicide offenders must be given the opportunity to reform. In his words: "By denying the defendant the right to reenter the community, the state makes an irrevocable judgment about that person's value and place in society. . . . This judgment is not appropriate in light of a juvenile nonhomicide offender's capacity for change and limited moral culpability."

Chief Justice Roberts concurred but would have decided such cases on a case-by-case basis and emphasized that "Some crimes are so heinous, and some juvenile offenders so highly culpable, that a sentence of life without parole may be entirely justified under the Constitution." Justice Thomas dissented, joined by Justices Scalia and Alito.

Notably, on the same day *Graham v. Florida* came down, the Court upheld the constitutionality of the Adam Walsh Child Protection and Safety Act of 2006, which authorizes the indefinite civil commitment of mentally ill, sexual federal offenders, even if they have served their sentences, in *United States v. Comstock*, 130 S.Ct. 1949 (2010). Similar state laws were upheld in *Kansas v. Hendricks*, 521 U.S. 346 (1997), which rejected a due process challenge. Writing for the Court, Justice Breyer held that Congress had the authority under Article I's necessary and proper clause, reasoning that: "As a federal custodian, it has the constitutional power to act in order to protect nearby (and other) communities from the danger federal prisoners may pose. . . . Neither Congress's power to criminalize conduct, nor its power to imprison individuals who engage in that conduct, nor its power to enact laws governing prisons and prisoners, is explicitly mentioned in the Constitution. But Congress nonetheless possesses broad authority to do each of those things." In addition, the majority rejected a Tenth Amendment challenge to the law for infringing on states' rights in holding that the statute did not invade states' interests. Justices Kennedy and Alito each wrote concurring opinions, agreeing with the result but expressing reservations about the majority's broad reading of the necessary and proper clause and congressional power. Justices Scalia and Thomas dissented.

B | *Capital Punishment*

In a sharply fragmented ruling, the Court concluded that the most common method of execution by lethal injection does not violate the Eighth Amendment. The vote was seven to two in *Baze v. Rees* (excerpted below), but the opinion for the Court failed to commend a majority. Writing for a plurality, joined by only Justices Kennedy and Alito, Chief Justice Roberts adopted as a standard for assessing the validity of an execution method whether it poses a "substantial risk of serious harm," and rejected the death row inmate's claim that the standard should be "unnecessary risk." Chief Justice Roberts' opinion left open the possibility of further challenges to the use of lethal drugs under a specific procedure of other states; lethal injection is used in thirty-five other states and the federal government. Notably, he observed that states are free to choose a procedure for carrying out executions so long as they are shown to be "feasible, readily implemented, and in fact significantly reduce a substantial risk of severe pain." But Chief Justice Roberts also added that "if a state refuses to adopt such an alternative in the face of these documented advantages, without a legitimate penological justification for adhering to its current method of execution, then a state's refusal to change its method can be viewed as 'cruel and unusual punishment' under the Eighth Amendment." In a concurring opinion, Justice Stevens contended that the ruling, instead of ending the controversy over the use of a three-drug protocol injection, would only invite more litigation. He also noted that based on his experience the imposition of capital punishment constituted a pointless and needless extinction of life with only negligible social benefits. Still, he would abide by the Court's precedents upholding capital punishment. In separate concurring opinions, Justices Scalia, Thomas, and Alito took issue with both Chief Justice Roberts' and Justice Stevens' opinions. Justice Ginsburg, joined by Justice Souter, filed a dissenting opinion.

In an even more sharply divided ruling, a bare majority struck down death penalty laws in Louisiana and five other states that imposed capital punishment for crimes like child rape. Writing for the majority in *Kennedy v. Louisiana* (2008) (excerpted below), Justice Kennedy categorically ruled out the death penalty for individual crimes "where the victim's life was not taken," but did not rule out capital punishment for "offenses against the state" such as treason, terrorism, or espionage. The Court had previously overruled laws imposing the death penalty for the crime of rape of an adult woman as disproportionate to the offense, in *Coker v. Georgia*, 433 U.S. 548 (1977). Justice Kennedy based the decision on "evolving standards of decency" and the Court's "own independent judgment." Writing for the dissenters, Justice Alito, joined by Chief Justice Roberts and Justices Scalia and Thomas, sharply criticized the majority's reasoning and maintained that the issue should be left to the states.

Baze v. Rees
128 S.Ct. 1530 (2008)

Ralph Baze and another death row inmate challenged the constitutionality of Kentucky's method of lethal injection by a three-drug protocol on the ground that it did not necessarily ensure a painless execution. A state court rejected the claim, and the Kentucky Supreme Court affirmed, though noting that a method of execution violates the Eighth Amendment if it "creates a substantial risk of wanton and unnecessary infliction of pain, torture, or lingering death." Baze appealed that decision and the Supreme Court granted *certiorari*.

The state supreme court's decision was affirmed by a seven-to-two vote. Chief Justice Roberts delivered the opinion for the Court, which only Justices Kennedy and Alito joined. Justices Stevens, Scalia, Thomas, and Alito filed separate concurring opinions. Justice Ginsburg, joined by Justice Souter, filed a dissenting opinion.

☐ *CHIEF JUSTICE ROBERTS announced the judgment of the Court and delivered the opinion, in which Justice KENNEDY and Justice ALITO join.*

Like 35 other States and the Federal Government, Kentucky has chosen to impose capital punishment for certain crimes. As is true with respect to each of these States and the Federal Government, Kentucky has altered its method of execution over time to more humane means of carrying out the sentence. That progress has led to the use of lethal injection by every jurisdiction that imposes the death penalty.

Petitioners in this case—each convicted of double homicide—acknowledge that the lethal injection procedure, if applied as intended, will result in a humane death. They nevertheless contend that the lethal injection protocol is unconstitutional under the Eighth Amendment's ban on "cruel and unusual punishments," because of the risk that the protocol's terms might not be properly followed, resulting in significant pain. They propose an alternative protocol, one that they concede has not been adopted by any State and has never been tried. . . .

By the middle of the 19th century, "hanging was the 'nearly universal form of execution' in the United States." *Campbell v. Wood*, 511 U.S. 1119 (1994). In 1888, following the recommendation of a commission empaneled by the Governor to find " 'the most humane and practical method known to modern science of carrying into effect the sentence of death,' " New York became the first State to authorize electrocution as a form of capital punishment. *Glass v. Louisiana*, 471 U.S. 1080 (1985). By 1915, 11 other States had followed suit, motivated by the "well-grounded belief that electrocution is less painful and more humane than hanging." *Malloy v. South Carolina*, 237 U.S. 180 (1915).

Electrocution remained the predominant mode of execution for nearly a century, although several methods, including hanging, firing squad, and lethal gas were in use at one time. Following the 9-year hiatus in executions that ended with our decision in *Gregg v. Georgia*, 428 U.S. 153 (1976), however, state legislatures began responding to public calls to reexamine electrocution as a means of assuring a humane death. A total of 36 States have now adopted lethal injection as the exclusive or primary means of implementing the death penalty, making it by far the most prevalent method of execution in the United States. It is also the method used by the Federal Government.

Of these 36 States, at least 30 (including Kentucky) use the same combination of three drugs in their lethal injection protocols. The first drug, sodium thiopental (also known as Pentathol), is a fast-acting barbiturate sedative that induces a deep, comalike unconsciousness when given in the amounts used for lethal injection. The second drug, pancuronium bromide (also known as Pavulon), is a paralytic agent that inhibits all muscular-skeletal movements and, by paralyzing the diaphragm, stops respiration. Potassium chloride, the third drug, interferes with the electrical signals that stimulate the contractions of the heart, inducing cardiac arrest. The proper administration of the first drug ensures that the prisoner does not experience any pain associated with the paralysis and cardiac arrest caused by the second and third drugs.

Kentucky replaced electrocution with lethal injection in 1998. The Kentucky statute does not specify the drugs or categories of drugs to be used during an execution, instead mandating that "every death sentence shall be executed by continuous intravenous injection of a substance or combination of substances sufficient to cause death." . . .

Kentucky's execution facilities consist of the execution chamber, a control room separated by a one-way window, and a witness room. The warden and deputy warden remain in the execution chamber with the prisoner, who is strapped to a gurney. The execution team administers the drugs remotely from the control room through five feet of IV tubing. If, as determined by the warden and deputy warden through visual inspection, the prisoner is not unconscious within 60 seconds following the delivery of the sodium thiopental to the primary IV site, a new 3-gram dose of thiopental is administered to the secondary site before injecting the pancuronium and potassium chloride. In addition to assuring that the first dose of thiopental is successfully administered, the warden and deputy warden also watch for any problems with the IV catheters and tubing.

A physician is present to assist in any effort to revive the prisoner in the event of a last-minute stay of execution. By statute, however, the physician is prohibited from participating in the "conduct of an execution," except to certify the cause of death. . . .

The Eighth Amendment to the Constitution, applicable to the States through the Due Process Clause of the Fourteenth Amendment, see *Robinson v. California*, 370 U.S. 660 (1962), provides that "[e]xcessive bail shall not be required, nor excessive fines imposed, nor cruel and unusual punishments inflicted." We begin with the principle, settled by *Gregg*, that capital punishment is constitutional. It necessarily follows that there must be a means of carrying it out. Some risk of pain is inherent in any method of execution—no matter how humane—if only from the prospect of error in following the required procedure. It is clear, then, that the Constitution does not demand the avoidance of all risk of pain in carrying out executions.

Petitioners do not claim that it does. Rather, they contend that the Eighth Amendment prohibits procedures that create an "unnecessary risk" of pain. Specifically, they argue that courts must evaluate "(a) the severity of pain risked, (b) the likelihood of that pain occurring, and (c) the extent to which alternative means are feasible, either by modifying existing execution procedures or adopting alternative procedures." Petitioners envision that the quantum of risk necessary to make out an Eighth Amendment claim will vary according to the severity of the pain and the availability of alternatives, but that the risk must be "significant" to trigger Eighth Amendment scrutiny.

Kentucky responds that this "unnecessary risk" standard is tantamount to a requirement that States adopt the "'least risk'" alternative in carrying out an execution, a standard the Commonwealth contends will cast recurring constitutional doubt on any procedure adopted by the States. Instead, Kentucky urges the Court to approve the "'substantial risk'" test used by the courts below.

This Court has never invalidated a State's chosen procedure for carrying out a sentence of death as the infliction of cruel and unusual punishment. In *Wilkerson v. Utah*, 99 U.S. 130 (1879), we upheld a sentence to death by firing squad imposed by a territorial court, rejecting the argument that such a sentence constituted cruel and unusual punishment. We noted there the difficulty of "defin[ing] with exactness the extent of the constitutional provision which provides that cruel and unusual punishments shall not be inflicted." Rather than undertake such an effort, the *Wilkerson* Court simply noted that "it is safe to affirm that punishments of torture, . . . and all others in the same line of unnecessary cruelty, are forbidden" by the Eighth Amendment. . . .

We carried these principles further in *In re Kemmler*, 136 U.S. 436 (1890). There we rejected an opportunity to incorporate the Eighth Amendment against the States in a challenge to the first execution by electrocution, to be carried out by the State of New York. In passing over that question, however, we observed that "[p]unishments are cruel when they involve torture or a lingering death; but the punishment of death is not cruel within the meaning of that word as used in the Constitution. It implies there something inhuman and barbarous, something more than the mere extinguishment of life." We noted that the New York statute adopting electrocution as a method of execution "was passed in the effort to devise a more humane method of reaching the result."

Petitioners do not claim that lethal injection or the proper administration of the particular protocol adopted by Kentucky by themselves constitute the cruel or wanton infliction of pain. Quite the contrary, they concede that "if performed properly," an execution carried out under Kentucky's procedures would be "humane and constitutional." . . . Instead, petitioners claim that there is a significant risk that the procedures will not be properly followed—in particular, that the sodium thiopental will not be properly administered to achieve its intended effect—resulting in severe pain when the other chemicals are administered. . . .

Simply because an execution method may result in pain, either by accident or as an inescapable consequence of death, does not establish the sort of "objectively intolerable risk of harm" that qualifies as cruel and unusual. In *Louisiana ex rel. Francis v. Resweber*, 329 U.S. 459 (1947), a plurality of the Court upheld a second attempt at executing a prisoner by electrocution after a mechanical malfunction had interfered with the first attempt. The principal opinion noted that "[a]ccidents happen for which no man is to blame," and concluded that such "an accident, with no suggestion of malevolence," did not give rise to an Eighth Amendment violation.

As Justice FRANKFURTER noted in a separate opinion based on the Due Process Clause, however, "a hypothetical situation" involving "a series of abortive attempts at electrocution" would present a different case. In terms of our present Eighth Amendment analysis, such a situation—unlike an "innocent misadventure"—would demonstrate an "objectively intolerable risk of harm" that officials may not ignore. In other words, an isolated mishap alone does not give rise to an Eighth Amendment violation, precisely because such an event, while regrettable, does not suggest cruelty, or that the procedure at issue gives rise to a "substantial risk of serious harm." . . .

Petitioners contend that there is a risk of improper administration of thiopental because the doses are difficult to mix into solution form and load into syringes; because the protocol fails to establish a rate of injection, which could lead to a failure of the IV; because it is possible that the IV catheters will infiltrate into surrounding tissue, causing an inadequate dose to be delivered to the vein; because of inadequate facilities and training; and because Kentucky has no reliable means of monitoring the anesthetic depth of the prisoner after the sodium thiopental has been administered.

As for the risk that the sodium thiopental would be improperly prepared, petitioners contend that Kentucky employs untrained personnel who are unqualified to calculate and mix an adequate dose, especially in light of the omission of volume and concentration amounts from the written protocol. The state trial court, however, specifically found that "[i]f the manufacturers' instructions for reconstitution of Sodium Thiopental are followed, . . . there would be minimal risk of improper mixing, despite converse testimony that a layperson would have difficulty performing this task." We cannot say that this finding is clearly erroneous, particularly when that finding is substantiated by expert testimony. . . .

Likewise, the asserted problems related to the IV lines do not establish a sufficiently substantial risk of harm to meet the requirements of the Eighth Amendment. Kentucky has put in place several important safeguards to ensure that an adequate dose of sodium thiopental is delivered to the condemned prisoner. The most significant of these is the written protocol's requirement that members of the IV team must have at least one year of professional experience as a certified medical assistant, phlebotomist, EMT, paramedic, or military corpsman. . . .

In addition, the presence of the warden and deputy warden in the execution chamber with the prisoner allows them to watch for signs of IV problems, including infiltration. . . .

The dissent believes that rough-and-ready tests for checking consciousness—calling the inmate's name, brushing his eyelashes, or presenting him with strong, noxious odors—could materially decrease the risk of administering the second and third drugs before the sodium thiopental has taken effect. Again, the risk at issue is already attenuated, given the steps Kentucky has taken to ensure the proper administration of the first drug. Moreover, the scenario the dissent posits involves a level of unconsciousness allegedly sufficient to avoid detection of improper administration of the anesthesia under Kentucky's procedure, but not sufficient to prevent pain. There is no indication that the basic tests the dissent advocates can make such fine distinctions. If these tests are effective only in determining whether the sodium thiopental has entered the inmate's bloodstream, the record confirms that the visual inspection of the IV site under Kentucky's procedure achieves that objective.

The dissent would continue the stay of these executions (and presumably the many others held in abeyance pending decision in this case) and send the case back to the lower courts to determine whether such added measures redress an "untoward" risk of pain. But an inmate cannot succeed on an Eighth Amendment claim simply by showing one more step the State could take as a failsafe for other, independently adequate measures. This approach would serve no meaningful purpose and would frustrate the State's legitimate interest in carrying out a sentence of death in a timely manner.

Reasonable people of good faith disagree on the morality and efficacy of capital punishment, and for many who oppose it, no method of execution would ever be acceptable. But as Justice FRANKFURTER stressed in *Resweber*, "[o]ne must be on guard against finding in personal disapproval a reflection of more or less prevailing condemnation." This Court has ruled that capital punishment is not prohibited under our Constitution, and that the States may enact laws specifying that sanction. "[T]he power of a State to pass laws means little if the State cannot enforce them." *McCleskey v. Zant*, 499 U.S. 467 (1991).

Kentucky has adopted a method of execution believed to be the most humane available, one it shares with 35 other States. Petitioners agree that, if administered as intended, that procedure will result in a painless death. The risks of maladministration they have suggested—such as improper mixing of chemicals and improper setting of IVs by trained and experienced personnel—cannot remotely be characterized as "objectively intolerable." . . .

Throughout our history, whenever a method of execution has been challenged in this Court as cruel and unusual, the Court has rejected the challenge. Our society has nonetheless steadily moved to more humane methods of carrying out capital punishment. The firing squad, hanging, the electric chair, and the gas chamber have each in turn given way to more humane methods, culminating in today's consensus on lethal injection. The broad framework of the Eighth Amendment has accommodated this progress toward more humane methods of execution, and our approval of a particular method in the past has not precluded legislatures from taking the steps they deem appropriate, in light of new developments, to ensure humane capital punishment. There is no reason to suppose that today's decision will be any different.

The judgment below concluding that Kentucky's procedure is consistent with the Eighth Amendment is, accordingly, affirmed.

☐ *Justice ALITO, concurring.*

I join the plurality opinion but write separately to explain my view of how the holding should be implemented. The opinion concludes that "a State's refusal to change its method [of execution] can be viewed as 'cruel and unusual' under the Eighth Amendment" if the State, "without a legitimate penological justification," rejects an alternative method that is "feasible" and "readily" available and that would "significantly reduce a substantial risk of severe pain." Properly understood, this standard will not, as Justice THOMAS predicts, lead to litigation that enables "those seeking to abolish the death penalty . . . to embroil the States in never-ending litigation concerning the adequacy of their execution procedures." . . .

☐ *Justice BREYER, concurring in the judgment.*

Assuming the lawfulness of the death penalty itself, petitioners argue that Kentucky's method of execution, lethal injection, nonetheless constitutes a constitutionally forbidden, "cruel and usual punishmen[t]." In respect to how a court should review such a claim, I agree with Justice GINSBURG. She highlights the relevant question, whether the method creates an untoward, readily avoidable risk of inflicting severe and unnecessary suffering. I agree that the relevant factors—the "degree of risk," the "magnitude of pain," and the "availability of alternatives"—are interrelated and each must be considered. At the same time, I believe that the legal merits of the kind of claim presented must inevitably turn not so much upon the wording of an intermediate standard of review as upon facts and evidence. And I cannot find, either in the record in this case or in the literature on the subject, sufficient evidence that Kentucky's execution method poses the "significant and unnecessary risk of inflicting severe pain" that petitioners assert. . . .

☐ *Justice STEVENS, concurring in the judgment.*

When we granted *certiorari* in this case, I assumed that our decision would bring the debate about lethal injection as a method of execution to a close.

It now seems clear that it will not. The question whether a similar three-drug protocol may be used in other States remains open, and may well be answered differently in a future case on the basis of a more complete record. Instead of ending the controversy, I am now convinced that this case will generate debate not only about the constitutionality of the three-drug protocol, and specifically about the justification for the use of the paralytic agent, pancuronium bromide, but also about the justification for the death penalty itself. . . .

In *Gregg v. Georgia*, 428 U.S. 153 (1976), we explained that unless a criminal sanction serves a legitimate penological function, it constitutes "gratuitous infliction of suffering" in violation of the Eighth Amendment. We then identified three societal purposes for death as a sanction: incapacitation, deterrence, and retribution (joint opinion of STEWART, POWELL, and STEVENS, JJ.). In the past three decades, however, each of these rationales has been called into question.

While incapacitation may have been a legitimate rationale in 1976, the recent rise in statutes providing for life imprisonment without the possibility of parole demonstrates that incapacitation is neither a necessary nor a sufficient justification for the death penalty. Moreover, a recent poll indicates that support for the death penalty drops significantly when life without the possibility of parole is presented as an alternative option. And the available sociological evidence suggests that juries are less likely to impose the death penalty when life without parole is available as a sentence.

The legitimacy of deterrence as an acceptable justification for the death penalty is also questionable, at best. Despite 30 years of empirical research in the area, there remains no reliable statistical evidence that capital punishment in fact deters potential offenders. In the absence of such evidence, deterrence cannot serve as a sufficient penological justification for this uniquely severe and irrevocable punishment.

We are left, then, with retribution as the primary rationale for imposing the death penalty. And indeed, it is the retribution rationale that animates much of the remaining enthusiasm for the death penalty. Our Eighth Amendment jurisprudence has narrowed the class of offenders eligible for the death penalty to include only those who have committed outrageous crimes defined by specific aggravating factors. It is the cruel treatment of victims that provides the most persuasive arguments for prosecutors seeking the death penalty. A natural response to such heinous crimes is a thirst for vengeance.

At the same time, however, as the thoughtful opinions by THE CHIEF JUSTICE and Justice GINSBURG make pellucidly clear, our society has moved away from public and painful retribution towards ever more humane forms of punishment. State-sanctioned killing is therefore becoming more and more anachronistic. In an attempt to bring executions in line with our evolving standards of decency, we have adopted increasingly less painful methods of execution, and then declared previous methods barbaric and archaic. But by requiring that an execution be relatively painless, we necessarily protect the inmate from enduring any punishment that is comparable to the suffering inflicted on his victim. This trend, while appropriate and required by the Eighth Amendment's prohibition on cruel and unusual punishment, actually undermines the very premise on which public approval of the retribution rationale is based. . . .

Our decisions in 1976 upholding the constitutionality of the death penalty relied heavily on our belief that adequate procedures were in place that would avoid the danger of discriminatory application identified by Justice

DOUGLAS' opinion in *Furman*, of arbitrary application identified by Justice STEWART, and of excessiveness identified by Justices BRENNAN and MARSHALL. In subsequent years a number of our decisions relied on the premise that "death is different" from every other form of punishment to justify rules minimizing the risk of error in capital cases. Ironically, however, more recent cases have endorsed procedures that provide less protections to capital defendants than to ordinary offenders. . . .

In sum, just as Justice WHITE ultimately based his conclusion in *Furman* on his extensive exposure to countless cases for which death is the authorized penalty, I have relied on my own experience in reaching the conclusion that the imposition of the death penalty represents "the pointless and needless extinction of life with only marginal contributions to any discernible social or public purposes. A penalty with such negligible returns to the State [is] patently excessive and cruel and unusual punishment violative of the Eighth Amendment."

The conclusion that I have reached with regard to the constitutionality of the death penalty itself makes my decision in this case particularly difficult. It does not, however, justify a refusal to respect precedents that remain a part of our law. This Court has held that the death penalty is constitutional, and has established a framework for evaluating the constitutionality of particular methods of execution. Under those precedents, whether as interpreted by THE CHIEF JUSTICE or Justice GINSBURG, I am persuaded that the evidence adduced by petitioners fails to prove that Kentucky's lethal injection protocol violates the Eighth Amendment. Accordingly, I join the Court's judgment.

☐ *Justice SCALIA, with whom Justice THOMAS joins, concurring in the judgment.*

I join the opinion of Justice THOMAS concurring in the judgment. I write separately to provide what I think is needed response to Justice STEVENS' separate opinion.

Justice STEVENS concludes as follows: "[T]he imposition of the death penalty represents the pointless and needless extinction of life with only marginal contributions to any discernible social or public purposes. A penalty with such negligible returns to the State [is] patently excessive and cruel and unusual punishment violative of the Eighth Amendment."

This conclusion is insupportable as an interpretation of the Constitution, which generally leaves it to democratically elected legislatures rather than courts to decide what makes significant contribution to social or public purposes. Besides that more general proposition, the very text of the document recognizes that the death penalty is a permissible legislative choice. The Fifth Amendment expressly requires a presentment or indictment of a grand jury to hold a person to answer for "a capital, or otherwise infamous crime," and prohibits deprivation of "life" without due process of law. The same Congress that proposed the Eighth Amendment also enacted the Act of April 30, 1790, which made several offenses punishable by death. There is simply no legal authority for the proposition that the imposition of death as a criminal penalty is unconstitutional other than the opinions in *Furman v. Georgia*, 408 U.S. 238 (1972), which established a nationwide moratorium on capital punishment that Justice STEVENS had a hand in ending four years later in *Gregg*. . . .

According to Justice STEVENS, the death penalty promotes none of the purposes of criminal punishment because it neither prevents more crimes than alternative measures nor serves a retributive purpose. He argues that "the recent rise in statutes providing for life imprisonment without the possibility of parole" means that States have a ready alternative to the death penalty. Taking the points together, Justice STEVENS concludes that the availability of alternatives, and what he describes as the unavailability of "reliable statistical evidence," renders capital punishment unconstitutional. In his view, the benefits of capital punishment—as compared to other forms of punishment such as life imprisonment—are outweighed by the costs.

These conclusions are not supported by the available data. Justice STEVENS' analysis barely acknowledges the "significant body of recent evidence that capital punishment may well have a deterrent effect, possibly a quite powerful one." . . .

But even if Justice STEVENS' assertion about the deterrent value of the death penalty were correct, the death penalty would yet be constitutional (as he concedes) if it served the appropriate purpose of retribution. I would think it difficult indeed to prove that a criminal sanction fails to serve a retributive purpose—a judgment that strikes me as inherently subjective and insusceptible of judicial review. Justice STEVENS, however, concludes that, because the Eighth Amendment "protect[s] the inmate from enduring any punishment that is comparable to the suffering inflicted on his victim," capital punishment serves no retributive purpose at all. The infliction of any pain, according to Justice STEVENS, violates the Eighth Amendment's prohibition against cruel and unusual punishments, but so too does the imposition of capital punishment without pain because a criminal penalty lacks a retributive purpose unless it inflicts pain commensurate with the pain that the criminal has caused. In other words, if a punishment is not retributive enough, it is not retributive at all. To state this proposition is to refute it, as Justice STEVENS once understood. "[T]he decision that capital punishment may be the appropriate sanction in extreme cases is an expression of the community's belief that certain crimes are themselves so grievous an affront to humanity that the only adequate response may be the penalty of death." *Gregg.*

Justice STEVENS' final refuge in his cost-benefit analysis is a familiar one: There is a risk that an innocent person might be convicted and sentenced to death—though not a risk that Justice STEVENS can quantify, because he lacks a single example of a person executed for a crime he did not commit in the current American system. His analysis of this risk is thus a series of sweeping condemnations that, if taken seriously, would prevent any punishment under any criminal justice system. . . .

But of all Justice STEVENS' criticisms of the death penalty, the hardest to take is his bemoaning of "the enormous costs that death penalty litigation imposes on society," including the "burden on the courts and the lack of finality for victim's families." Those costs, those burdens, and that lack of finality are in large measure the creation of Justice STEVENS and other Justices opposed to the death penalty, who have "encumber[ed] [it] . . . with unwarranted restrictions neither contained in the text of the Constitution nor reflected in two centuries of practice under it"—the product of their policy views "not shared by the vast majority of the American people."

But actually none of this really matters. As Justice STEVENS explains, "'objective evidence, though of great importance, [does] not wholly determine the controversy, for the Constitution contemplates that in the end our own judgment will be brought to bear on the question of the acceptability of the death penalty under the Eighth Amendment.'" "I have relied on my own experience in reaching the conclusion that the imposition of the death penalty" is unconstitutional.

Purer expression cannot be found of the principle of rule by judicial fiat. In the face of Justice STEVENS' experience, the experience of all others is, it appears, of little consequence. The experience of the state legislatures and the Congress—who retain the death penalty as a form of punishment—is dismissed as "the product of habit and inattention rather than an acceptable deliberative process." The experience of social scientists whose studies indicate that the death penalty deters crime is relegated to a footnote. The experience of fellow citizens who support the death penalty is described, with only the most thinly veiled condemnation, as stemming from a "thirst for vengeance." It is Justice STEVENS' experience that reigns over all.

I take no position on the desirability of the death penalty, except to say that its value is eminently debatable and the subject of deeply, indeed passionately, held views—which means, to me, that it is preeminently not a matter to be resolved here. And especially not when it is explicitly permitted by the Constitution.

☐ *Justice THOMAS, with whom Justice SCALIA joins, concurring in the judgment.*

Although I agree that petitioners have failed to establish that Kentucky's lethal injection protocol violates the Eighth Amendment, I write separately because I cannot subscribe to the plurality opinion's formulation of the governing standard. As I understand it, that opinion would hold that a method of execution violates the Eighth Amendment if it poses a substantial risk of severe pain that could be significantly reduced by adopting readily available alternative procedures. This standard—along with petitioners' proposed "unnecessary risk" standard and the dissent's "untoward risk" standard—finds no support in the original understanding of the Cruel and Unusual Punishments Clause or in our previous method-of-execution cases; casts constitutional doubt on long-accepted methods of execution; and injects the Court into matters it has no institutional capacity to resolve. Because, in my view, a method of execution violates the Eighth Amendment only if it is deliberately designed to inflict pain, I concur only in the judgment.

The Eighth Amendment's prohibition on the "inflict[ion]" of "cruel and unusual punishments" must be understood in light of the historical practices that led the Framers to include it in the Bill of Rights. . . .

That the Constitution permits capital punishment in principle does not, of course, mean that all methods of execution are constitutional. In English and early colonial practice, the death penalty was not a uniform punishment, but rather a range of punishments, some of which the Framers likely regarded as cruel and unusual. Death by hanging was the most common mode of execution both before and after 1791, and there is no doubt that it remained a permissible punishment after enactment of the Eighth Amendment. In addition to hanging, which was intended to, and often did, result in a quick and painless death, "[o]fficials also wielded a set of tools capable of intensifying a death sentence," that is, "ways of producing a punishment worse than death."

One such "tool" was burning at the stake. Because burning, unlike hanging, was always painful and destroyed the body, it was considered "a form of super-capital punishment, worse than death itself." Reserved for offenders whose crimes were thought to pose an especially grave threat to the social order—such as slaves who killed their masters and women who killed their husbands—burning a person alive was so dreadful a punishment that sheriffs sometimes hanged the offender first "as an act of charity." Other methods of intensifying a death sentence included "gibbeting," or hanging the condemned in an iron cage so that his body would decompose in public view, and "public dissection," a punishment Blackstone associated with murder, 4 W. Blackstone, *Commentaries* (1769). But none of these was the worst fate a criminal could meet. That was reserved for the most dangerous and reprobate offenders—traitors. "The punishment of high treason," Blackstone wrote, was "very solemn and terrible," and involved "embowelling alive, beheading, and quartering." . . .

The principal object of these aggravated forms of capital punishment was to terrorize the criminal, and thereby more effectively deter the crime. Their defining characteristic was that they were purposely designed to inflict pain and suffering beyond that necessary to cause death. These "superadded" circumstances "were carefully handed out to apply terror where it was thought to be most needed," and were designed "to ensure that death would be slow and painful, and thus all the more frightening to contemplate."

Although the Eighth Amendment was not the subject of extensive discussion during the debates on the Bill of Rights, there is good reason to believe that the Framers viewed such enhancements to the death penalty as falling within the prohibition of the Cruel and Unusual Punishments Clause.

Moreover, the evidence we do have from the debates on the Constitution confirms that the Eighth Amendment was intended to disable Congress from imposing torturous punishments. . . .

Consistent with the original understanding of the Cruel and Unusual Punishments Clause, this Court's cases have repeatedly taken the view that the Framers intended to prohibit torturous modes of punishment akin to those that formed the historical backdrop of the Eighth Amendment. . . .

In the first case, *Wilkerson v. Utah*, 99 U.S. 130 (1879), the Court rejected the contention that death by firing squad was cruel and unusual. . . . Similarly, when the Court in *In re Kemmler*, 136 U.S. 436 (1890), unanimously rejected a challenge to electrocution, it interpreted the Eighth Amendment to prohibit punishments that "were manifestly cruel and unusual, as burning at the stake, crucifixion, breaking on the wheel, or the like." . . . Finally, in *Louisiana ex rel. Francis v. Resweber*, 329 U.S. 459 (1947), the Court rejected the petitioner's contention that the Eighth Amendment prohibited Louisiana from subjecting him to a second attempt at electrocution, the first attempt having failed when "[t]he executioner threw the switch but, presumably because of some mechanical difficulty, death did not result." . . .

We have never suggested that a method of execution is "cruel and unusual" within the meaning of the Eighth Amendment simply because it involves a risk of pain—whether "substantial," "unnecessary," or "untoward"—that could be reduced by adopting alternative procedures. And for good reason. It strains credulity to suggest that the defining characteristic of burning at the stake, disemboweling, drawing and quartering, beheading, and the like was that they involved risks of pain that could be eliminated by using alternative methods of execution. Quite plainly, what defined these punishments was that they were designed to inflict torture as a way of enhancing a death sentence; they were intended to produce a penalty worse than death, to accomplish something "more than the mere extinguishment of life." The evil the Eighth Amendment targets is intentional infliction of gratuitous pain, and that is the standard our method-of-execution cases have explicitly or implicitly invoked. . . .

In short, I reject as both unprecedented and unworkable any standard that would require the courts to weigh the relative advantages and disadvantages of different methods of execution or of different procedures for implementing a given method of execution. To the extent that there is any comparative element to the inquiry, it should be limited to whether the challenged method inherently inflicts significantly more pain than traditional modes of execution such as hanging and the firing squad.

Judged under the proper standard, this is an easy case. It is undisputed that Kentucky adopted its lethal injection protocol in an effort to make capital punishment more humane, not to add elements of terror, pain, or disgrace to the death penalty. And it is undisputed that, if administered properly, Kentucky's lethal injection protocol will result in a swift and painless death. As the Sixth Circuit observed in rejecting a similar challenge to Tennessee's lethal injection protocol, we "do not have a situation where the State has any intent (or anything approaching intent) to inflict unnecessary pain; the complaint is that the State's pain-avoidance procedure may fail because the executioners may make a mistake in implementing it." But "[t]he risk of negligence in implementing a death-penalty procedure . . . does not establish a cognizable Eighth Amendment claim." Because Kentucky's lethal injection protocol is designed to eliminate pain rather than to inflict it, petitioners' challenge must fail. I accordingly concur in the Court's judgment affirming the decision below.

☐ *Justice GINSBURG, with whom Justice SOUTER joins, dissenting.*

It is undisputed that the second and third drugs used in Kentucky's three-drug lethal injection protocol, pancuronium bromide and potassium chloride, would cause a conscious inmate to suffer excruciating pain. Pancuronium bromide paralyzes the lung muscles and results in slow asphyxiation. Potassium chloride causes burning and intense pain as it circulates throughout the body. Use of pancuronium bromide and potassium chloride on a conscious inmate, the plurality recognizes, would be "constitutionally unacceptable."

The constitutionality of Kentucky's protocol therefore turns on whether inmates are adequately anesthetized by the first drug in the protocol, sodium thiopental. Kentucky's system is constitutional, the plurality states, because "petitioners have not shown that the risk of an inadequate dose of the first drug is substantial." I would not dispose of the case so swiftly given the character of the risk at stake. Kentucky's protocol lacks basic safeguards used by other States to confirm that an inmate is unconscious before injection of the second and third drugs. I would vacate and remand with instructions to consider whether Kentucky's omission of those safeguards poses an untoward, readily avoidable risk of inflicting severe and unnecessary pain.

The Court has considered the constitutionality of a specific method of execution on only three prior occasions. Those cases, and other decisions cited by the parties and *amici*, provide little guidance on the standard that should govern petitioners' challenge to Kentucky's lethal injection protocol [*Wilkerson, Kemmler, Resweber*]. . . . No clear standard for determining the constitutionality of a method of execution emerges from these decisions. Moreover, the age of the opinions limits their utility as an aid to resolution of the present controversy. The Eighth Amendment, we have held, "'must draw its meaning from the evolving standards of decency that mark the progress of a maturing society.'" *Atkins v. Virginia*, 536 U.S. 304 (2002) (quoting *Trop v. Dulles*, 356 U.S. 86 (1958). *Wilkerson* was decided 129 years ago, *Kemmler* 118 years ago, and *Resweber* 61 years ago. Whatever little light our prior method-of-execution cases might shed is thus dimmed by the passage of time.

Further phrases and tests can be drawn from more recent decisions, for example, *Gregg v. Georgia*, 428 U.S. 153 (1976). Speaking of capital punishment in the abstract, the lead opinion said that the Eighth Amendment prohibits "the unnecessary and wanton infliction of pain"; the same opinion also cautioned that a death sentence cannot "be imposed under sentencing proce-dures that creat[e] a substantial risk that it would be inflicted in an arbitrary and capricious manner." . . .

Other than using qualified and trained personnel to establish IV access, however, Kentucky does little to ensure that the inmate receives an effective dose of sodium thiopental. After siting the catheters, the IV team leaves the execution chamber. From that point forward, only the warden and deputy warden remain with the inmate. Neither the warden nor the deputy warden has any medical training.

The warden relies on visual observation to determine whether the inmate "appears" unconscious. In Kentucky's only previous execution by lethal injection, the warden's position allowed him to see the inmate best from the waist down, with only a peripheral view of the inmate's face. No other check for consciousness occurs before injection of pancuronium bromide. . . .

Nor does Kentucky monitor the effectiveness of the sodium thiopental using readily available equipment, even though the inmate is already connected to an electrocardiogram (EKG). . . .

Recognizing the importance of a window between the first and second drugs, other States have adopted safeguards not contained in Kentucky's pro-tocol. . . . In California, a member of the IV team brushes the inmate's eye-lashes, speaks to him, and shakes him at the halfway point and, again, at the completion of the sodium thiopental injection. In Alabama, a member of the execution team "begin[s] by saying the condemned inmate's name. If there is no response, the team member will gently stroke the condemned inmate's eyelashes. If there is no response, the team member will then pinch the con-demned inmate's arm." In Indiana, officials inspect the injection site after administration of sodium thiopental, say the inmate's name, touch him, and use ammonia tablets to test his response to a noxious nasal stimulus.

These checks provide a degree of assurance—missing from Kentucky's protocol—that the first drug has been properly administered. They are simple and essentially costless to employ, yet work to lower the risk that the inmate will be subjected to the agony of conscious suffocation caused by pancuron-ium bromide and the searing pain caused by potassium chloride. The record contains no explanation why Kentucky does not take any of these elementary measures. . . .

"The easiest and most obvious way to ensure that an inmate is uncon-scious during an execution," petitioners argued to the Kentucky Supreme Court, "is to check for consciousness prior to injecting pancuronium [bromide]." The court did not address petitioners' argument. I would therefore remand with instructions to consider whether the failure to include readily available safe-guards to confirm that the inmate is unconscious after injection of sodium thio-pental, in combination with the other elements of Kentucky's protocol, creates an untoward, readily avoidable risk of inflicting severe and unnecessary pain.

Kennedy v. Louisiana
128 S.Ct. 2641 (2008)

In 1995 Louisiana extended the death penalty to the crime of rape of a child under the age of twelve. Five other states—Georgia, Montana,

Oklahoma, South Carolina, and Texas—followed, though they required that defendants have a prior rape conviction or other aggravating factor for imposing the death penalty. In 2003 Patrick Kennedy was convicted and sentenced to death for raping his eight-year-old stepdaughter. The state supreme court affirmed and Kennedy appealed that decision.

The state supreme court's decision was reversed by a five-to-four vote. Justice Kennedy delivered the opinion of the Court. Justice Alito filed a dissenting opinion, which Chief Justice Roberts and Justices Scalia and Thomas joined.

☐ *Justice KENNEDY delivered the opinion of the Court.*

The Eighth Amendment, applicable to the States through the Fourteenth Amendment, provides that "[e]xcessive bail shall not be required, nor excessive fines imposed, nor cruel and unusual punishments inflicted." The Amendment proscribes "all excessive punishments, as well as cruel and unusual punishments that may or may not be excessive." *Atkins* [*v. Virginia*, 536 U.S. 304 (2002)]. The Court explained in *Atkins*, and *Roper* [*v. Simmons*, 543 U.S. 551 (2005)], that the Eighth Amendment's protection against excessive or cruel and unusual punishments flows from the basic "precept of justice that punishment for [a] crime should be graduated and proportioned to [the] offense." *Weems v. United States*, 217 U.S. 349 (1910). Whether this requirement has been fulfilled is determined not by the standards that prevailed when the Eighth Amendment was adopted in 1791 but by the norms that "currently prevail." The Amendment "draw[s] its meaning from the evolving standards of decency that mark the progress of a maturing society." *Trop v. Dulles*, 356 U.S. 86 (1958). This is because "[t]he standard of extreme cruelty is not merely descriptive, but necessarily embodies a moral judgment. The standard itself remains the same, but its applicability must change as the basic mores of society change." *Furman v. Georgia*, 408 U.S. 238 (1972).

Evolving standards of decency must embrace and express respect for the dignity of the person, and the punishment of criminals must conform to that rule. As we shall discuss, punishment is justified under one or more of three principal rationales: rehabilitation, deterrence, and retribution. It is the last of these, retribution, that most often can contradict the law's own ends. This is of particular concern when the Court interprets the meaning of the Eighth Amendment in capital cases. When the law punishes by death, it risks its own sudden descent into brutality, transgressing the constitutional commitment to decency and restraint.

For these reasons we have explained that capital punishment must "be limited to those offenders who commit 'a narrow category of the most serious crimes' and whose extreme culpability makes them 'the most deserving of execution.'" *Roper*. Though the death penalty is not invariably unconstitutional, see *Gregg v. Georgia*, 428 U.S. 153 (1976), the Court insists upon confining the instances in which the punishment can be imposed.

Applying this principle, we held in *Roper* and *Atkins* that the execution of juveniles and mentally retarded persons are punishments violative of the Eighth Amendment because the offender had a diminished personal responsibility for the crime. The Court further has held that the death penalty can be disproportionate to the crime itself where the crime did not result, or was not intended to result, in death of the victim. In *Coker*, for instance, the Court held it would be unconstitutional to execute an offender who had raped an adult woman. On the other hand, in *Tison v. Arizona*, 481 U.S. 137 (1987), the Court allowed the defendants' death sentences to stand where they did not themselves kill the victims but their involvement in the events leading up to the murders was active, recklessly indifferent, and substantial.

In these cases the Court has been guided by "objective indicia of society's standards, as expressed in legislative enactments and state practice with respect to executions." The inquiry does not end there, however. Consensus is not dispositive. Whether the death penalty is disproportionate to the crime committed depends as well upon the standards elaborated by controlling precedents and by the Court's own understanding and interpretation of the Eighth Amendment's text, history, meaning, and purpose.

Based both on consensus and our own independent judgment, our holding is that a death sentence for one who raped but did not kill a child, and who did not intend to assist another in killing the child, is unconstitutional under the Eighth and Fourteenth Amendments.

The existence of objective indicia of consensus against making a crime punishable by death was a relevant concern in *Roper, Atkins, Coker* [*v. Georgia*, 433 U.S. 584 (1997)], and *Enmund* [*v. Florida*, 458 U.S. 782 (1982)], and we follow the approach of those cases here. The history of the death penalty for the crime of rape is an instructive beginning point.

In 1925, 18 States, the District of Columbia, and the Federal Government had statutes that authorized the death penalty for the rape of a child or an adult. Between 1930 and 1964, 455 people were executed for those crimes.

In 1972, *Furman* invalidated most of the state statutes authorizing the death penalty for the crime of rape; and in Furman's aftermath only six States reenacted their capital rape provisions. Three States—Georgia, North Carolina, and Louisiana—did so with respect to all rape offenses. Three States—Florida, Mississippi, and Tennessee—did so with respect only to child rape. Louisiana reintroduced the death penalty for rape of a child in 1995. Under the current statute, any anal, vaginal, or oral intercourse with a child under the age of 13 constitutes aggravated rape and is punishable by death. Mistake of age is not a defense, so the statute imposes strict liability in this regard. Five States have since followed Louisiana's lead: Georgia, Montana, Oklahoma, South Carolina, and Texas. Four of these States' statutes are more narrow than Louisiana's in that only offenders with a previous rape conviction are death eligible.

By contrast, 44 States have not made child rape a capital offense. As for federal law, Congress in the Federal Death Penalty Act of 1994 expanded the number of federal crimes for which the death penalty is a permissible sentence, including certain nonhomicide offenses; but it did not do the same for child rape or abuse. . . .

Definitive resolution of state-law issues is for the States' own courts, and there may be disagreement over the statistics. It is further true that some States, including States that have addressed the issue in just the last few years, have made child rape a capital offense. The summary recited here, however, does allow us to make certain comparisons with the data cited in the *Atkins, Roper*, and *Enmund* cases.

When *Atkins* was decided in 2002, 30 States, including 12 noncapital jurisdictions, prohibited the death penalty for mentally retarded offenders; 20 permitted it. When *Roper* was decided in 2005, the numbers disclosed a similar division among the States: 30 States prohibited the death penalty for juveniles, 18 of which permitted the death penalty for other offenders; and 20 States authorized it. Both in *Atkins* and in *Roper,* we noted that the practice of executing mentally retarded and juvenile offenders was infrequent. Only five States had executed an offender known to have an IQ below 70 between 1989 and 2002, and only three States had executed a juvenile offender between 1995 and 2005.

The statistics in *Enmund* bear an even greater similarity to the instant case. There eight jurisdictions had authorized imposition of the death penalty solely for participation in a robbery during which an accomplice committed murder, and six defendants between 1954 and 1982 had been sentenced to death for felony murder where the defendant did not personally commit the homicidal assault. These facts, the Court concluded, "weigh[ed] on the side of rejecting capital punishment for the crime."

The evidence of a national consensus with respect to the death penalty for child rapists, as with respect to juveniles, mentally retarded offenders, and vicarious felony murderers, shows divided opinion but, on balance, an opinion against it. Thirty-seven jurisdictions—36 States plus the Federal Government— have the death penalty. As mentioned above, only six of those jurisdictions authorize the death penalty for rape of a child. Though our review of national consensus is not confined to tallying the number of States with applicable death penalty legislation, it is of significance that, in 45 jurisdictions, petitioner could not be executed for child rape of any kind. That number surpasses the 30 States in *Atkins* and *Roper* and the 42 States in *Enmund* that prohibited the death penalty under the circumstances those cases considered. . . .

We conclude on the basis of this review that there is no clear indication that state legislatures have misinterpreted *Coker* to hold that the death penalty for child rape is unconstitutional. The small number of States that have enacted this penalty, then, is relevant to determining whether there is a consensus against capital punishment for this crime. . . .

There are measures of consensus other than legislation. Statistics about the number of executions may inform the consideration whether capital punishment for the crime of child rape is regarded as unacceptable in our society. These statistics confirm our determination from our review of state statutes that there is a social consensus against the death penalty for the crime of child rape.

Nine States—Florida, Georgia, Louisiana, Mississippi, Montana, Oklahoma, South Carolina, Tennessee, and Texas—have permitted capital punishment for adult or child rape for some length of time between the Court's 1972 decision in *Furman* and today. Yet no individual has been executed for the rape of an adult or child since 1964, and no execution for any other nonhomicide offense has been conducted since 1963.

Louisiana is the only State since 1964 that has sentenced an individual to death for the crime of child rape; and petitioner and Richard Davis, who was convicted and sentenced to death for the aggravated rape of a 5-year-old child by a Louisiana jury in December 2007, are the only two individuals now on death row in the United States for a nonhomicide offense.

After reviewing the authorities informed by contemporary norms, including the history of the death penalty for this and other nonhomicide crimes, current state statutes and new enactments, and the number of executions since 1964, we conclude there is a national consensus against capital punishment for the crime of child rape. As we have said in other Eighth Amendment cases, objective evidence of contemporary values as it relates to punishment for child rape is entitled to great weight, but it does not end our inquiry. "[T]he Constitution contemplates that in the end our own judgment will be brought to bear on the question of the acceptability of the death penalty under the Eighth Amendment." We turn, then, to the resolution of the question before us, which is informed by our precedents and our own understanding of the Constitution and the rights it secures.

It must be acknowledged that there are moral grounds to question a rule barring capital punishment for a crime against an individual that did not result in death. These facts illustrate the point. Here the victim's fright, the sense of betrayal, and the nature of her injuries caused more prolonged physical and mental suffering than, say, a sudden killing by an unseen assassin. The attack was not just on her but on her childhood. For this reason, we should be most reluctant to rely upon the language of the plurality in *Coker*, which posited that, for the victim of rape, "life may not be nearly so happy as it was" but it is not beyond repair. Rape has a permanent psychological, emotional, and sometimes physical impact on the child.

It does not follow, though, that capital punishment is a proportionate penalty for the crime. The constitutional prohibition against excessive or cruel and unusual punishments mandates that the State's power to punish "be exercised within the limits of civilized standards." *Trop.* Evolving standards of decency that mark the progress of a maturing society counsel us to be most hesitant before interpreting the Eighth Amendment to allow the extension of the death penalty, a hesitation that has special force where no life was taken in the commission of the crime. It is an established principle that decency, in its essence, presumes respect for the individual and thus moderation or restraint in the application of capital punishment.

To date the Court has sought to define and implement this principle, for the most part, in cases involving capital murder. One approach has been to insist upon general rules that ensure consistency in determining who receives a death sentence. At the same time the Court has insisted, to ensure restraint and moderation in use of capital punishment, on judging the "character and record of the individual offender and the circumstances of the particular offense as a constitutionally indispensable part of the process of inflicting the penalty of death." *Woodson* [*v. North Carolina*, 428 U.S. 280 (1976)]. . . .

Our response to this case law, which is still in search of a unifying principle, has been to insist upon confining the instances in which capital punishment may be imposed.

Our concern here is limited to crimes against individual persons. We do not address, for example, crimes defining and punishing treason, espionage, terrorism, and drug kingpin activity, which are offenses against the State. As it relates to crimes against individuals, though, the death penalty should not be expanded to instances where the victim's life was not taken. We said in *Coker* of adult rape: "We do not discount the seriousness of rape as a crime. It is highly reprehensible, both in a moral sense and in its almost total contempt for the personal integrity and autonomy of the female victim . . . . Short of homicide, it is the 'ultimate violation of self.' . . . [But] [t]he murderer kills; the rapist, if no more than that, does not. . . . We have the abiding conviction that the death penalty, which 'is unique in its severity and irrevocability,' is an excessive penalty for the rapist who, as such, does not take human life."

The same distinction between homicide and other serious violent offenses against the individual informed the Court's analysis in *Enmund*, where the Court held that the death penalty for the crime of vicarious felony murder is disproportionate to the offense. The Court repeated there the fundamental, moral distinction between a "murderer" and a "robber," noting that while "robbery is a serious crime deserving serious punishment," it is not like death in its "severity and irrevocability."

Consistent with evolving standards of decency and the teachings of our precedents we conclude that, in determining whether the death penalty is excessive, there is a distinction between intentional first-degree murder on the one hand and nonhomicide crimes against individual persons, even including child rape, on the other. The latter crimes may be devastating in their harm, as here, but "in terms of moral depravity and of the injury to the person and to the public," *Coker*, they cannot be compared to murder in their "severity and irrevocability." . . .

Our decision is consistent with the justifications offered for the death penalty. *Gregg* instructs that capital punishment is excessive when it is grossly out of proportion to the crime or it does not fulfill the two distinct social purposes served by the death penalty: retribution and deterrence of capital crimes.

As in *Coker*, here it cannot be said with any certainty that the death penalty for child rape serves no deterrent or retributive function. . . . [Yet, the] incongruity between the crime of child rape and the harshness of the death penalty poses risks of over punishment and counsels against a constitutional ruling that the death penalty can be expanded to include this offense.

The goal of retribution, which reflects society's and the victim's interests in seeing that the offender is repaid for the hurt he caused does not justify the harshness of the death penalty here. In measuring retribution, as well as other objectives of criminal law, it is appropriate to distinguish between a particularly depraved murder that merits death as a form of retribution and the crime of child rape.

There is an additional reason for our conclusion that imposing the death penalty for child rape would not further retributive purposes. . . .

It is not at all evident that the child rape victim's hurt is lessened when the law permits the death of the perpetrator. Capital cases require a long-term commitment by those who testify for the prosecution, especially when guilt and sentencing determinations are in multiple proceedings. In cases like this the key testimony is not just from the family but from the victim herself. During formative years of her adolescence, made all the more daunting for having to come to terms with the brutality of her experience, L. H. was required to discuss the case at length with law enforcement personnel. In a public trial she was required to recount once more all the details of the crime to a jury as the State pursued the death of her stepfather. And in the end the State made L. H. a central figure in its decision to seek the death penalty, telling the jury in closing statements: "[L. H.] is asking you, asking you to set up a time and place when he dies."

Society's desire to inflict the death penalty for child rape by enlisting the child victim to assist it over the course of years in asking for capital punishment forces a moral choice on the child, who is not of mature age to make that choice. The way the death penalty here involves the child victim in its enforcement can compromise a decent legal system; and this is but a subset of fundamental difficulties capital punishment can cause in the administration and enforcement of laws proscribing child rape.

There are, moreover, serious systemic concerns in prosecuting the crime of child rape that are relevant to the constitutionality of making it a capital offense. The problem of unreliable, induced, and even imagined child testimony means there is a "special risk of wrongful execution" in some child rape cases. This undermines, at least to some degree, the meaningful contribution of the death penalty to legitimate goals of punishment. . . .

With respect to deterrence, if the death penalty adds to the risk of non-reporting, that, too, diminishes the penalty's objectives. Underreporting is a common problem with respect to child sexual abuse. Although we know little about what differentiates those who report from those who do not report, one of the most commonly cited reasons for nondisclosure is fear of negative consequences for the perpetrator, a concern that has special force where the abuser is a family member. As a result, punishment by death may not result in more deterrence or more effective enforcement.

In addition, by in effect making the punishment for child rape and murder equivalent, a State that punishes child rape by death may remove a strong incentive for the rapist not to kill the victim. . . . Assuming the offender behaves in a rational way, as one must to justify the penalty on grounds of deterrence, the penalty in some respects gives less protection, not more, to the victim, who is often the sole witness to the crime. It might be argued that, even if the death penalty results in a marginal increase in the incentive to kill, this is counterbalanced by a marginally increased deterrent to commit the crime at all. Whatever balance the legislature strikes, however, uncertainty on the point makes the argument for the penalty less compelling than for homicide crimes. . . .

Our determination that there is a consensus against the death penalty for child rape raises the question whether the Court's own institutional position and its holding will have the effect of blocking further or later consensus in favor of the penalty from developing. The Court, it will be argued, by the act of addressing the constitutionality of the death penalty, intrudes upon the consensus-making process. By imposing a negative restraint, the argument runs, the Court makes it more difficult for consensus to change or emerge. The Court, according to the criticism, itself becomes enmeshed in the process, part judge and part the maker of that which it judges.

These concerns overlook the meaning and full substance of the established proposition that the Eighth Amendment is defined by "the evolving standards of decency that mark the progress of a maturing society." *Trop.* Confirmed by repeated, consistent rulings of this Court, this principle requires that use of the death penalty be restrained. The rule of evolving standards of decency with specific marks on the way to full progress and mature judgment means that resort to the penalty must be reserved for the worst of crimes and limited in its instances of application. In most cases justice is not better served by terminating the life of the perpetrator rather than confining him and preserving the possibility that he and the system will find ways to allow him to understand the enormity of his offense. Difficulties in administering the penalty to ensure against its arbitrary and capricious application require adherence to a rule reserving its use, at this stage of evolving standards and in cases of crimes against individuals, for crimes that take the life of the victim.

The judgment of the Supreme Court of Louisiana upholding the capital sentence is reversed.

☐ *Justice ALITO, with whom THE CHIEF JUSTICE, Justice SCALIA, and Justice THOMAS join, dissenting.*

The Court today holds that the Eighth Amendment categorically prohibits the imposition of the death penalty for the crime of raping a child. This is so, according to the Court, no matter how young the child, no matter how many times the child is raped, no matter how many children the perpetrator rapes, no matter how sadistic the crime, no matter how much physical or psychological trauma is inflicted, and no matter how heinous the perpetrator's prior criminal record may be. The Court provides two reasons for this sweeping conclusion: First, the Court claims to have identified "a national consensus" that the death penalty is never acceptable for the rape of a child; second, the Court concludes, based on its "independent judgment," that imposing the death penalty for child rape is inconsistent with "'the evolving standards of decency that mark the progress of a maturing society.'" Because neither of these justifications is sound, I respectfully dissent.

I turn first to the Court's claim that there is "a national consensus" that it is never acceptable to impose the death penalty for the rape of a child. The Eighth Amendment's requirements, the Court writes, are "determined not by the standards that prevailed" when the Amendment was adopted but "by the norms that 'currently prevail.'" In assessing current norms, the Court relies primarily on the fact that only 6 of the 50 States now have statutes that permit the death penalty for this offense. But this statistic is a highly unreliable indicator of the views of state lawmakers and their constituents. As I will explain, *dicta* in this Court's decision in *Coker v. Georgia*, 433 U.S. 584 (1977), has stunted legislative consideration of the question whether the death penalty for the targeted offense of raping a young child is consistent with prevailing standards of decency. The *Coker dicta* gave state legislators and others good reason to fear that any law permitting the imposition of the death penalty for this crime would meet precisely the fate that has now befallen the Louisiana statute that is currently before us, and this threat strongly discouraged state legislators—regardless of their own values and those of their constituents—from supporting the enactment of such legislation.

As the Court correctly concludes, the holding in *Coker* was that the Eighth Amendment prohibits the death penalty for the rape of an "'adult woman,'" and thus *Coker* does not control our decision here. . . .

Because of the effect of the *Coker dicta*, the Court is plainly wrong in comparing the situation here to that in *Atkins* or *Roper v. Simmons*, 543 U.S. 551 (2005). Atkins concerned the constitutionality of imposing the death penalty on a mentally retarded defendant. Thirteen years earlier, in *Penry v. Lynaugh*, 492 U.S. 302 (1989), the Court had held that this was permitted by the Eighth Amendment, and therefore, during the time between *Penry* and *Atkins*, state legislators had reason to believe that this Court would follow its prior precedent and uphold statutes allowing such punishment.

The situation in *Roper* was similar. *Roper* concerned a challenge to the constitutionality of imposing the death penalty on a defendant who had not reached the age of 18 at the time of the crime. Sixteen years earlier in *Stanford v. Kentucky*, 492 U.S. 361 (1989), the Court had rejected a similar challenge, and therefore state lawmakers had cause to believe that laws allowing such punishment would be sustained.

When state lawmakers believe that their decision will prevail on the question whether to permit the death penalty for a particular crime or class of offender, the legislators' resolution of the issue can be interpreted as an expression of their own judgment, informed by whatever weight they attach to the values of their constituents. But when state legislators think that the enactment of a new death penalty law is likely to be futile, inaction cannot reasonably be interpreted as an expression of their understanding of prevailing societal values. In that atmosphere, legislative inaction is more likely to evidence acquiescence.

If anything can be inferred from state legislative developments, the message is very different from the one that the Court perceives. In just the past few years, despite the shadow cast by the *Coker dicta*, five States have enacted targeted capital child-rape laws. If, as the Court seems to think, our society is "[e]volving" toward ever higher "standards of decency," these enactments might represent the beginning of a new evolutionary line.

Such a development would not be out of step with changes in our society's thinking since *Coker* was decided. During that time, reported instances of child abuse have increased dramatically; and there are many indications of growing alarm about the sexual abuse of children. In 1994, Congress enacted the Jacob Wetterling Crimes Against Children and Sexually Violent Offender Registration Program, which requires States receiving certain federal funds to establish registration systems for convicted sex offenders and to notify the public about persons convicted of the sexual abuse of minors. All 50 States have now enacted such statutes. In addition, at least 21 States and the District of Columbia now have statutes permitting the involuntary commitment of sexual predators, and at least 12 States have enacted residency restrictions for sex offenders. . . .

In light of the points discussed above, I believe that the "objective indicia" of our society's "evolving standards of decency" can be fairly summarized as follows. Neither Congress nor juries have done anything that can plausibly be interpreted as evidencing the "national consensus" that the Court perceives. State legislatures, for more than 30 years, have operated under the ominous shadow of the *Coker dicta* and thus have not been free to express their own understanding of our society's standards of decency. And in the months following our grant of certiorari in this case, state legislatures have had an additional reason to pause. Yet despite the inhibiting legal atmosphere that has prevailed since 1977, six States have recently enacted new, targeted child-rape laws.

I do not suggest that six new state laws necessarily establish a "national consensus" or even that they are sure evidence of an ineluctable trend. In terms of the Court's metaphor of moral evolution, these enactments might have turned out to be an evolutionary dead end. But they might also have been the beginning of a strong new evolutionary line. We will never know, because the Court today snuffs out the line in its incipient stage.

The Court is willing to block the potential emergence of a national consensus in favor of permitting the death penalty for child rape because, in the end, what matters is the Court's "own judgment" regarding "the acceptability of the death penalty." Although the Court has much to say on this issue, most of the Court's discussion is not pertinent to the Eighth Amendment question at hand. And once all of the Court's irrelevant arguments are put aside, it is apparent that the Court has provided no coherent explanation for today's decision. . . .

A major theme of the Court's opinion is that permitting the death penalty in child-rape cases is not in the best interests of the victims of these crimes and society at large. In this vein, the Court suggests that it is more painful for child-rape victims to testify when the prosecution is seeking the death penalty. The Court also argues that "a State that punishes child rape by death may remove a strong incentive for the rapist not to kill the victim," and may discourage the reporting of child rape.

These policy arguments, whatever their merits, are simply not pertinent to the question whether the death penalty is "cruel and unusual" punishment. The Eighth Amendment protects the right of an accused. It does not authorize this Court to strike down federal or state criminal laws on the ground that they are not in the best interests of crime victims or the broader society. . . .

The Court also contends that laws permitting the death penalty for the rape of a child create serious procedural problems. Specifically, the Court maintains that it is not feasible to channel the exercise of sentencing discretion in child-rape cases, and that the unreliability of the testimony of child victims creates a danger that innocent defendants will be convicted and executed. Neither of these contentions provides a basis for striking down all capital child-rape laws no matter how carefully and narrowly they are crafted. . . .

After all the arguments noted above are put aside, what is left? What remaining grounds does the Court provide to justify its independent judgment that the death penalty for child rape is categorically unacceptable? I see two.

The first is the proposition that we should be "most hesitant before interpreting the Eighth Amendment to allow the extension of the death penalty." But holding that the Eighth Amendment does not categorically prohibit the death penalty for the rape of a young child would not "extend" or "expand" the death penalty. Laws enacted by the state legislatures are presumptively constitutional, and until today, this Court has not held that capital child rape laws are unconstitutional. Consequently, upholding the constitutionality of such a law would not "extend" or "expand" the death penalty; rather, it would confirm the status of presumptive constitutionality that such laws have enjoyed up to this point. . . .

The Court's final—and, it appears, principal—justification for its holding is that murder, the only crime for which defendants have been executed since this Court's 1976 death penalty decisions, is unique in its moral depravity and in the severity of the injury that it inflicts on the victim and the public. But the Court makes little attempt to defend these conclusions.

With respect to the question of moral depravity, is it really true that every person who is convicted of capital murder and sentenced to death is more morally depraved than every child rapist? Consider the following two cases. In the first, a defendant robs a convenience store and watches as his accomplice shoots the store owner. The defendant acts recklessly, but was not the triggerman and did not intend the killing. See, e.g., *Tison v. Arizona*, 481 U.S. 137 (1987). In the second case, a previously convicted child rapist kidnaps, repeatedly rapes, and tortures multiple child victims. Is it clear that the first defendant is more morally depraved than the second?

The Court's decision here stands in stark contrast to *Atkins* and *Roper*, in which the Court concluded that characteristics of the affected defendants—mental retardation in *Atkins* and youth in *Roper*—diminished their culpability. Nor is this case comparable to *Enmund v. Florida*, 458 U.S. 782 (1982), in which the Court held that the Eighth Amendment prohibits the death penalty where the defendant participated in a robbery during which a murder was committed but did not personally intend for lethal force to be used. I have no doubt that, under the prevailing standards of our society, robbery, the crime that the petitioner in *Enmund* intended to commit, does not evidence the same degree of moral depravity as the brutal rape of a young child. Indeed, I have little doubt that, in the eyes of ordinary Americans, the very worst child rapists—predators who seek out and inflict serious physical and emotional injury on defenseless young children—are the epitome of moral depravity. . . .

In summary, the Court holds that the Eighth Amendment categorically rules out the death penalty in even the most extreme cases of child rape even though: (1) This holding is not supported by the original meaning of the Eighth Amendment; (2) neither *Coker* nor any other prior precedent commands this result; (3) there are no reliable "objective indicia" of a "national consensus" in support of the Court's position; (4) sustaining the constitutionality of the state law before us would not "extend" or "expand" the death penalty; (5) this Court has previously rejected the proposition that the Eighth Amendment is a one-way ratchet that prohibits legislatures from adopting new capital punishment statutes to meet new problems; (6) the worst child rapists exhibit the epitome of moral depravity; and (7) child rape inflicts grievous injury on victims and on society in general.

The party attacking the constitutionality of a state statute bears the "heavy burden" of establishing that the law is unconstitutional. *Gregg.* That burden has not been discharged here, and I would therefore affirm the decision of the Louisiana Supreme Court.

12

THE EQUAL PROTECTION OF THE LAWS

By a six-to-three vote in *Engquist v. Oregon Department of Agriculture*, 128 S.Ct. 2146 (2008), the Court held that government employees who claim that they were singled out for arbitrary, irrational, or vindictive treatment by supervisors may not claim that they are a "class of one" and protected by the equal protection clause; they must claim that their mistreatment was due to discrimination based on race, sex, or another protected category. Writing for the Court, Justice Roberts held that the "class-of-one theory of equal protection" was "simply a poor fit in the public employment context" because government needs "broad discretion" to make "subjective and individualized" decisions about employees. In his words: "To treat employees differently is not to classify them in a way that raises equal protection concerns. . . . A challenge that one has been treated individually in this context, instead of like everyone else, is a challenge to the underlying nature of the governmental action." The chief justice added, "The federal court is not the appropriate forum in which to review the multitude of personnel decisions that are made daily by public agencies." Anup Engquist, a native of India, had experienced problems with laboratory co-workers and management over ten years and was effectively laid off in 2002 after being given the choice to move to another position, for which she was deemed unqualified, or accept a demotion, which she denied to accept. In response, Engquist brought a "class-of-one" equal protection suit, alleging that she dismissed for "arbitrary, vindictive, and malicious reasons," and not because she was a member of an identified class protected by the equal protection clause. Justice Stevens, joined by Justices Souter and Ginsburg, dissented, contending that the majority "carves a novel exception out of state employees' constitutional rights" and that there is a "clear distinction between an exercise of discretion and an arbitrary decision."

C | *Affirmative Action and Reverse Discrimination*

In an important affirmative action decision in *Ricci v. DeStefano*, 129 S.Ct. 2658 (2009), a bare majority reversed an appellate court's ruling upholding a New Haven, Connecticut, decision to disregard test scores for promotions of firefighters because no African Americans passed the tests and the city feared a discrimination lawsuit under Section VII of the Civil Rights Act of 1964 for using a test that had a "disparate impact" on minorities. The city was sued by white firefighters who passed the test but were denied promotions. Writing for the Court, Justice Kennedy avoided a Fourteenth Amendment equal protection challenge and ruled narrowly on statutory grounds that under Section VII employees must have a "strong basis in evidence" that a test is deficient and discriminatory, rather than just "raw racial statistics." Justice Kennedy observed that, "The process was open and fair. . . . The problem, of course, is that after the tests were completed, the raw racial results became the predominant rationale for the city's refusal to certify the results. . . . Fear of litigation [brought by minorities] alone cannot justify an employer's reliance on race to the detriment of individuals who passed the examinations and qualified for promotions." Concurring Justice Scalia, however, added that "The war between disparate impact and equal protection will be waged sooner or later, and it behooves us to begin thinking about how—and on what terms—to make peace between them." By contrast, writing for dissenting Justices Stevens, Souter, and Breyer, Justice Ginsburg countered that "Congress and, until the decision just announced, this Court regarded Title VII's dual prescriptions on intentional and disparate impact as complementary. . . . Standing on equal footing, both provisions aim to end workplace discrimination and promote genuinely equal opportunity."

D | *Nonracial Classifications and the Equal Protection of the Law*

(1) Gender-Based Discrimination

In its 2010–2011 term the Court will consider whether the Immigration and Nationality Act's (INA) residency requirement, which applies to U.S. citizen fathers but not to U.S. mothers, violates equal protection, in *Flores-Villar v. United States* (No. 09-5801). The INA requires that to establish citizenship of a child born abroad and out of wedlock, the parent with citizenship must have been a resident of the United States for not less than ten years, five of which must have been after the age of fourteen. If the mother is the parent with U.S. citizenship, however, the child's citizenship is presumed, regardless of the duration of residency. Flores-Villar was born in Tijuana, Mexico, to a noncitizen mother and a citizen father. Yet, Flores-Villar's father was sixteen at the time of Flores-Villar's birth and could not have been a resident for five years after the age of fourteen. Flores-Villar was deported, and then charged with being a deported alien found in the United States. A trial court granted the government's motion to exclude evidence of derivative citizenship based on the Act's residence requirement, and found him guilty. A federal district court affirmed and the Court of Appeals for the Ninth Circuit affirmed the conviction, holding that intermediate scrutiny applied to gender-based classifications, and that the classification furthers governmental interests of assuring that a biological relationship exists, along with the fact that mothers and fathers are not similarly situated in this respect. Flores-Villar appealed that decision and challenged the age and gender residence requirement under the equal protection component of the Fifth Amendment.

(4) *Alienage and Age*

■ The Development of Law

Recent Rulings on Age Discrimination

CASE	VOTE	RULING
Gomez-Perez v. Potter, Postmaster General, 128 S.Ct. 1931 (2008)	6:3	Writing for the Court, Justice Alito held that under the Age Discrimination in Employment Act federal employees may not be

subjected to retaliation because of their complaints about age discrimination. Chief Justice Roberts and Justices Thomas and Scalia dissented.

| *CBOCS West v. Humphries,* 128 S.Ct. 1951 (2008) | 7:2 | Writing for the Court, Justice Breyer held that employment-related retaliation claims are per- |

missible under Title VII of the Civil Rights Act of 1964. Humphries had alleged that CBOCS terminated his employment because he is black and had complained that a black co-worker was also dismissed based on race. Justice Thomas and Scalia dissented.

| *Gross v. FBL Financial Services, Inc.,* 129 S.Ct. 2343 (2009) | 7:2 | Writing for the Court, Justice Thomas held that age, by a preponderance of evidence, must be the "but for" cause of adverse em- |

ployment action under the Age Discrimination Employment Act of 1967 (ADEA). In doing so, Justice Thomas made clear that companies may not be held to age discrimination suits of mixed motives because (1) that standard had proven over the years difficult to articulate to juries, and (2) even though Congress has extended mixed motive standards to many disparate treatment claims, it failed to do so with respect to age discrimination. Justices Stevens, Souter, Ginsburg, and Breyer dissented.

INDEX OF CASES

Cases printed in boldface are excerpted on the page(s) printed in boldface.

Other Books by David M. O'Brien

Storm Center:
The Supreme Court in American Politics
8th ed.

Constitutional Law and Politics:
Vol. 1. *Struggles for Power and Governmental Accountability*
Vol. 2. *Civil Rights and Civil Liberties*
7th ed.

Congress Shall Make No Law: The First Amendment,
Unprotected Expression, and the U.S. Supreme Court

Animal Sacrifice and Religious Freedom:
Church of Lukumi Babalu Aye v. City of Hialeah

To Dream of Dreams:
Religious Freedom and Constitutional Politics in Postwar Japan

Judicial Roulette

What Process Is Due?
Courts and Science-Policy Disputes

The Public's Right to Know:
The Supreme Court and the First Amendment

Privacy, Law, and Public Policy

Judges on Judging: Views from the Bench
3rd ed. (editor)

The Lanahan Readings on Civil Rights aqnd Civil Liberties
3rd ed. (editor)

Abortion and American Politics
(co-author)

Judicial Independence in the Age of Democracy:
Critical Perspectives from Around the World
(co-editor)

The Politics of Technology Assessment:
Institutions, Processes and Policy Disputes
(co-editor)

Views from the Bench:
The Judiciary and Constitutional Politics
(co-editor)

The Politics of American Government
3d ed.
(co-author)

Government by the People
22nd ed.
(co-author)

Courts and Judicial Policymaking
(co-author)